ASIAN
DEPARTMENT
STORES

ConsumAsiaN Book Series
edited by
Brian Moeran and Lise Skov

The ConsumAsiaN book series examines the way in which things and ideas about things are consumed in Asia, the role of consumption in the formation of attitudes, experiences, lifestyles and social relations, and the way in which consumption relates to the broader cultures and societies of which it is a part. The series consists of both single-authored monographs and edited selections of essays, and is interdisciplinary in approach. While seeking to map current and recent consumer trends in various aspects of Asian cultures, the series pays special attention to the interactions and influences among the countries concerned, as well as to the region as a whole in a global context. The volumes in the series apply up-to-date theoretical arguments frequently developed in Europe and America to non-western societies – both in order to analyse how consumption practices in Asia compare to those found elsewhere, and to develop new theories that match a specific Asian context.

Women, Media and Consumption in Japan
Edited by Lise Skov and Brian Moeran
Published 1995

A Japanese Advertising Agency
An Anthropology of Media and Markets
Brian Moeran
Published 1996

Contemporary Japan and Popular Culture
Edited by John Whittier Treat
Published 1996

Packaged Japaneseness
Weddings, Business and Brides
Ofra Goldstein-Gidoni
Published 1997

Australia and Asia
Cultural Transactions
Edited by Maryanne Dever
Published 1997

ASIAN
DEPARTMENT
STORES

Edited by
Kerrie L. MacPherson

CURZON

First published in 1998
by Curzon Press
15 The Quadrant, Richmond
Surrey, TW9 1BP

© 1998 Kerrie L. MacPherson

Typeset in Times by LaserScript Ltd, Mitcham
Printed and bound in Great Britain by
Biddles Ltd, Guildford and King's Lynn

British Library Cataloguing in Publication Data
A catalogue record for this book is available from the British Library

ISBN 0–7007–0332–2

CONTENTS

v

PREFACE

This volume in the *ConsumAsiaN* series on the origins and development of Asian department stores grew out of a lively discussion at a seminar given by Kaoru Sugihara on 'Intra-Asian Trade and Japan's Industrialization' at the newly established Department of Japanese Studies at The University of Hong Kong, ably directed by its first Swire Professor, Brian Moeran. Originally conceived to include not only China (including Hong Kong) and Japan, but also Korea, Taiwan and Singapore, the scope of the volume changed due to the problems faced by researchers in accessing company archives in their respective regions.

We have focused here in the first section of the volume, 'Overseas Chinese Entrepreneurs, Department Store Culture, and the State', on the historical rise and interrelationships of these large enterprises in Hong Kong and China, and on their 'offshoots' in Australia that grew out of long-established overseas Chinese trading networks in Southeast Asia. The role of these entrepreneurs, together with the development of enterprise culture within colonial and semi-colonial political frameworks and the emergence of a modern state in China, highlights the trajectory of Chinese capitalism and consumption before 1949. The section closes with a chapter on the continued role of the department store as a viable concern under communism in China, now transformed into a 'state department store', and the re-emergence of enterprise culture as a unifying force in the face of major economic reforms since 1978.

In the second section, 'Visions of Modernism and Japanese Department Stores', we examine the synchronous rise of department stores in Japan and their modern incarnations. Although there are many parallels between the origins and rise of Japanese and Chinese stores, unlike the chapters on Chinese department stores that stress the role of the entrepreneur, the focus here is on the 'aesthetics of consumption', that is the consumer experience tied to 'image making' within the

vii

context of Japanese economic development since the turn of the century.

The final section of the volume, 'A Japanese Entrepreneur in China and Hong Kong', on the more recent and successful expansion of Yaohan, a Japanese retailing firm in Hong Kong and China, examines not only its global strategies, but also the importance of entrepreneurship and the role of enterprise culture in achieving its goals in competition with other newly established 'overseas' Japanese trading networks.

These studies do not constitute a comprehensive survey of Asian department stores, but a collection of chapters linked together in significant ways by the thematic continuity of shared histories and cultures. We hope that the works presented here will encourage continuing research on and analysis of these enterprises throughout Asia, moving towards a more integrated view of Asian consumption and economic development that takes into account the environment and cultural factors which gave rise to them.

This volume owes its existence to the inspiration and hard work of many individuals. Foremost among them are Brian Moeran and Lise Skov, general editors of the *ConsumAsiaN* book series, who were instrumental in sustaining the transformation of the original concept into its final form. Their encouragement and help were invaluable. Brian's own contribution on the origins of Japanese department stores, and his translation and adaptation of Ueno Chizuko's originally much lengthier study, strengthened and supported the discursive flow that illuminates the chapters on Japanese department stores from the turn of the century to the present. I wish to express my appreciation to Qian Jiang, through whose wide knowledge of Chinese history and many scholarly contacts in China I was introduced to Professors Guo and Liu at the Beijing Institute of Business, who contributed a chapter on the Wangfujing Department Store for this volume, one of the first studies of a department store under socialism in China. I wish to gratefully acknowledge the timely and important editorial assistance in sorting out problems of translation provided by Yeung Wingyu, Lolo Young and A. H. Y. Lin. I also wish to thank John Bradford for his swift reproduction of the illustrations for the introduction. Finally, it was a pleasure to work with Marie Lenstrup who copy edited the book with skill, patience and a propitious sense of humour, a true professional who made my editorial burden a light one.

I have to end my prefatory remarks with a sad epistle. Dr. John Dragon Young, who contributed a seminal chapter on Sun Yatsen and the department store, died tragically during the preparation of this volume. His pioneering book *Confucianism and Christianity: the first encounter* (1983, Hong Kong: The University of Hong Kong Press), as well as his other numerous publications, won him the respect and admiration of scholars internationally. An abiding concern of John's intellectual journey was the dialogue and interaction between east and west, a theme that he was bringing to fruition before his untimely death, by re-evaluating Sun Yatsen's role in the modernization of China. We are most fortunate, therefore, to be able to publish a small portion of this promising research posthumously. To honour his memory, I wish to dedicate this volume to John, with my respect and love.

Kerrie L. MacPherson

EDITOR'S NOTE

The problem of representing the Chinese and Japanese languages in romanized form is a familiar and tedious one to researchers in the field. We have opted here to represent the *pinyin* (the system now used in China) transliteration for all Chinese names and terms, whilst noting the original Cantonese-dialect spellings where historically appropriate. In some cases, well-known individuals such as Sun Yatsen remains as he styled himself in English, as is the case for the overseas Chinese in Australia. Japanese names and terms are transliterated according to the modified Hepburn system (with the use of macrons).

Every effort has been made to trace the copyright holders of the illustrations in this book. The editor and publishers would be pleased to hear from any copyright holders whom they have been unable to contact, and to print due acknowledgements in the next edition.

INTRODUCTION

ASIA'S UNIVERSAL PROVIDERS

Kerrie L. MacPherson

'The Only IDEAL STORE in the town offering High Quality, Good Service, Reasonable Price', promised the Sun Sun Co., Ltd. (Xinxin gongsi) in an advertisement published in a Shanghai guidebook in the 1930s (*All about Shanghai and Environs* 1934–5:31) (*Figure 1*). Established there in 1926, Sun Sun Co. was one of the 'big four' department stores in Shanghai along with Dah Sun (Daxin gongsi, established in 1936), and the venerable Sincere (Xianshi gongsi, 1917) and Wing On (Yong'an gongsi, 1918) companies (Shanghai baihuo gongsi et al. 1988). These department stores vied for the expanding market of a growing Chinese middle-class clientele in China's largest and most cosmopolitan city. Located on Shanghai's version of New York's Fifth Avenue, Nanjing Road, arguably one of the world's busiest streets, the architecture, ambiance and sheer number of goods for sale from the 'cheapest to the highest grade' was a powerful mix of western and Asian tastes purveyed with a bewildering variety of services, from roof-top tea gardens and afternoon dancing parties to attached hotels. Sincere's Oriental Hotel, we are told in another local guidebook, was offering 114 rooms – Chinese-style from $1 to $2.50 a day or foreign-style from $2 to $6 a day (Darwent 1920:14; Xianshi gongsi 1924[?]). At Sincere's opening in 1917, it was heralded as 'the largest and most up-to-date Chinese-owned store in Shanghai, at which everything from a needle to an elephant (toy) can be obtained', but not for long. Opposite Sincere, its rival Wing On (like Macy's and Gimbel's in New York, or Mitsukoshi and Shirokiya on opposite ends of the Nihonbashi bridge in Tōkyō) offered competitive prices and services. Wing On's attached Great Eastern Hotel, although smaller than Sincere's, boasted a complex that included four theatres and music halls that stayed opened until 2am, attracting 30,000 people there in a twenty-four hour period (*North-China Herald* 1917; Macmillan 1923:491).

1

Figure I.1 Advertisement of the Sun Sun Company Ltd. (Xinxin gongsi), one of the 'big four' department stores in Shanghai, from the guidebook *All About Shanghai and Environs* (1934-5:31).

Located in the relative security and profitability of the International Settlements of Shanghai, on the Bund bordering the foreign enclave of Shamian in Guangzhou or in the British Colony of Hong Kong, areas controlled by foreigners but overwhelmingly populated by Chinese, these department stores in concept and origin were derived from the west, but their capitalization, ownership and management were exclusively Chinese.[1]

In Japan at the turn of the century, the western-inspired commercial revolution was pioneered by the Japanese entrepreneurs of Mitsukoshi and its rival, Shirokiya, Tōkyō's first and largest department stores, offering their version of 'modern life' or *modan raifu*. Retailing novelties or curiosities from abroad, along with local products, in a novel and foreign way – selling almost everything under one roof, departmentalized and displayed behind glass-counters for a fixed price – by the post-earthquake era (1923) they stood literally as beacons (multi-storied above the horizontal lines of the city) of the changes that were transforming all aspects of Japanese life, going 'the whole distance toward becoming what the Japanese had observed in New York and London', if not surpassing them (Seidensticker 1991:29–30). Merchandising, entertainment and culture, now 'unregulated and open to anyone (including, increasingly, women)', fused in these thriving centres (*sakariba*) in the new 'national' capital that had doubled its population to almost four million people between the Sino-Japanese War (1895) and the eve of the great Kantō earthquake (Smith 1978:69–71).

Department Stores East and West

The scope of this book concerns the origin and development of Asian department stores in China, Japan, Hong Kong and Australia from the late nineteenth century to their most recent incarnations, in distinction to notable western transplants in Asia or to European owned and managed emporiums that originated in Asia. Examples of these 'departmental stores' are Whiteaway & Laidlaw and Co., Ltd., with 50 branches scattered across Asia and Africa by 1923, 'organized and operated with special reference to the characteristics and idiosyncracies of its particular centre of trade' but keeping its books balanced by a 'strict adherence to cash trade'; Hong Kong's Lane Crawford opened in a 'matshed' in 1850, becoming a leader in controlling the European retail trade in the Far East from Columbo to Yokohama, a veritable 'barometer of the unceasing evolution in the productions of the great industrial centres beyond the seas'; Shanghai's Hall & Holtz, Ltd. established in 1843 from modest beginnings as a bakery; or A.H. Jacques & Co., opening in 1901 in Tianjin, and regarded as the local 'Whiteley's', modeled on London's first 'Universal Provider' (Wright 1908:650, 742; Macmillan 1923:362–3, 381, 464–5, 467) (*Figure 2*).

Due recognition is given to the importance of these western owned and managed stores in Asia as comparative examples and competitors – questions as to how or why they differed from their Asian owned and managed counterparts, in management styles, types of goods for sale, displays, clienteles, and the diversification of their operations would sharpen our understanding of the development of department stores generally, but they fall outside the purview of this book. Nevertheless, we hope that the line of inquiry and analysis pursued by the collection presented here will encourage continuing investigation in what constitutes an under-researched field.

We have concentrated on Chinese and Japanese owned and managed entities because they were outstanding leaders in developing this new

Figure I.2 Views of some of Shanghai's prominent department stores, adapted from Zhou Shixun 1933 *Shanghai daguan* (The Grand Sights of Shanghai), Shanghai: Wenhua meishu tushu gongsi.

1. Wing On Co., Ltd. (Yong'an gongsi); 2. Sincere Co., Ltd. (Xianshi gongsi); 3. Sun Sun Co., Ltd. (Xinxin gongsi); 4. Fook On Co. (Fu'an gongsi), a smaller departmental store located at the east gate of the old walled city; 5. Whiteaway, Laidlaw and Company, a British owned department store and the first to operate in Shanghai; 6. Hall & Holtz, a keen competitor of Whiteaway's.

4

form of retail trade within their own respective cultures; in the scale, sophistication and innovation of their business strategies; as well as in their continued expansion and viability throughout the region. Moreover, by focusing on these enterprises, the particular historical circumstances giving rise to them, the culturally specific responses to modernization – often simplistically viewed as 'westernization' – in the Asian context, and their role as interpreters and retailers of an emerging and ambivalent modernity, the authors have gone far in defining what an Asian department store might be. However, there is some evidence of indigenous 'general merchants' in Thailand, like the Oriental Stores, Ltd., Rangoon's Burmese Favourite Co., 'the leading native firm of general outfitters', or the Straits Settlements Buan Soon Lee & Co established in 1915 by Straits-born Chinese who gained their experience in Malaya (Wright 1908:141, 178). Whether they constitute analogous institutions, or gave rise to modern department stores in their respective regions clearly in evidence today, are questions awaiting the attention of modern scholarship (Lee 1984).

Asian department stores, as demonstrated in the chapters presented in this volume, were stimulated originally by the expansion of the west in East and Southeast Asia. In China, Japan, Hong Kong, and in the overseas Chinese communities in Australia (in a slightly different context), this was effected through the establishment of colonial outposts or treaty ports as well as the introduction of modern western influences in a variety of guises in the second half of the nineteenth and early twentieth centuries. In this context, it is worth reviewing the essential features that define a department store and the conditions that made possible their rise, first in London, Paris, and New York, and then replicated in less grandiose metropolises dotted across Europe and the United States, and in places linked to them in the nineteenth century.

From city to city, they reflected variations in management or in the organization of distribution and supply, as custom and history dictated, that left them their discrete identities, adding 'distinctive touches to the emergence of a new mode of retailing' (Barth 1980:110). Yet, they all shared defining features that shaped new shopping behaviour and experiences that departed from traditional merchandising practices of the past. First, the organization of a broad spectrum of goods in departmentalized sections under one roof; second, the visible display of goods available, usually in glass-windowed counters; third, fixed and marked prices (often touted as 'fair') that favored high turnover by shortening the selling process. Furthermore, the quality and price of the goods for sale were guaranteed by a return or exchange policy which in turn encouraged consumption 'through price and service innovations'. As Miller (1981:24) suggests in his study of the Parisian Bon Marché, entrance to the department store, unlike traditional shops, entailed no obligation to buy, thereby facilitating a new kind of shopping behaviour.

No matter how substantial their differences, operating as it were in differing cultural milieus, department stores were analogous institutions. Across the western world, the department store was a product of clearly identifiable general trends in social and economic conditions born out of nineteenth century industrialization. The mass merchandizing of department stores was directly linked to the mass production of the factory, to urbanization, revolutions in technology, communications, transportation, information systems and new financial instruments capable of supporting this mass retailing (Lambert 1938; Ferry 1960; Barth 1980:110; Miller 1981).

The nineteenth century constituted the 'age of great cities'. The emergence of the 'million-peopled cities' and the striking increase in their numbers were phenomena generally associated with the extension of liberal capitalism in its varied configurations throughout the world. Urbanization, that is the demographic shift from the countryside to the city, was a trend statistically verifiable in the west by the turn of the century.[2] Although both China and Japan were highly urbanized even by pre-modern standards before the coming of the west, their cities served as agricultural service centres, as agricultural dependencies, or as solely local cultural, religious, or administrative centres, rather than as integral parts of national industrial economies (Elvin 1974:2–11). The introduction of foreign investments in production, transport and communications, as well as the flow of ideas and non-economic institutions that conditioned the emergence of national markets, processes best described as 'modernization', was abetted by western imperialism, the 'unequal treaties' that opened China's coastal cities to foreign trade and residence in 1842, followed by those with Japan in 1859. It is interesting to note that in 1871, China signed a treaty of amity with Japan which opened their respective treaty ports to mutual trade, though China refused to allow Japanese merchants access to the interior or to extend the 'most favoured nation' clause, rights enjoyed by western nations. However discrete their individual reactions to the challenges that modernization posed, great growth did occur, first in these new conurbations, or 'beachheads' of western contact.[3] The department store was a uniquely urban institution as Gunther Barth (1980:110) reminds us, with 'the modern city providing the economic incentive and the physical setting for new enterprise'.

Cities, Transportation and the Asian Department Store

The city linked its citizens above and below the streets, and with other cities across the globe, through new technologies in communications and transportation. The telegraph, the railroad and the steamship were conquering time and distance. Such advances brought the world marketplace within reach of increasingly affluent urbanites and made possible the rationalization, coordination and control of production, supply and distribution of mass goods. In Asia this was first effected by the advances made in oceanic and riverine shipping, the latter particularly important in China as its major rivers were also its major highways into the interior. But it was also a field of fierce competition amongst Chinese and foreign shipping concerns, including the Japanese, whose principal item of invisible income derived from China by 1933 was interest on investments and revenue from shipping services. The first Chinese department stores set up in the British colony and entrepôt of Hong Kong in the first decade of the twentieth century were dependent on the steamship and on these shipping networks as they quickly expanded, both in the size and breadth of their operations, to other port cities like Guangzhou and Shanghai. Founded by 'overseas' Chinese entrepreneurs living in Australia hailing from the same native district (Xiangshan) in South China with shared familial and business connections, they gained their business acumen by organizing and then mastering the supply and distribution of commodities, some highly perishable like fruit, throughout Southeast Asia.

The coming of the railroad in both China and Japan accelerated the flow of goods, people and ideas, transforming the scale and location of commercial activities. If in China the steamship brought the coal mine and in turn required a railroad, as John King Fairbank et al. (1989) remind us, railroad development was stalled in the late nineteenth century by the government's policy of circumventing foreign exploitation by avoiding foreign financed and run railways, a policy which failed by 1898. Foreign-controlled lines – Russian and Japanese in the northeast, German in Shandong, French in Yunnan – and the railways nominally under government control which were financed by foreign banking syndicates who built and managed them and who held the first mortgages as security on the loans, meant that China was 'entering the railway age with foreign financiers awaiting the profits' (Fairbank et al. 1989:737). The troubled history of railway development in China, whether viewed as a product of the 'economic tools of imperialism' or as a less successful competitor to the older, cheaper and well

7

established coastal and river transport systems, did not influence the location of department stores until after the Second World War, leaving them in the central business districts, along the rivers and harbors of the port cities.

Japanese railway development, on the other hand, was predicated on national goals, a state-centred ambitious program of forced modernization carried out initially by the Ministry of Industry (Kōbushō) from 1870. The potent combination of nationalism and western borrowing meant that the hundred or so British technicians and engineers employed by the ministry at the height of the railway construction program would impart their knowledge to Japanese counterparts and depart swiftly once the transfer was successfully completed (Morris-Suzuki 1994:73–4). In a country with few good roads and navigable rivers, railroads proved immediately profitable. In due course, the development of railroads came to be closely linked to that of the department store. As Brian Moeran points out in this volume, a new style of department store – the 'terminal *depāto*' – was first founded by the railway companies at the station terminals to capture the new commuter market. With the building of the Tōkyō subway in the early 1930s, older established stores like Mitsokoshi, Shirokiya and Matsuya financed the construction of their own stations in order to encourage commuter traffic to their doors.

Consumption and Urban Lifestyles

Consumption expanded beyond the basic requirements of life. What passed for a luxury in a rural setting became a necessity in the urban environment. Some of the themes explored in this volume are the tensions between traditional practices, well-established in such highly organized and urban consumer societies as China and Japan, and the adoption of new techniques in retailing (and thereby consumption) derived from the west within a colonial or semi-colonial setting. It should be noted however, that even after the formal exposure to modern western influences in China's coastal cities, or in Japan, local urban markets and the retail shops selling well-known brands organized along traditional lines, that is similar products purveyed in the same location, did not lose their vitality (Hamilton and Lai 1989). They continued to flourish and expand as these cities rapidly grew beyond their traditional boundaries between 1842 and 1925. Shanghai, to take one example, grew from a modest marketing town, in the traditional Chinese urban hierarchy, of less than 300,000 people, to a metropolis of 1.5 million, in the meantime establishing a municipal government and embracing what passed in China and the west at that time as a modern urban infrastructure (MacPherson 1987). The bustle of the local market where daily necessities were purchased by the ever increasing numbers of urban inhabitants, along with the incessant and protracted haggling over prices and other hallmarks of traditional habits, were not immediately threatened by the introduction of the 'fair' fixed price of the department store. Most of Shanghai's urbanites may have known about but rarely visited Nanjing Road where these large emporiums were located (Lu 1995).

The small neighborhood shops and local markets continued to coexist with this new retail institution and in notable examples in Japan, some of these specialty shops transformed themselves into department stores. Thus, in the last decades of Meiji, Mitsui dry-goods store, established in Edo (Tōkyō) in the seventeenth century, led the commercial revolution by becoming Mitsukoshi in 1904, moving in 1914 into grand new premises, a five-storey renaissance-style building, replete with elevators, escalator, central heating and a roof garden. On the opposite end of the Nihonbashi Bridge its rival, Shirokiya, had built its new premises three years earlier, four storeys high with a tower, housing in addition to the 'one hundred goods' (*hyakkaten* or department store literally meaning 'one hundred goods' store) a game room and the first exhibition halls that, according to Edward Seidensticker (1983:110–4), gave 'the modern Japanese department store certain aspects of a museum and amusement park'.

Women, whether poor or rich, who had once monopolized modest household purchases, became participants in, and helped to revolutionize, the retail trade. In China and Japan, department stores tutored them in the essentials of a modern lifestyle. They not only brought them the 'dietetic resources of the world', but also the latest styles from London or Paris, and 'lace and silk garments from the factories of Guangzhou and other Chinese cities'.

Many of them were now employed in new industrial enterprises like textiles, churning out the semi-processed materials that fueled the manufacturing industry. Shanghai's rise as a major industrial centre came at the end of the Sino-Japanese War and the signing of the Treaty of Shimonoseki (1895), which gave foreigners the right to build factories in China's treaty ports. Two-thirds of of the total industrial work force in Shanghai were women, and they constituted the majority of the work force employed in the most modern of industrial enterprises, the cotton mills, over half of which were owned by British and Japanese capitalists (Honig 1986:1–3). Although many of the women arrived at the factory gates dressed in the styles and customs of their home villages, a fashionable (westernized) outfit was a prerequisite for obtaining and keeping a job in some of the Japanese owned mills, prompting female employees to forgo eating well, or purchasing other necessities, in order to maintain the dress standard. The Wing On Company, having diversified into the textile industry operating its Number Three Mill in Yangshupu, faced a somewhat different problem. The trend for wearing new and fashionable styles among its female employees prompted the management to publish dress regulations forbidding the wearing of leather high heels, and prohibiting permanent waves and rouge on the grounds of safety and hygiene (Honig 1986:138–9). Rising expectations and new desires infected more than the solid middle-classes with disposable income.

By the turn of the century, in the west, women would replace men as clerks and sales staff in this new kind of store packed with a variety of conveniently displayed goods, served with a smile. As Wellington Chan points out in his chapter, traditionally women worked only in small family-run shops in China, so that when Sincere opened their new premises in Hong Kong in 1900, the fashionably dressed salesgirls (including the owner's wife and sister-in-law) caused a sensation, disrupted business and after a few months were laid off. It was not until the late 1930s that women sales clerks became an accepted and common feature of China's department store business.[4]

In Japan, the replacing of men in the retail trade by shop girls in the 1920s deserves some mention, as it relates to problems of modernity in another cultural context (cf. Skov and Moeran 1995:16–22). 'The question of the shop girl and whether or not she was ideally liberated', as Edward Seidensticker (1991:32–4) recounts, was connected to the first multiple-storey fire in Tōkyō in 1932 and the 'worst department store fire anywhere since one in Budapest late in the nineteenth century'. It happened in Shirokiya's eight-storey building constructed after the earthquake, a fire that evidently needlessly claimed thirteen deaths from falling or jumping. The shop girls, who wore traditional Japanese dress and underclothes, attempted for the sake of modesty to slide down the safety ropes while at the same time holding their skirts to keep them from flying open, and fell to their deaths. In 1933, Shirokiya paid its shop girls subsidies for wearing foreign dress and required that they wear western-style underpants.

The department store emerged with changing urban lifestyles and an expanding appetite for consumption, and it also emerged to herald the new building technologies and architectural aesthetics of the industrial age. The department store invariably rose multi-storied, grandly facaded, and constructed to stream customers from the street-curbs of the central city to the top floors, circulating around well-organized and glass-countered displays selling a plethora of goods, at a fixed price with no obligation to buy, all conveniently located under one roof. In Shanghai, the successive openings of the Sincere, Wing On, Sun Sun and Dah Sun companies on Nanjing Road occasioned something of an architectural event. Sincere's architects, Lester, Johnson and Moriss, were praised in the local press for designing a 'well-balanced and accurately designed' reinforced concrete building in the 'English Renaissance style', faced with blue Ningbo stone to the first floor level and granite-chip cement above, 'carved out by Japanese', and finished with a flourish of columns, cornices and dressings of patent stone (*North-China Herald* 1917). Wing On's premises were designed by the firm of Palmer and Turner of Hong Kong (architects of the Hong Kong and Shanghai Bank) where the 'ventilation, lighting and all other facilities are arranged after the most approved methods' (*Far Eastern Review* 1918:424–5). The Sun Sun Co., opening in 1926 and rising seven storeys on Nanjing Road, had Shanghai's first ballroom and radio station which greatly facilitated the advertisement of the company (Gan 1987:92–3). The parallels between these stores and Japanese stores, in terms of their built form and the combination of retailing and the provision of amenities, as well as cultural activities – roof-top gardens, restaurants, theatres, entertainment areas – are striking. In fact, the Dah Sun Co., opened in 1936, was said to have been modeled on Osaka's Daimaru department store. It boasted Shanghai's first escalators as well as air-conditioning on every floor (Lin 1986:9; Shanghai baihuo gongsi et al. 1988:106–7). A feature common to all of these stores was the extensive provisions made for fire-proofing, in materials, design and equipment, in addition to the oft mentioned modernized and spacious lavatory facilities (*North-China Herald* 1917, 1918, 1926).

Nationalism and the Department Store

To some, the impact of the encounter with a modernizing west created a 'new negative' in these Asian societies, by enhancing a traditional assertion of a 'self-sufficient and self-satisfied identity' and a firm resistance to foreign models (Murphey 1974; MacPherson and Yearley 1987).[5] To others, the impact created a new nationalistic, but modern urban sector, limited by and large to the coastal treaty ports (or colonial

Hong Kong) with little or no significant impact on the rural interior (Bergère 1979, 1989:13–62). Japan, as Sakakibara (1997:80) reminds us, was an example of an Asian nation that succeeded in modernizing without losing its culture and religion, 'fusing western capitalism with pre-modern but nonetheless well-developed Asian global commercialism'.

The growing nationalism and debates over cultural identity in the late nineteenth and early twentieth centuries in Asia were reflected in the commercial strategies of these large businesses. The geo-political picture was a complicated one and differed from place to place. The rise of Japan as an imperial power in the early twentieth century, its colonization of Korea and the Chinese province of Taiwan, as well as its status as a treaty power in China with industrial rights by 1895, provided another commercial conduit that intensified the complex workings of business, cultural and political interactions. Western imperialism helped to spawn Asian nationalism, and Japanese nationalism led to dreams of an Asian empire. The success and failure of department stores in Asia was dependent on more than national economic growth.

In China, their advent coincided with a rapid expansion of Chinese capitalism in response to external factors, specifically the world economic situation before and after the Great War, creating a 'golden age' (*huangjin shiqi*) of national industrialization between 1910 and 1920. This era of economic opportunity for Chinese entrepreneurs, when the foreign powers were less occupied with their colonial footholds in Asia, was also the era of political revolution. The goals of the Republican revolution in China were linked: to rid China of imperialism so blatantly symbolized by the treaty ports, and to make China into a strong and modern nation-state (Bergère 1989:64–98).

As John D. Young points out in the first chapter in this volume, Sun Yatsen, father of the Chinese revolution, not only invested in the Wing On Company but also promoted the idea of the department store (*baihuo gongsi*, literally the 'one hundred goods' company) as one way to realize his modernization program for China. The use of this term to denote the department store is significant in this context. Although the term 'baihuo', meaning numerous kinds of goods, dates back almost three thousand years to the classical Zhou dynasty, and the term 'gongsi', meaning a company with shared capital, dates back to the mid-Qing, the evolution of the concept is veiled in mystery, only coming into common usage in both China and Japan after the First

World War. The first shop actually using the term in its name following Japanese usage (hyakkaten) was the Fumei Baihuo Shangdian in Shanghai in 1921 (Shanghai baihuo gongsi et al. 1988:27). The term *'baihuo shangdian'* first appeared in a 'Daily Encyclopedia' (*Riyong baike quanshu*) published in Shanghai in 1923. The description is of some interest since it conveys the somewhat ambivalent attitude towards this new form of retailing, particularly in relationship with traditional shops (*dian*) dealing in daily goods:

> Those businesses engaged in large-scale retailing of daily articles are known as baihuo shangdian. The stores are divided into departments headed by supervisors (*zhuren*). All the daily articles are drawn together in one place which greatly facilitates the shopping of the customers. Business of this kind is highly profitable, but the surrounding retail shops are always substantially affected.
>
> (Chen 1923:1)[6]

In a series of short items published in the newspaper *Huazi ribao* in 1907, extolling Sincere's new style of retailing and management, it was never referred to as a 'baihuo gongsi' or department store, though the term in English, 'universal provider' was blazoned across the outside of the building. Its usage became important not only to distinguish these modern enterprises from older stores that sold well-known goods crafted in Southern China (*guanghuo*), but also for them to distance themselves as purveyors of foreign goods (*yanghuo*) in increasingly nationalistic times. It was a singularly Chinese adaptation, the use of a classical term 'baihuo' culturally significant but politically neutral, and the term 'gongsi' representing modern business organization (Shanghai baihuo gongsi et al. 1988:27).

As John D. Young argues, to Sun Yatsen, the 'free flow' of the 'one hundred goods' would take not only railroads, new harbors and industrialization linking newly built or redeveloped and modernized cities, but would also embrace and transform rural China. It would entail a thorough re-evaluation of the merchant class, away from the traditional view that stereotyped them as parasitic and unproductive, to one that gave them due recognition as prime movers in economic development, the success of the department store in fomenting a commercial revolution being a case in point. National Reconstruction (*guojia jianshe*) might be based on ideas of science and democracy originating in the west, but like the department store, to Sun they embodied 'universal' principles.

Early Chinese Department Stores

If many of Sun Yatsen's ideas can be traced to his formative years as a native of Xiangshan (Zhongshan) and his sojourn overseas where he was directly exposed to modern western influences, the merchants and entrepreneurs who developed the department store in Asia shared a similar journey. As Yen Ching-hwang demonstrates in his chapter on the Wing On Company, in China, Southeast Asia, and Australia, these businesses drew upon the commercial intelligence and expertise of well-established overseas Chinese trading networks, as well as on their capital. Wing On and the other three great stores of Shanghai, for example, were direct products of these networks funded by the fortunes made by overseas Chinese entrepreneurs, their sons, and familial and native place connections in the 'southern seas' (Nanyang) (Godley 1981; Yen 1982; see also Wellington K. K. Chan's chapter in this volume).

For Yen, the entrepreneurial spirit of the Guo brothers, as traced through their history, business organization, management styles, diversifications, and risk-taking behavior, should be seen not just in Schumpeterian terms, but as the product of two cultures, Chinese and western, creating a new type of entrepreneurship in modern China – that of the 'overseas Chinese entrepreneur'. No longer the 'marginal men' from overseas, like the department store they founded, they became the *avant-garde* of a modern and innovative force for change.

Wellington Chan discusses both Wing On and Sincere (founded by Ma Yingbiao) in comparative perspective focusing on the role of Chinese cultural values in shaping their entrepreneurship and ability to successfully read and capitalize on a volatile market in politically fragile times. Having tested their fortunes in the Australian state of New South Wales where both the Guos and Ma were suitably impressed by the western business methods and acumen of successful department stores such as Sydney's Anthony Hodern's & Son, they established their first ventures in the British Crown Colony of Hong Kong, and subsequently extended their operations to Guangzhou and Shanghai. Ranking as two of the largest companies in China, adapting western managerial, accounting and selling methods to their own culturally specific needs, introducing foreign products 'hitherto unknown to the Chinese people' as well as local products often produced in their numerous factories in Hong Kong, Guangzhou and Shanghai, they evinced a cosmopolitanism remarkable in their historical context.

Although primarily established as 'universal providers', they expanded their field of operations into hotels, the entertainment business, real estate, insurance, banking and manufacturing, providing goods and services 'the demand for which is even now immense and capable of infinite increase as time and good government bring peace and prosperity to China' (Xianshi gongsi 1924[?]:4). Cultivating good relations with the revolutionary government in Guangzhou by subsidizing public undertakings like schools, Sincere and Wing On continued to rely on their overseas networks for capital to fund their expansions, since financial institutions in Guangzhou never assisted them in their business undertakings. And until 'good government' appeared, Sincere's banking system provided security for remittances sent to and from any part of the interior.

The directors of Sincere, heartened by the initial success of the Hong Kong store opened in 1900, and hoping to play 'an important part in the uplift of the Chinese, both commercially and socially', established their first mainland emporium, rising five storeys on the Bund in the revolutionary capital of Guangzhou in the first year of the Republic of China (1912), followed by a Shanghai branch in 1917 (Xianshi gongsi 1924[?]:4). Wing On, having a larger capitalization than Sincere, soon followed, opening its Hong Kong store in 1907, to gratifyingly immediate success, then opening its main store in Shanghai in 1918. But the revolution brought disruption to Sincere's and Wing On's business, and forced changes in management and commodities. The patriotic May Fourth Movement of 1919, targeting imperialism as obstructing China's national and economic sovereignty, resulted in boycotts against the importation of foreign goods (western and Japanese), substantial quantities of which were on sale in Sincere's and Wing On's stores. Both stores were forced to close in Shanghai for a part of June, and their employees organized against the management. Sincere's Guangzhou store was destroyed by fire in 1921 and the continual political disturbances in that year forced the closure of both the Guangzhou and Nanning branches.[7]

Both emporiums faced fierce opposition from increasingly organized and politicized workers and students. In response to the May Thirtieth Incident in Shanghai in 1925, patriotic strikes and boycotts lasting for twenty-five days were spearheaded by workers and students demanding social justice, better working conditions and an end to foreign imperialism, specifically British interests in China. In the British colony of Hong Kong, the seamen's strike lasted an entire year, disrupting business and eliciting a promise from the companies to stop importing British goods (Motz 1972; Clifford 1979). The Second World War brought an end to foreign imperialism, but the victory of the

Communist Party over the nationalists, and the establishment of the People's Republic of China in 1949, brought the end of capitalism. Wing On's and Sincere's businesses in the mainland were nationalized and the companies retreated to their original base in Hong Kong to rebuild their enterprises.

Less well known, but an equally important influence on these enterprises, was the experience gained by their compatriots (the Xiangshanese as Yen Ching-hwang dubs them) who established and operated small Chinese department stores in Sydney and rural areas of New South Wales. As Janis Wilton points out in her chapter on 'Chinese Stores in Rural Australia', the interconnectedness of the Chinese-Australian networks, maintained through business partnerships, investments, savings, employment, visits, and marriages, sustained Australian 'off-shoots' or 'cousins' of the larger emporiums in Hong Kong and China.

If these more modest ventures in Australia share common characteristics with their compatriots' more substantial undertakings in Asia, Wilton explores the extent to which these stores were shaped by a distinctively Australian environment, where they faced a set of challenges different from those faced by Asian department stores in China. If, on the one hand, traditional practices and customs, and, on the other hand, a growing nationalism aiming to detach the notion of 'westernization' from 'modernization' tested western-inspired business models and the sale of western-made products in China, the problem of introducing and gaining acceptance of Chinese practices in a western context challenged their 'cousins' in Australia.

Selling Chinese Goods

Looked at another way, if Wing On and Sincere were partly founded to introduce and then tap the potential for foreign goods in China and Hong Kong, as well as significant overseas communities in Singapore and Malaysia, the China Products Co., Ltd., established in Hong Kong in 1938, was to tap the same market, the foreign expatriate communities, as well as increasing numbers of tourists, for Chinese made products.

Originally leasing a two storey building on Des Voeux Road Central, not far from Wing On's flagship store, China Products Co. did a flourishing business with branches established in Kowloon in 1939, and in the Portuguese colony of Macau in 1940. The Japanese invasion and occupation of Hong Kong during the Pacific war disrupted their local business and supply of goods from the mainland. Unlike Lane Crawford's store in Central that became Matsuzakaya, the China Products Co. remained intact (Hahn 1987:411). But the sacking of their main stores by mobs, as well as the requisitioning of their Wanchai warehouse by the Japanese army, temporarily closed down their operations. After 'making many representations to the quarters concerned', the main store reopened in 1942, and struggled on with a reduced staff of 60, opening for only five hours of business each day.

It was only after the founding of the People's Republic of China and the 'constant development of socialist construction of our country', proclaimed the company, that their business expanded, though British recognition of the new communist regime in China, and Hong Kong's liberal trade policies, no doubt smoothed the course of commerce.

Any tourist visiting Hong Kong today probably visits this self-proclaimed 'Shopping Mecca', now housed in three major locations selling products of mainland origin alongside products made in Hong Kong, Taiwan, Japan and other countries. From the 1980s onwards, the company has branched out from the retail business and now includes a department promoting wholesale trade of Chinese-made shoes to the world market, an Overseas Trading Department handling mail orders and entrepôt trade, as well as a service, pioneered by Wing On and Sincere in their remittance business in the 1920s and 1930s, for the purchase and payment of electronic goods in Hong Kong for collection in the mainland (*Zhongguo guohuo youxian gongsi jianjie* 1988:28–31).

The history of the China Products Co. and its competitive struggle with Sincere and Wing On, especially during the radical years of the Great Proletarian Cultural Revolution in China (1966–69) that inspired the riots of 1967 in Hong Kong, has yet to be studied. If Hong Kong's *hoi polloi* (the majority of whom were refugees fleeing the mainland between October 1949 and May 1950 – an estimated 700,000 people) were shooed away from the likes of Lane Crawford by imposing Sikh doormen, or intimidated by the bourgeois upwardly-mobile ambiance of Wing On and Sincere, they were just as afraid to patronize the China Products Co. for fear, as local rumor had it, of being labeled communist sympathizers during those troubled years. National politics and the department store shared common ground, the reciprocity of relationships historically complex enough to warrant the considerable attention of researchers as evidenced in this volume.

What then is the socialist department store? With the establishment of the PRC in 1949, the systematic elimination of private property, and the move towards 'productive' rather than 'consumer' society and economy, the department store did not wither away contrary to expectations, but was transformed by the state (Solinger 1984:41–2) (*Figure 3*). Guo Hongchi and Liu Fei in their chapter on Beijing's Wangfujing Department Store give us insight into its identity. The politics of commercialism in a socialist state are revealed in their discussion of the problems of making a profit, gaining access to state controlled resources, and the imperatives of up-grading marketing and management in line with international (and therefore capitalist) standards. So too, are the old nagging problems of customer service standards (one of the innovations of Sincere and Wing On), partly related to staff training – instilling the Wangfujing 'blazing spirit' in their employees – in addition to the linked problem of staff incentives.

The history of Beijing's Wangfujing Department Store parallels studies detailing the shift from state owned and managed enterprises to state owned but enterprise managed entities since the change in national economic policy in 1978, allowing for limited but encouraging experimentation in market economies. Profit as incentive, or the control of profit at the enterprise level, in some regards could be viewed as a 'back to the future' for the Chinese department store. Whether this socialist department store with Chinese characteristics will lead to a

Figure I.3 Satirical commentary in China on the problems faced by consumers under socialism in the 1950s. (*People's Tribune* 1956 no. 23 (December).)

second commercial revolution is a moot point, but clearly it heralds changes to come, reflecting social desires and the rising expectations and demands for better standards that have marked the historical development of Asian department stores.[8]

Retailing in Japan

Japan may have lost the war, so goes the cliché, but won the battle, at least where its postwar economic recrudescence is concerned. The economic and civil victory of the Japanese in creating a dynamic industrial, then post-industrial economy and a strong constitutional and highly urbanized state has left the western world gasping and the rest of Asia envious and cautious. Historians and other scholars are familiar with the complex causes of its modern development. It is a picture within which the evolution and transformation of the Japanese department store constitutes more than just a few brush strokes – for they were more than just by-products of urbanization, modernization, westernization and material affluence. They were, in turn, interpreters and shapers of cultural change for a profit, and were uniquely positioned for that role because of their history since the nineteenth century of translating what was western or modern to a society reaching for acceptance, then leadership beyond the confines of their island nation.

Brian Moeran in his contribution to this volume on the birth of the Japanese department store provides a historically relevant analysis, away from the traditional stereotype that depicts the Japanese as a nation of imitators. The concept of the department store may have been a foreign importation, but it was never a question of unreflective copying, involving as it did selectivity and adaptation to suit Japanese needs. Moeran shows how and why Japanese department stores, particularly Mitsukoshi, became 'emblems of modernization', tracing their development from its prototype in the *kankōba* stores or bazaars to its links with innovations in industry and technology transforming Japanese life, like the railways, creating a national market and a revolution in marketing. The department store grew up with and 'imaged' the embourgeoisement of Japanese urban life.

Encouraging an interest in new commodities and their consumption went beyond the novel display of goods within the new multi-storeyed and glass-windowed stores built to house them. The practice of reaching new clienteles and keeping them as regular customers was pioneered by Japanese entrepreneurs, like Takahashi of Mitsukoshi, by creating new fashions, introduced at regular intervals, like the great fashion emporiums of Paris. Starting out by designing and dying *kimono* to suit different seasons and social contexts, Takahashi popularized the Mitsukoshi brand, as Moeran points out, 'by the clever marketing strategy of issuing local Shinbashi *geisha* with Mitsukoshi-made kimono . . . and then ensuring that they wore them when dancing at parties they attended'. This advertising strategy was quickly imitated by Mitsukoshi's competitors and matured into an entire spectrum of sales campaigns, advertising in the mass media, and public relations ploys targeting their respective clienteles that had patronized them in their pre-modern forms as drapery and dry goods stores. After the great Kantō earthquake in 1923, the department stores increasingly appealed to and cultivated the lower-middle class customers that formed the bulk of the new urban masses. The department stores, like their counterparts in the west and China, provided entertainment – restaurants, roof gardens, and in Kyōto's Daimaru store even a roof-top skating rink, and 'enlightenment' through arts and crafts, educational exhibitions, and musical concerts that went beyond their commercial function, contributing to the panoply and ambiance of urban life.

As mentioned earlier in this introduction, the railway and the department store formed natural links in the chain of industrialization, a reciprocity of mutually reinforcing relationships allowing the 'free flow' of the 'one hundred goods', stimulating the mass productions of the factory, and their consumption, mediated by the department store. In some regards, as Moeran points out, department stores like Mitsukoshi abetted Japan's entry into the modern era through consumption. Yet, the question of cultural identity, variously addressed by the contributors to this volume, is an important one. In Japan, the department stores were places where the 'domestication' of foreign things, or the creation of what Moeran calls a 'hybrid cultural creole form', took place. As Morris-Suzuki (1995:4–5) argues, in the Japanese context, 'imitation' and 'invention' are not 'radically opposed alternatives' but are in reality 'two ends of a spectrum along which outside inspiration and innate creativity are combined in many complex ways'.

As for the postwar period, Ueno Chizuko examines the new structures produced by Japanese department stores. Because of their size and showplaces before the war, they were able to bring in material goods during a time of scarcity after the Second World War, and were well positioned to expand their operations after the occupation forces lifted commodity controls in 1950. In the ensuing years of rapid economic growth there were enormous profits to be made selling 'modernization', now called 'internationalization' by government-led programmes to rebuild Japan. As Ueno demonstrates in her chapter, the mass society and mass consumption characterizing this period produced the structure and functioning of the new department store, which in turn struggled to shape and stay ahead of a fast-changing market. Ueno examines the Seibu Saison Group and the Seibu Department Store to focus on trends emerging in postwar Japanese consumerism, specifically what she calls the 'breakdown' of Japan's mass market in the 1970s and 80s, coinciding with a strong economy and experimental marketing strategies using mass media to capture special markets aimed at the new urban consumers (and commuters) in the Tōkyō-Kantō metropolis.

Internal re-organization and new marketing strategies targeting the newly affluent youth born at the beginning of the economic boom were one part of the transformation of the department store, but image-making through the mass media aimed at winning the cut-throat competition between the more conservative department stores and the new super-discount stores and supermarkets in the 1960s influenced the situation. The decline of the department store was heralded as imminent. Seibu, confronting its own 'identity crisis', faced this challenge by a process of devolution, moving away from the older established concept of 'one hundred goods' under one roof, drawing customers in for services, entertainment and special events, as well as selling commodities. By diversifying the functions of the department store, by creating dozens of new specialized business ventures, this strategy reduced Seibu Department Store's turnover to only one-third of the total turnover of the Seibu Saison Group. More importantly however, the Seibu Saison Group was able to move away from just selling goods to other activities attached to notions of value (as when they opened a museum) and ephemeral concepts of lifestyles to overtake economy-oriented organizations, and successfully compete in what Ueno calls 'the amoebae-like changes in the Japanese market'. Adding up the various businesses of the Seibu Saison Group, it could be viewed therefore as recreating the 'one hundred goods' under one corporate umbrella, an identity flexible enough for survival in a perplexing market, thus giving us insight into the very nature of modern Japanese capitalism.

Millie Creighton brings us back to the question of modern identity and Japanese department stores in the postwar period by examining Seibu's commercial foray into the realm of philosophical issues that they perceive as informing their customers' lives.[9] As Creighton and other contributors point out, the role of the department store in upholding social values by performing educational and 'enlightening' services was historically well-developed since the emergence of these stores in the late Meiji period. The affluence of Japan in recent times, or, from a different perspective, the saturation of the consumer market, led Seibu's Chairman in the 1980s to redefine the goals of the department store in line with his view of consumers' desire to go beyond material goods, in search of a valuable and meaningful life. To Tsutsumi Seiji, helping consumers to 'transcend' material values (though not necessarily material goods) and to seek 'psychological self-fulfillment' was the new goal of the retail industry.

Creighton traces this process through a fascinating look at the different branches of Seibu, its 'theme stores' espousing different aspects of the concept of a 'Life Worthy of Human Beings' aimed at a fast-aging population with concerns for health and security, along with the need to provide educational opportunities for life-long education. The latter concern resulted in Seibu annexing to its main store a community college with over 400 course offerings. The Yūrakuchō Seibu, located in the old commercial district of the Ginza in Tōkyō, opened in 1985, not as a department store per se, but as an 'information centre' providing information on services not necessarily provided by the Seibu Saison Group. They also established the first 'Foreign Customer Liaison Office' to assist non-Japanese in navigating the complex world of Japanese commerce, as well as providing information services not related to sales.

In the same year, Seibu opened its Tsukuba store, an area planned as a national research community, coinciding with the International Science Exposition, Expo '85, an event described as heralding Japan's emergence as a leading scientific innovator no longer dependent on western scientific advances. Dedicated to service-oriented technology, the store remained after the Expo ended, to deliver the message to its major customers, mainly rural farm families, that technological advances did not threaten, but rather enhanced their traditional lifestyles. From lifestyles to 'the meaning of life', the Seibu Seed Department Store, opened in 1986, offered consumerism as a creative process, like its biological metaphor, providing its customers with a medium for personal growth. These are examples of ways in which, instead of simply selling goods, Japanese department stores have concentrated on becoming 'life style' stores by offering their customers a comprehensive aesthetic experience. Japanese department stores, like the reality of contemporary Japan, continually promise that 'something more'.

From Japan to China via Hong Kong

The department store as mediator between culture and consumption has its Asian face. The historical relationship between politics and economics in Asia, particularly between China and Japan since the first Sino-Japanese War (1894–5), has continued to influence this process of mediation. The expansion of the innovative Japanese department stores in Asia since the Second World War buries some political considerations, but not all. We come full circle with the last chapters in this volume that examine the strategies, structure, process and impact by which Japanese retailers entered the Hong Kong and China markets.

Lonny Carlile traces the roots of internationalization of Japanese retailing by examining the early experiences of these large enterprises overseas. This includes Seibu's Los Angeles venture, deemed a failure and underscoring the view that Japanese retailers were not competitive in the mature mass markets of advanced industrialized nations, and Daimaru's Hong Kong venture that catered to a growing Japanese expatriate community and Japanese tourist clientele (the same goods were cheaper in Hong Kong than in Japan), and procured mainland Chinese goods for sale back home in Japan. But it was not until the 1980s, when the appreciation of the yen made labor and real estate costs attractive in Southeast Asia, and when new markets were opened to foreign investments, at the same time as Japanese domestic consumer demand saw a relative stagnation, that the overseas 'colonization' by Japan's retail industry took off.

In Taiwan (a former colony of Japan from 1895–1945), for example, Japanese department stores are now doing booming business. Sogō opened its first retail store in Taibei in 1987, and by 1994 claimed 20 percent of all department store sales in Taiwan's largest city. Of the twenty large stores in the city, five are Japanese joint ventures, and locally owned stores have revamped their image to copy their marketing style (Underwood 1995).

Carlile focuses on the Yaohan Group because of the centrality of its overseas strategies and its decision to enter the China market, a market undergoing liberalization but still importantly guided by national and nationalistic economic goals. Attuning its corporate strategy to the development strategy of the host government, lessons learned in its ventures in Brazil and Singapore, and by cultivating personal connections or '*guanxi*' with Chinese economic elites in Hong Kong and China, as Carlile points out, the 'Sinicization' of Yaohan was a 'de-Japanization' of the enterprise – another example of cultural hybridization that uniquely positioned Yaohan in the China market.

Wong Heung Wah, in his anthropological study 'From Japanese Supermarket to Hong Kong Department Store', aptly points out that the success of Yaohan was closely tied to the attitudes of Hong Kong Chinese towards the Japanese occupation of Hong Kong and their activities in China during the Second World War which shaped local responses to this Japanese 'department store'.[10] In turn, the venture's foray into the China market was also conditioned on political attitudes expressed by the company's owner.

Matzusakaya, Mitsukoshi, Sogō, and Daimaru, for example, all have solid, impressive imprimaturs in Hong Kong located substantially in Causeway Bay, with the exception of Seibu, a more recent arrival in Hong Kong, and Yaohan located in the new towns. The Chinese department stores, such as Wing On, Sincere, and China Products Co., continue to retain their original sites in the Central district, though they also have other locations around Hong Kong. These large emporiums co-exist in Hong Kong's 'little Japan' with numerous small retail outlets selling Japanese goods scattered throughout Causeway Bay's narrow side-streets. Japanese 'image-making', visible on the backs of Hong Kong's youth, in the considerable market for Japanese pop music, movies (one Japanese movie ran for so long it set a new record, probably due to its theme of a family's unbridled pursuit of money), sushi bars, and karaoke lounges, certainly has great staying power and appeal.

Even the controversy that erupted over the Diaoyu Islands between China and Japan in 1996, appealing as it did to notions of a 'greater' China composed of the PRC, Taiwan, and Hong Kong, resulted in only a few minor incidents of local protest against these Japanese concerns. Cultural shifts are notoriously difficult to document, but Japanese department stores as disseminators of Japanese culture in Hong Kong were seemingly liberated in the popular mind from nationalistic policy.

Wong gives us one explanation. The success of Yaohan in Hong Kong, and the company's later ventures into China, were partly conditioned on the owner's very public renunciation of Japanese aggression during the Second World War. Equally timely, but somewhat frivolous, was his assertion that when China regained sovereignty over Hong Kong on 1 July 1997, ending 155 years of colonial rule, then if the Chinese Government saw fit to nationalize his business he would view it as just compensation for Japan's wartime transgressions.

Another factor in the venture's success besides its business diversification in Hong Kong (similar to the Seibu Saison Group in Japan) was the local perception of the 'supermarket' as a department store. In some measure, this was a product of its location away from the cluster of Japanese department stores selling up-market goods in Causeway Bay and other tourist areas, to the new towns, mostly consisting of public housing built for Hong Kong's working classes. Reflecting local cultural perceptions and habits of consumerism, unlike the situation in Japan, the 'one-stop shopping' of the 'supermarket' and its spacious ambiance made it recognizable as a department store in Hong Kong, in distinction to the cramped supermarkets that essentially sell foodstuffs. Local cultural perceptions were also shaped by the fact that in Hong Kong, department stores traditionally sold provisions, a feature still retained by the China Products Co.[11]

Conclusion

Asian department stores, though founded on the same principles as their western predecessors as 'universal providers', diverge from that model in important ways. The introduction of western business techniques and western products, arising as they did from the particular economic and social development of the west, made the transplantation of the department store in Asia culturally specific. The history of the political and economic relations of the west in Asia was problematical, raising questions of cultural identity even as Asians embraced what they perceived to be the hallmarks of modernity. Chinese and Japanese entrepreneurs established department stores to make a profit by offering people new and exciting alternatives to traditional ways of providing goods. Judging by the continued commercial success of Wing On, its recent expansion on the mainland in partnership with Japan's giant Seiyū Group, rising expectations and slowly increasing affluence, there are many Chinese urbanites eager to participate in this ongoing commercial revolution. The same could be said of Japan, of Mitsukoshi, or Shirokiya in leading the Meiji commercial transformation early in this century. Revolutionaries and modernizers like Sun Yatsen could even promote the idea of the department store as one part of the overall package of national reconstruction by equating modernization not with 'westernization' but with universal principles, while his revolutionary cohorts could close down these department stores at least temporarily in the name of patriotism. The department store was politicized no matter the context. Although not on the same scale as Wing On or Sincere, their Chinese 'cousins' in Australia suffered similar problems of cultural specificity in reverse, having to overcome Australian resistance to perceived Chinese practices.

The China Products Co., founded in the British colony of Hong Kong in direct response to the challenge of the west in Asia, responded by selling at first exclusively Chinese made products to compatriots and foreigners alike, though marketed and managed according to the models pioneered by Wing On and Sincere. After 'liberation' of the mainland in 1949, and the elimination of capitalism and 'capitalist-roaders', the department store was transformed into a state-run socialist institution of the new China. Almost thirty years of anti-development economic policies brought recognition of their failure to promote modernization. In 1978, the new reforms heralded a commitment to 'open up to the outside world'. For Beijing's Wangfujing Department Store this meant a competitive market and profit-oriented approach to retailing that led back to the problem of identity and the question of what customers want, rather than just what they are perceived to need.

In Japan, both before and after the Second World War, department stores reacted to modernization both as 'imitators' and 'innovators', creating a new hybrid culture that captured the popular imagination and aspirations by re-packaging and re-inventing Japanese identity, at the same time scrambling to keep ahead of their competition from large discount stores and supermarkets that took an ever-increasing share of a fast-changing market born out of postwar economic and industrial strength.

If the west in Asia created a crisis of identity, the Japanese attempt to build a Greater East Asian Co-Prosperity Sphere in the first half of the twentieth century left it own legacy. The expansion and investment of Japanese business in the postwar era, viewed through the prism of department store ventures in Hong Kong or in China, still had to address the concerns of former victims of Japanese expansionism. Although Hong Kong, Taiwan and, to a limited extent, China have openly embraced the internationalization of Japanese culture, con-sidering the popularity and profit of their commodities purveyed in their department store transplants, goodwill can be bought with a judicious use of humble pie. When, not if, the Japanese government makes a fulsome and formal apology and restitution to its Asian neighbors for its wartime activities, this will no doubt facilitate the course of commercial intercourse. In the meantime, as we have seen, one Japanese entrepreneur has beat the competition.

The authors of the chapters presented in this volume on Asian department stores have opened up a field of inquiry of abiding interest across disciplines of historical and current import. One of the themes explored is the tension between traditional practices and the adoption of new techniques of retailing (and thereby consumption) derived from the west within a colonial or semi-colonial setting. In both Japan and China the imperatives of nationalism, modernization, and the debates over cultural identity in the first half of the twentieth century were reflected in the commercial strategies, the successes and failures of these large businesses. The continued role of the department store as a viable concern under communism in China, now transformed as the 'state department store' is examined. Finally, and more recently, the spread of Japanese department stores throughout the entire region provides important insights into the global economy in what has been styled the 'Pacific century'.

These chapters furthermore contribute to current re-evaluations of theoretical assumptions of economic organization and the nature of Asian capitalism and economic institutions that do not fully take into account the Asian environment, its history and cultures. We refer here to the seminal works of Brown (1995) and Orru et al. (1997), for example, that propose an 'institutional theory' of economic life derived from Weberian sociology. Although proponents of this view vary considerably in their approaches to explaining organizational functions and structures, overall they recognize the equivalency between social and economic actions, 'the embeddedness of economic activity in institutional settings, institutional logic as a crucial concept, and the necessarily multilevel nature of an institutional argument' (Orru et al. 1997:21). Thus, Asian department stores are not defined by the authors as merely objective artifacts, the outcome of material forces or economic rationality, but as socially and historically constructed organizations that influence, and in turn are influenced by, the multiple and interlocking networks into which they fit.

Tracing the development and functioning of Chinese owned and managed department stores, Chan, Yen and Wilton illustrate this premise by emphasizing the role of entrepreneurs and entrepreneurship built upon long established familial and ethnic trading networks throughout South Asia.[12] They stress the importance of cultural values as significant factors in explaining the form and operation of economic activity, whether it is located within the same cultural zone or, as

Wilton shows in her study of the smaller Chinese department stores or 'offshoots' of Wing On and Sincere in Australia, in a strikingly different dominant culture. Similarly, Carlile and Wong in their studies of Yaohan and its expansion into Hong Kong and China, explain its global strategies as conditioned not only by familism but also by the religious beliefs embraced by the Wada family and transformed into the company's ideology.[13] Indeed, the construction of enterprise culture or spirit proved to be a unifying force instrumental in the expansion and continued viability of these enterprises. As Guo and Liu show, 'the blazing spirit' based on the work experiences of one individual in a state-owned company became a commercial model and driving force of the Beijing Wangfujing Department Store, supporting its modernization and transition from socialism to capitalism. In post-war Japan, a well developed capitalist society supported by a variety of civic institutions, as Ueno and Creighton show in their examination of the Seibu Saison Group, the links between enterprise culture and consumption, consumption and productivity, marketing strategies and consumer needs, state attitudes and societal wishes have clearly been 'produced socially and culturally maintained' (Orru et al 1997:20). The department store, as Creighton argues, is not only a product of economic rationality, but a mediator between culture and consumption.

A final point that bears repeating is the pioneering establishment of urban infrastructures supporting the rise of the modern city in China and Japan that both ensured and invigorated commercial activities and civic institutions. The origin of department stores in Japan, as Moeran points out, was inseparable from the development of technologies, from transportation to public health, that underpinned the economic, political and social systems. In China, as Young makes explicit, Sun Yatsen's programme for modernization of the nation, physically and culturally, was dependent on the extension of infrastructure such as railroads throughout the country producing and amplifying new commercial organizations like department stores, which in turn would improve and transform the livelihood of the people – a 'revolution' in living.

Outside a clutch of articles, many written by contributors to this book, and company festschrifts, there is a dearth of analysis and research on the rise of department stores in Asia and their modern transformation. The authors have gone a considerable distance in defining what constitutes Asian department stores. As generators of consumption as well as disseminators of cultural tastes, department stores are critical to our understanding of economic development and expansion, historically, in those non-western states struggling for greater measures of modernization or economic viability, as well as in the present context of rapid and sustained Asian economic growth.

Notes

1 Over 80 per cent of the products sold in Sincere and Wing On were imported, reflecting a Chinese preference for what were viewed as superior goods. The estimated turnover rates for all goods amounted to an astonishing HK$ 3,600,000 for Sincere in 1918 and HK$ 4,550,000 for Wing On in 1919.

2 The remark was made by John Garwood (1853), editor of the *London City Mission Magazine*, describing London as 'a world in itself, and its records embrace a world's history. See also Weber (1899) for the first study that statistically verified this demographic shift.

3 In China, the treaty port city, with one late exception, arose beside the existing city, with a similar environment provided in Japan by the building of foreign quarters in the opened cities, such as the Tsukiji Settlement in Tōkyō. Ishizuka Hiromichi (1981) sees this as an indication that 'Tōkyō's emerging urban structure was then essentially "semi-colonial" in form'. For China, see Murphey (1974).

4 For women and the department store, see McBride (1978), and for a more recent look at women as arbiters of taste, see Silverman (1986).

5 For an insightful discussion of the nature of anti-foreignism in Southern China, see Ho (1991).

6 By 1930, the department store's competitive advantages over small local retailers, particularly their innovations of the 'fixed price' and 'one hundred goods' was critiqued in a Guangzhou newspaper *(Guangzhou minguo ribao* 1930.)

7 The Versailles Peace Treaty conference at the close of the First World War raised Chinese hopes for full recognition by the foreign powers, and abrogation of their treaty rights and privileges gained over the preceding century. Instead, Japan was recognized as a leading power and was given control of the former German concessions in Shandong province. For an overview of the growing labor movement and the strikes and boycotts of this period, see Motz (1972), Chan (1975), and Clifford (1979).

8 For observations of the China market and the future of commercialism since the reforms of 1978, see Keuh (1992). To promote the study of business and commercial enterprises in China, a field neglected during the Maoist years, The Institute of Economics of the Shanghai Academy of Social Sciences (Shanghai shehui kexueyuan) established a Resource Center for Chinese Business History in 1992.

9 In the post-war years of rapid economic growth there were enormous profits to be made selling 'modernization', but also losses that had to be counted. Creighton has argued (in an unpublished paper 'Pre-industrial dreaming in post-industrial Japan: department stores and the commoditization of community traditions') that the department stores took an active role in addressing growing perceptions of cultural loss, of replacing what seemed to be a fading sense of community and village traditions brought about by

these transformative processes. The government may have led society firmly down the road of 'internationalization', but popular culture was consumed by a fascination with Japanese 'traditions' and engrossed by a nostalgia for an idealized pre-industrial past. This created what retailers called the 'retro boom' in the 1980s and 90s, a thirst for neo-nostalgic products and consumer events tied to the rhythm of agricultural and village-based life, even inventing some new traditions in the process.

The 'retro boom' has reached Hong Kong with the opening of Shanghai Tang Department Store, Ltd, stocked with nostalgic products ranging from Chinese female gowns (*qipao*) to Sun Yatsen-style jackets and traditional long gowns (*changpao*) for men from the 'golden age' of Shanghai's past, circa 1920s and 30s. The products, we are assured, are 'made by Chinese', this being emblazoned (in English) on the bright green and orange shopping bags. For an excellent discussion of 'culture' and its meanings, see Morris-Suzuki (1995).

10 Hong Kong fell to Japan on 8 December 1941 and the Japanese military, amongst other activities, ruthlessly reduced the local population principally by sending an estimated 1 million people back to Guangdong province (Endacott 1958).

11 There is little published work on the Japanese department store in Hong Kong, but see Tang (1990), Hung (1991), Wada (1992), and Phillips et al. (1992).

12 This is what Wong (1988:170–1) has described as 'entrepreneurial familism'.

13 Just as this book is going to press, Yaohan Japan has filed for insolvency protection with outstanding debts of HK$10.32 billion attributed to over-expansion. This sparked rumours that Kazuo Wada would resign as chairman of Yaohan Japan and Yaohan International Holdings (YIH), and the Wada family would sell its Hong Kong assets (*South China Morning Post* 1997:9:19).

Part I

Overseas Chinese Entrepreneurs, Department Store Culture, and the State

SUN YATSEN AND THE DEPARTMENT STORE

An Aspect of National Reconstruction

by John D. Young

In a number of letters dated between 1914 and 1917 now preserved in his native home in Cuiheng Village, Zhongshan County, Sun Yatsen, father of the 1911 Revolution, wrote about various matters of family finance to his first wife Lu Muzhen (*Aomen ribao* 1991).[1] Mostly details on domestic issues, Sun discussed amounts of monthly allowances he was sending her (Sun married Song Qingling in Japan on 25 October 1915), their son Sun Ke's loan for building a house, and charity work related to schools and relatives. In a letter dated 16 December 1916, Sun specifically referred to her earlier correspondence concerning the purchase of Wing On Company stocks, and expressed his agreement with her decision. He ended his basically business-oriented letter by referring to his own speedy recovery from a short illness.

The information contained in these short correspondences is too sketchy for any extensive conclusions to be drawn, except perhaps that Sun Yatsen was keen to perform his family duties amidst his political activities. Madame Lu's interest in Wing On Company stocks and Sun Yatsen's concurrence might be a simple business matter, where they both believed that the investment would be a wise one. Or perhaps Wing On stocks were one of the few viable options available at the time.

Personal reasons aside, however, in the light of Sun Yatsen's overall commitment to China's modernization and national reconstruction, this chapter will attempt to show that it would have been out of character for him not to be interested in the Wing On Company, or what it represented to the New China he envisaged.[2] Indeed, other available evidence clearly shows that Sun Yatsen had always been interested in the department store, both as a concept and as a possibility, so much so that he wanted to establish such stores throughout China. To generate wealth and power for China, he wanted to build railways to link up all of China; he wanted department stores set up throughout China for much of the same reasons.

Unhindered Transportation of the 'Hundred Goods' (baihuo)

Sun Yatsen's 1894 petition[3] is one of the most widely cited sources on Sun Yatsen's early thoughts on 'reform' (Ng 1981:168–78; Young 1985:133–45; Chang and Gordon 1991:13–6). In this document, published in the September–October issue of the *Wanguo gongbao* (Review of the Times) (Sun 1894:14703–14715;14787–14793), one general interpretation notes that Sun mentioned the four themes of 'maximum use of human talent, the fullest exploitation of the benefits of land and resources, and the unrestricted flow of commodities' (Schriffin 1970:35), but that 'there was nothing new or revolutionary' (Schriffin 1970:36) about them. In short, this school argues that Sun's ideas were rather similar to the reformist thinking of the times, advanced by men like Feng Gueifen (1809–1874), Dr. He Qi (Ho Kai) (1859–1914), and Zheng Guanying (c.1841–1923) (Schriffin 1970:37–40).

There is no doubt that Sun did share similar ideas on how to solve many of China's problems with his reformist contemporaries, since he would otherwise not have approached Li Hongzhang in the first place. It is even possible that the petition itself went through some stylistic improvements, perhaps even suggested by Zheng Guangying who had close ties with the *Wanguo gongbao* monthly. But if Sun's real intention was to join the ranks of China's Confucian literati, then the question which needs to be asked is: Why did he choose to advocate what was basically a 'wholesale westernization' program for China? Or did he have other motives?

A complete reading of the petition shows, in fact, that Sun was rather uncompromising in his criticisms of 'Chinese' traditions. For example, he argued that citizens of western nations generally did not like to 'waste time', but that people in China 'worshipped ghosts and spirits' and that expenses for bringing back spirits, arranging temple fairs, and burning money for the dead cost millions and drained the entire country. These were indeed 'useless' activities which should be banned by the government (Sun 1894)!

In my view, one of the reasons why Sun's petition is difficult to comprehend is its vocabulary. Although Sun used rather traditional terms, those terms very often needed to be understood in the context of nineteenth-century commercialized Hong Kong and the Pearl River Delta region. Indeed, such a minor point as his medical qualification causes confusion. Schiffrin translated '*kaoshou Yingguo yishi*' as 'passed the English medical examination' (Schriffin 1970:37) whereas another translator suggests that Sun was 'awarded the British MD degree' (Sun 1894).[4] My own preferred translation is: 'was awarded a licentiate in western medicine by examination'. My consideration is two-fold: firstly to take into account the well-known fact that despite Sun's training in western medicine, he was never allowed to practice as a medical doctor in Hong Kong, and secondly to translate Sun's ideas as accurately as possible.

Indeed, when Sun discussed the 'men of talent', he was surely not thinking along traditional lines, certainly not the kind of 'true Confucianists' envisaged by men like Zeng Guofan or Li Hongzhang.[5] On the contrary, it is clear from this petition that Sun not only did not believe in the 'amateur ideal' (Levenson 1968:119–23), but that he was advocating a totally opposite position. China needed experts, officials who had specialized knowledge, who were trained in particular professions. It is therefore not surprising that Sun was critical of the civil service examination; and again it seems odd that Sun would be so openly hostile towards the examination system if what he really wanted was to join the ranks of those who became China's elites precisely because they had succeeded in composing 'eight-legged' essays (Buck 1953:43–44;[6] Schriffin 1970:36).

What Sun meant by 'maximum use of human talent' must be understood in the context of specialization (*zhuan*) a recurring theme which can be found in many of his writings. In this petition, Sun elaborated with plenty of examples, one of the major differences between China and the west being the latter's employment of specialization. For teaching, there were specialized teachers; research-ers had specialized fields; there were specialized learned societies and specialized journals; any individual who had the slightest talent had a 'specialty', and more likely than not, they were also employed in their fields of specialization. Even more importantly, regardless of speciality all specialists were equally rewarded by the state, and they all had equal status in society.

Thus, if China wanted to solve its flooding problems and improve its agricultural production, officials with specialized technical knowledge must be trained and recruited, and special bureaux (*zhuanguan*)[7] established for handling various technological ventures. The reason why floodings of the Ganges in India and the Mississippi in the United

States were eventually harnessed was to a large extent due to the fact that specialists with relevant professions were trained in specialized schools to tackle the required large-scale scientific undertaking. China urgently needed to give high priority to the creation of agricultural schools (Sun 1894:14712–3).

Sun's proposal that China's agriculture must be mechanized, his concerns for the issue of 'land' (both politically and scientifically), and perhaps his so-called peasant background have all been given due emphasis by scholars interested in his ideas about people's livelihood. So much so that there is a tendency for us to neglect Sun's urban background, and his belief in the vital role of trade and commerce in China's modernization efforts.

It is certainly accurate to say that Sun was not alone amongst his contemporaries in the call for improving the status of the merchant class and abolishing traditional discrimination measures against them, but Sun's overall evaluation of the importance of the merchants indicates that he did have first-hand knowledge of China's commercial situation, at least in South China. He went so far as to say that merchants were just as important as peasants and workers, the producers and manufacturers of the 'hundred goods', in that they 'relieve shortage in one area with surplus from another'. To be sure, the lives of merchants were harsh and difficult as they often had to leave their homes to trade for small profits in strange places, sometimes ending up starving. In the west, governments protected their merchants, while in China 'the government exploits them, inflicts losses on them, and restrains and suppresses them'. Sun might have had a somewhat negative view of capitalism and capitalists in the 1920s, a point much emphasized by Chinese mainland scholars,[8] but in the 1890s, Sun was asking the question, 'How can those intent on strengthening the nation not begin by protecting our merchants immediately?'

Furthermore, when western nations 'protected' their merchants, special taxation measures were also taken into consideration. After import taxes had been imposed, goods were subject to no further taxes within the country, and were shipped without any hindrance. In China, customs stations posted in various provinces levied abusive taxes, and petty officials openly collected bribes. A country like America, Sun pointed out, enjoyed tremendous wealth and 'the credit belongs to the merchants who engage in trade and shipping'; once again, in China, both natural resources and man-made goods were wasted.

Thus what Sun meant by the 'free flow' of commodities basically involved a number of measures centred around China's due recognition of the status of the merchant class. Merchants should not only be acknowledged as people of talent who had special skills, but their success should be accepted as vital for a nation to acquire wealth and power. Low taxation and railways were essential in that they would enable the merchants to develop trade and commerce throughout China, and throughout the world. Sun proposed that railroads must first be built in rich, prosperous regions like 'Guangzhou, Xianggang [Hong Kong], Suzhou, Shanghai, Tianjin, and Dingzhou' so that quick profits could be realized. Here, it is clear that Sun's interest in building railroads had its specific purpose: to assist in the unrestricted transportation of commodities. And the final result would be that China would become rich. 'Taking into consideration China's population and financial resources, if China follows in the footsteps of the west, adopts news methods', Sun predicted, 'China will catch up and surpass Europe in twenty years' time' (Sun 1894:14789).

Whilst some studies have unnecessarily exaggerated Sun's obsession with the importance of railroads, another extreme approach has been to explain Sun's optimism in terms of his naïvety. Sun's 1894 Petition – his belief in the urgency of 'unrestricted' transportation of the 'hundred goods' – demonstrates Sun's commitment to modernization as a panacea. The proper formula, and the proper dosage, had worked in the west and would work in China. In Sun's view, all problems were solvable because human beings in the late nineteenth-century world had unlocked the secrets of the universe; in other words, there was every reason to be optimistic since nothing could stand in the way of human progress. Just identify the difficulty, apply the correct prescription (one was always available), and cure the ailment.[9] And one of those universal cures was the establishment of department stores in China.

Foreign Investments and Department Stores

It would surely be erroneous to suggest that somehow Sun Yatsen had something to do with the founding of China's two best-known department stores, Sincere in 1900 and Wing On in 1907. But something can be said about the fact that both companies started out in Hong Kong, the place which generated many of Sun's ideas for his 1894 Petition. Both companies, the histories of which have been ably studied by Yen (1995) and Chan (1982, 1993; see also Shanghai jindai baihuo gongsi et al. 1988), also prospered in Shanghai, where Sun spent much time writing on China's industrial-financial needs after 1911.

Even more interesting is the fact that the founders of both department stores also came from the same district as Sun Yatsen, Xiangshan County, now known as Zhongshan County.

At around the time that Sun Yatsen was trying to persuade Li Hongzhang to join his cause, Guo Quan, one of the founders of Wing On, went to stay in Hawaii for three years, learning English and dabbling in small-scale businesses, before returning to China in 1897. Two years and two children later, Guo left for Australia, where he first engaged in the retail business and learned first-hand about department stores (see the chapter by Yen in this book for a detailed account of the business history of the Guo brothers). Sun Yatsen arrived in Hawaii in January 1896, after the failure of his first revolutionary 'uprising' in Guangdong. There, not only did he persuade his elder brother Sun Mei to look after his family and their mother, but also managed to enlist financial commitments from Sun Mei (who had sent Sun back to Hong Kong in 1884 because of his interest in becoming a Christian). At the time, the elder Sun owned a 'general store' and other properties, and if he had not had a revolutionary for a brother, or if he had met Guo Quan, he might also have succeeded as an overseas entrepreneur. On the other hand, if Sun Yatsen had not had a brother who supported him and shouldered his family responsibilities (Sun had three children by now, all living in Hawaii with their mother), his revolutionary career might have ended before he went to London and was kidnapped.[10]

But despite his brother's personal sacrifices, Sun seldom seemed successful in raising enough money to finance his military plans, and other related revolutionary activities. Commenting on some of Sun's letters now preserved at the Hoover Institution at Stanford University, historian J. Y. Wong suggests that 'they are full of grammatical errors' (Wong 1986:175–6).[11] The letters were of such a personal nature, some written in code language, that I wonder if Sun cared much about his English grammar. Interestingly, though, some of the letters addressed to him by his American and English friends also contained 'grammatical' inaccuracies. What is important about all these correspondences, which surely need to be further analyzed, is what they reveal about Sun's priorities, his personal thoughts, his assessment of China (plenty of comments on Yuan Shikai, for instance), and his single-mindedness in pursuing his goals.[12]

At any rate, from the handwriting of the letters themselves, it is clear that Sun relied on his English secretaries rather heavily; some letters were typed, but Sun's own signature was always distinctive, although those sent from Japan (between 1905 and 1910) were signed 'Chung Shan' while usually he simply put down 'Y.S. Sun' or 'Sun Yat Sen'. In one letter, he explained his tardiness in replying by saying that his English secretary, Song Ailing, had just gotten married!

These letters show that he was interested in a variety of issues ranging from railways to aviation warfare to helping his friend Homer Lea secure a translator for his book, *The Day of the Saxon*. But the letters certainly indicate that Sun's main preoccupation was with raising money. In a letter dated 4 September 1910 to Charles B. Boothe, an American businessman who he appointed 'sole foreign financial agent' for the so-called 'Federal Association of China', Sun wrote that,

> If you think that our project of raising the funds will be surely succeeded and final settlement is only a question of time, I should like you would advance me a sum of $50,000 American dollars from your own account for the preparatory work . . . If you would advance this sum, when the project is succeeded, you may have twice of it back as interest for the risk you run.

Boothe's original job, according to the appointment letter in which Sun called himself President (and, in Chinese, Zongli of the Tongmenghui) and signed in both English and Chinese, was to negotiate loans and receive monies. In a letter to Homer Lea dated 7 November 1910 and sent from Penang, Sun stated that,

> Of course I will not wait if any opportunity turn up, but it is very difficult to push matter forward without the necessary means. Since I been here I have improved the condition of the preparatory work in many ways. And now we can make a sure success with far less money than we first proposed. I think even a tenth of our original sum would be enough. Can you get that any way quick? I am going try to raise some money here.

Sun's equally ambitious efforts to raise money from Chinese communities all over the world are well-known and need not be repeated here.

Of course, Sun's interest in money had more to do with his modernization plans than with personal considerations; money seems to have been a practical dimension of his optimism. His overwhelming attention to raising funds for his ultimate goals probably also conditioned his political concerns which he sometimes viewed as pragmatic considerations, such as his belief in the importance of

foreign investments in China's industrial and infrastructural development. In a letter dated 27 June 1912 to Homer Lea's wife, besides the
usual family news (Sun Ke was going to study at the University of
California, Berkeley), Sun announced that,

> I have tried to eschew politics as much as possible, I intend to
> devote all my energies to develop the natural resources of this
> country, and particularly to the construction of railways. I hope to
> succeed.

In another letter dated 13 October 1912 from Shanghai to 'General'
Homer Lea, a title conferred by Sun before the 1911 Revolution, Sun
told Lea that,

> some of the Shansi bankers have approached me to see whether it
> would be possible to start an industrial bank. It is hoped that they
> would raise five million dollars for the purpose. I am now
> exchanging letters with General Yen of Shansi on the matter.

Indeed, for the realization of his nationalistic goals, Sun was prepared
to work with anyone. Towards the last days of his life he might have
become rather outspoken in his anti-imperialist and anti-colonial stand,
but before that he was a staunch advocate of Chinese and foreign joint-
ventures and international economic co-operation. In his *Memoirs of a
Chinese Revolutionary*, sub-titled *A programme of national reconstruction for China* (Sun 1918),[13] he summed up his views on why China
must have the support of foreign capital:

> Not so very long ago I presented to all the Governments my work
> on 'a plan for the development of Chinese industry through the
> medium of international co-operation'. I met with great
> sympathy from the American Government, and I trust that the
> other Governments also will follow its example in their opinion
> of my work. Chinese aspirations can be realised only when we
> understand that, to regenerate the State and to save the country
> from destruction at this critical moment, we must welcome the
> influx of large-scale foreign capital on the largest possible scale,
> and also must consider the question of attracting foreign
> scientific forces and highly-trained experts to work in our
> country and train us. Then in the course of the next ten years we
> shall create our own powerful large-scale industry and shall
> accumulate technical and scientific knowledge.
>
> (Sun 1918:173–4)

He went on to predict that,

> After these ten years it will be possible gradually to pay off the foreign loans and acquire complete independence in our work, possessing a complete equipment of the necessary knowledge. Then our national culture can be made literally the common property of all the Chinese. This will render possible the awakening of the slumbering forces and possibilities of China.
>
> (Sun 1918:174)

Sun believed that the Chinese people would be supportive of China's open door. He elaborated, saying that,

> The Chinese people will welcome the opening-up of the riches of our country, providing China is protected against the corrupting influence of the mandarins and will have a guarantee of normal intercourse with foreign states.
>
> (Sun 1918:179)

At the same time, in order to ensure that the foreign nations of Europe and America would not be too concerned with 'undesirable competition', Sun reiterated his plan for 'the organization of a new market in China, sufficiently extensive both to develop China's own productive forces and to absorb the industrial capacity of the foreign Powers'. This ten-point programme covered the development of railways, construction of new canals, organization of commercial harbours, and so forth. Referring to the building of modern cities, Sun (1918:180–1) noted that those cities must have 'social conveniences of all kinds, near all railway centres, principal stations, and harbours'.

One of those social conveniences will have been modern department stores. This western institution, or at least the idea of it, was one item which required large-scale foreign investment and which Sun had attempted to raise money for.

If, as historian Gunther Barth (1980:11) has suggested, 'the modern city, providing the economic incentive and the physical setting for new enterprise, produced the department store' (see also Ferry 1960; Leach 1993:15–38, 279–82), then Hong Kong at the time of Sun's medical training must have been a modern city. Hong Kong in the 1890s had stores like Lane Crawford & Co. and A. S. Watson & Co. Ltd. which sold goods ranging from umbrellas to rugs to cigars. Although they were known as 'general stores', they did provide the 'hundred goods' under one roof. They were certainly novelties to the local Chinese populace who were more used to shops which sold particular goods;

interestingly, there was no Chinese equivalent for the word 'store' and it was transliterated into Cantonese as '*si-door*'.

Exactly how Sun viewed the modern city of Hong Kong – and what his specific impressions of these general stores were – awaits further study.[14] Most likely, he simply saw the stores as part of the modernization package, to be taken for granted in a developed setting. Modern 'conveniences' had always fascinated him, and according to anecdotal accounts, he was the first Chinese person in his county to install a western-style bath-tub in his ancestral home.

There is no evidence to suggest that either Wing On or Sincere had any connections with Sun's revolutionary activities (if there was any interaction, there is no data to support it). But just around the time that Wing On and Sincere were raising capital amongst overseas Chinese for their further developments (Yen 1995:205–19), Sun Yatsen was also approaching some of his western friends in an attempt to finance the establishment of department stores in various parts of China. Apparently, his friend Boothe approached a number of people in California to look into the possibilities, and in one of his correspondences with Mrs. Homer Lea, Sun mentioned a certain Mr. J. Deitrick who had written him and offered to assist in investigating the details involved. Unfortunately, no other details are available on the outcome of Sun's venture into the business world, but his letter dated 13 September 1914 tells us why Sun had become interested in such a 'scheme':

> My plan of such a store is to relieve the financial straits and to facilitate Commerce in revolutionary time, for as you well know that China's finance is controlled entirely by the foreign banks. When war breaks out Commerce will be absolutely stagnant, thus the people will naturally suffer a great deal. My plan is to avert such sufferings, and it will not be opposed by any person.

The scheme was apparently an important one for Sun, or he would not have mentioned in the same letter that,

> I am pleased to tell you that my work is progressing favorably. I am confident that the time is near when the reactionary government will be crushed forever.[15]

Was Sun interested in the department store simply as a means to an end, to use it a tool to raise funds for his fight to bring down the Beijing 'warlord' regime? Or was he truly worried about the First World War's possible impact on the Chinese people? Whatever the hidden agenda, the simple fact is that Sun believed in the department store, that it would have a great influence on people's livelihood – and that foreign investments were a real possibility.

'Hundred Goods' and National Reconstruction

Like so many of Sun Yatsen's blueprints for national development, such as that for establishing China's first air-force corps, his attempt to raise funds for department stores never met with success. In any event, there were other more urgent priorities for him to attend to in his overall view of China's industrial undertakings; department stores must have been a footnote in those larger schemes generally considered by many as Sun's unrealistic and overly ambitious strategies aimed at national reconstruction.

This is not to suggest that Sun only had a passing interest in department stores, that they were merely something which caught his fancy in his frantic search for guns and foreign capital. He wanted to establish department stores in Chinese cities because the idea fitted well with aspects of his belief in what constituted the vital necessities for building a new China. It would be far-fetched to suggest that Sun wanted to start a department store company and manage the store himself, or that he wanted to become a business tycoon. For Sun, the department store was a symbol of possibilities; it was a smaller version of the railway. The department store would become a depot for the 'hundred goods' shipped freely throughout China via her new railway system. Commerce and national development would go hand in hand.

In his work *The Chineseness of China*, historian Wang Gungwu (1991: 288–89) suggests that Sun 'could have been a modern version of the Chinese intellectual'. To be sure, Sun was 'modern' because he was a southerner born near Macau and Hong Kong; he was educated abroad, he absorbed western ideas, and was encouraged by his teachers and friends to open more gates in the Chinese wall. Wang's observation is that 'Sun was China's first modern politician'. As far as his tactics and his nationalism were concerned, Sun could very well have been China's first modern politician. But in terms of his modernity,[16] his interest in the department store (a small but integral component of his commitment to international commerce and free flow of the 'hundred goods') seems to indicate that Sun fundamentally conceived of his modernization ideals as universal values; he absorbed 'western ideas' because to him they were also universal ideas. They might have originated in the west but, to his mind, they were universal principles.[17]

In the preface to his *Memoirs*, Sun reiterates his position on action and knowledge:

> I devoted myself to the study of the question of 'difficulty of action and easiness of knowledge'. I studied this question for several years, and finally came to the conviction that the old tradition was false: the exact opposite is the cause. I was happy because I had understood the cause of China's stagnation. It is due to the fact that the Chinese are ignorant of many things, and not at all because they cannot act. The fact that, even though they have knowledge, they do not act, is due to their misconception that knowledge is easy but action difficult.

> (Sun 1918:8)

Clearly, Sun's discussion here of knowledge and action had very little to do with Neo-Confucian philosophy, nor was he attempting to re-invigorate the Chinese tradition. What he meant by knowledge was modern, scientific, universal knowledge, such as that required in the operation of a twentieth-century 'hundred goods' store. In such a context, national reconstruction would surely involve the proliferation of department stores throughout a new China.

Notes

1 J. Epstein (1987:40) suggests that Sun Yatsen obtained 'an amicable divorce, legally certified' from Lu Muzhen partly because she 'was barely literate and little informed about the world'. Her interest in stocks, however, seems to indicate that Madame Lu was not completely isolated from the outside world.
2 For a general history of the Wing On Company, see Yen (1995:196–236).
3 The only complete English translation of this document is entitled 'A Plea to Li Hung-chang' and will be published in a translated volume of Sun's more important Chinese writings by the Hoover Institution. I am grateful to Professor Ramon Myers for lending me a copy of this translation which has been used in the preparation of this chapter.
4 Technically speaking, Sun never qualified to become a medical doctor as he did not receive the MD degree after his sojourn at the College of Medicine for Chinese in Hong Kong. Interestingly, though, the title of Dr. gradually came to be translated as doctor of philosophy (*boshi*), and in contemporary literature Sun is often referred to as Sun Yatsen boshi.
5 For a discussion of the traditional concept of 'men of talent', see Wright (1969:43–46).
6 No sources are cited in this work and it is hard to tell what kind of information Buck relied upon to write her book. She claimed that Charles Soong (Song Jiashu) had a role to play in Sun's decision to become a

revolutionary, but there is no evidence to support this observation.

7 Zhuangguan can mean individual officials with specialized skills, or it can mean a special bureau. Here it is difficult to ascertain Sun's exact usage.

8 See, for example, Ma (1992).

9 In recent times, some historians have argued that Sun Yatsen relied more on traditional ideas for his revolutionary program than on 'western' ideas. Some have even suggested that Sun was a 'Confucianist' in the 1890s. See, for example, Chang and Gordon (1991), and also the various chapters in Cheng (1989).

10 For the latest treatment of Sun's kidnapping in London, see Wong (1986).

11 Wong claims that the letters he saw were written between 1908 and 1910, but at the Hoover Institution archive I saw some written as late as the early 1920s, although to be accurate, Wong only cites the Charles Boothe Papers.

12 Unfortunately, it is impossible to cite the letters individually, as they are not in any chronological order. Some of my information is based on the Joshua Powers Papers, also at the Hoover Institution Archive. The archive also holds some interesting film footage of Sun Yatsen's funeral. I would like to take this opportunity to thank the Hoover Institution for allowing me access to the material.

13 Sun's preface is dated 30 December, 1918, but I am not sure whether this is the edition cited by Chang and Gordon (1991) (translated by Frank Price from Sun's *Jianguo fanglue* and published in 1918).

14 In recent years, Sun Yatsen has probably become the most studied man of Modern China – much more so than Mao Zedong, for example (in a recent letter to the editor of *Asia Magazine* (1996), Sebastian Lew of Singapore said that 'Sun Yatsen was the real hero of modern China, not Mao Zedong . . . Sun overthrew oppression but Mao caused immense suffering. Nothing will change that history'), but unfortunately, the number of primary sources available to study him has not increased significantly. Basically, most of the studies rely on the same materials which have been probed by scholars over the last two decades.

15 Sun Yatsen's letter to Mrs. Homer Lea, 13 September 1914 (Joshua Powers Collection, Hoover Institution Archive) (reproduced in *Figure 1.1*). Here I am giving a specific reference because of the importance of this letter to my arguments throughout this chapter.

16 I refrain from giving a definition of modernity here as the concept continues to be problematic in the field of modern Chinese intellectual history; basically I am adopting Wang's rather general usage in his description of Sun.

17 Certainly Sun's conversion to Christianity also substantiates my point that he did see some western values as universal (Treadgold 1973:70–98).

26 Reinanzaka,Akasaka,

Tokio,Japan.

Sept,13,1914.

My dear Mrs. Lea,

Your kind letter of Aug.3rd is at nand,

for which I desire to tender you my warmest thanks and

appreciation, especially for the great personal interest

you have shown in my scheme of a department store.

My plan of such a store is to relieve

the financial straits and to facilitate Commerce in revo-

lutionary time,for as you well know that China's finance

is controlled entirely by the foreign banks. When war

breaks out Commerce willbe absolutely stagnant,thus the

people will naturaly suffer a great deal.My plan is to

avert such sufferings and it willnot be opposed by any

person.

Our friend,Mr.J.Deitrick,has written

me recently and I have put the entire matter in his hands,

so I shall not trouble you anymore about this matter. I

am pleased to tellyou that my work is progressing favorably

I am confident that the time is near when the reactionary

government will be crushed forever.

As soon as you hear that I have succeeded in my undertaking

or that I have gained a footing in any part of China, I wish

and hope that you will come to the East as soon as possible

for I need your assistance in various matters of impor-

tance.

Again thanking you for your esteemed

letter, and with kindest regards and best wishes, I am,

Your sincerefriend,

2

WING ON AND THE KWOK BROTHERS

A Case Study of Pre-War Overseas Chinese Entrepreneurs[*]

Yen Ching-hwang

Albert Feuerwerker's (1958) and Marion J. Levy's and Shih Kuo-heng's (1949) ideas about the absence of Chinese entrepreneurship no longer hold sway among economic historians working on modern China. Hao Yen-ping (1970) was the first to identify compradors on the China coast as Schumpeterian entrepreneurs par excellence. Thomas Rawski (1975:208) and Sherman Cochran (1980:214) in their works have identified indigenous entrepreneurs, while Wellington K. K. Chan (1982:218–35) has identified Ma Yingbiao, founder of Sincere Department Store in Hong Kong, as a reformer of the traditional business structure and an overseas entrepreneur.

This study of the Wing On Department Stores in Hong Kong and Shanghai aims to show that the founders, Kwok Lock (Guo Le) and Kwok Chin (Guo Quan)[1], were among the modern type of entrepreneur – overseas Chinese who played an important role in transforming family-based companies into modern corporate conglomerates. This type of entrepreneur emerged in the second half of the 19th century when the western colonial involvement in Southeast Asia sparked off rapid economic development. Men like Oei Tjie Sien and his son Oei Tiong Ham of Java (Panglaykim and Palmer 1970a, 1970b), Yap Ah Loy of Kuala Lumpur (Middlebrook 1951; Wang 1958), and Zhang Bishi of Penang and Sumatra (Godley 1981) are just a few examples. Born during the same period, the Kwok brothers spent some years in

---

* This chapter was first published in the *Proceedings of the Conference on Eighty Years' History of the Republic of China 1912–1991* (Taipei, 1991), vol. TV, p. 77–117, subsequently in Yen Ching-wang 1995 *Studies in Modern Overseas Chinese History*, Times Academic Press: Singapore. It has been adapted for publication in this volume.

Australia before founding the Wing On Department Store in Hong Kong, which due to its status as a British Crown colony will be treated as an overseas Chinese area.

As overseas entrepreneurs, the position of the Kwok brothers was ambiguous. On the one hand, they had been immigrants and thus marginal men in Australia, with the desire for material gain and the will to succeed almost ingrained in the Chinese virtues of thrift and diligence. On the other hand, their business was able to take advantage of an efficient colonial government in Hong Kong while at the same time enjoying preferential treatment from the Chinese government. As overseas Chinese, they had wide contacts with foreigners and were not so steeped in traditional culture. Their thorough staff training programme and their management style, their ingenious marketing techniques, their mobilization of scattered overseas Chinese capital, and their extensive diversification strategies – which will all be discussed in detail later in this chapter – can be seen as an eclectic combination of Chinese and western business cultures. The Kwok brothers knew how to make use of kinship and local connections for business purposes in ways which may only have been available to them because of their overseas experience.

The brothers employed these connections in several different ways – to retain control of an efficient business organization by including family members and fellow Xiangshanese in the management, to create corporate spirit among the staff, to sustain good capital flows by attracting investing partners and small individual savings alike, and to secure a growing following of customers. In the next chapter in this volume, Wellington Chan argues that it was the brothers' ability to invoke these family networks, ethnic connections and other cultural formations which in the long run gave Wing On its competitive edge over Sincere. This chapter will explore how this business culture, embedded in broader Chinese culture, was built up through an account of the interconnectedness between the lives of the Kwok brothers and the company they founded and developed.

The Kwok Brothers

Kwok Lock and Kwok Chin came from the Chuk Sau Yuen village (Zhuxiuyuan), Xiangshan district (modern-day Zhongshan district) of Guangdong province. Kwok Lock was born in 1874 as the second of six brothers, while Kwok Chin was the third, born in 1880. Their father, Peixun, was a peasant tilling his land with the help of his children.

Chuk Sau Yuen was a small village in the Xiangshan district, predominantly inhabited by people with the surname Kwok (Wing On 1975:20–1). Most of its inhabitants were rice farmers supplementing their income with sales of vegetables, fruits and fish. The village was no different from thousands of other rural villages except for its proximity to Macau, the earliest western enclave in South China. Visiting their home villages during Chinese festivals, the inhabitants of Macau – predominantly from Xiangshan – kept the villagers informed about life in the colony. They brought news about the prosperity of the colony, the strange appearance and costumes of foreigners, the kidnapping of innocent people for the slave trade, the cruel treatment of coolies (Knt 1832–3:403–404; British Foreign Office n.d.:88a–b; Yen 1985:52–6), and above all, perhaps, opportunities in the colony and overseas. For centuries, Macau attracted tens of thousands of Xiangshanese to work in the colony, and stirred the imagination of thousands and thousands more.

For ambitious Xiangshanese, this western influence provided opportunities. Had Kwok Lock and Kwok Chin had connections with Christian missionaries, they might have studied in the west like Yung Wing (Rong Hong) who returned to China to become a mandarin (Yung Wing 1909). Had they had rich and influential relatives in the business world along the China coast, they might have become powerful compradors like Zheng Guanying, Tang Jingxing or Xu Run (Hao 1970, Hsu 1988:34–70). But the Kwok family belonged to the middle peasant class. The grain produced on the family-owned land with the help of the boys was enough to feed the members of the family, but not to create a surplus in lean years. The brothers appear to have received seven years of elementary education in the village school (Guo 1961). Like other village boys in Xiangshan, they must have heard many fascinating stories about the outside world where land was fertile and plentiful, and gold could be picked up from the roadside. They must have cherished the hope of becoming rich and wealthy by making money overseas.

In 1892, at the age of eighteen, Kwok Lock left his native village after a flood. With HK$280 in his pocket, he arrived in Sydney where his eldest brother, Kwok Ping Fai (Guo Binghui), had already been living for many years (Guo 1961:4, Zhu 1988:208–9). Two years later, the fifteen-year-old Kwok Chin went with a relative to Honolulu at the encouragement of his father (Guo 1961:2). With the help of another relative, he was employed as an office boy in a legal firm, and spent his free time studying English and the Hawaiian dialect. The following year, he started working at the British Consulate, but after a year's service decided to leave the foreign establishment. He had saved some money and started a small business, but his luck did not carry the day. Still, Kwok Chin's exposure to foreigners gave him not only the opportunity to learn English, but also some insight into western manners and habits which were to prove useful in his future enterprises. After three years in Hawaii, he returned home and married, but after the birth of his second child decided to try his luck overseas again, and in 1899 left his home village for Sydney to join his second brother (Guo 1961:3–4).

Wing On Fruit Store

Meanwhile in Sydney, the oldest brother had died from disease, and Kwok Lock was working as a shop assistant in Wing Sang & Co. (Yongsheng Zhuang) (Zhu 1988:209). Wing Sang which was partly owned by the Kwok brothers' cousin, George Kwok Bew (Guo Biao), was the first Chinese fruit and vegetables wholesale store in Sydney. Founded in 1890 by a group of Xiangshanese, it handled a large part of the banana trade between Queensland and Fiji (Yong 1977:56) and later expanded successfully into the general import-export trade. One of its founders and proprietors was Ma Yingbiao who later opened the famous Sincere Department Store in Hong Kong (Xianshi gongsi 1924[?]). Young Kwok Lock must have been impressed by the success of Wing Sang, and was clearly a quick learner. With only a few years' work experience and savings, he founded the Wing On Fruit Store in 1897 with two good friends, Leung Chong (Liang Chuang) and Ma Cho Seng (Ma Zuxing), and an initial capital of only £1,400 Australian (Guo 1961:4, Zhu 1988:209). In the following year, three of his younger brothers, Kwok Yik Fai (Guo Yihui), Kwok Yuen Fai (Guo Yuanhui), and the youngest Kwok Ho Fai (Guo Hehui), joined him in Sydney, where the last assisted him in the fruit store. When Kwok Chin arrived in 1899, the brothers were reunited overseas, and his presence helped strengthen the foundation of their business.

Wing On Fruit Store became a close business partner of Wing Sang. The banana trade was a lucrative business in which the Xiangshanese in Sydney occupied a predominant position (Yong 1965–6:28) as they effectively marketed their produce in Sydney, Melbourne, Adelaide and Perth through a network of distribution agencies which included both Wing Sang and Wing On (Yong 1977:48). The scope for the banana trade and other business was wide, so there was no need for Wing On and Wing Sang to compete, while kinship and local ties also held the two companies together, as all the proprietors came from neighbouring villages of Xiangshan and spoke the same dialect. As Kwok Lock had worked with Wing Sang for several years, he must have felt indebted to the company, and particularly to his cousin George Kwok Bew who was one of the proprietors (Zhu 1988:209). In 1902, Wing On, Wing Sang and another Xiangshanese controlled fruit store, Wing Tiy (Yong Tai), formed a partnership to cultivate bananas in Fiji. The name of the new company, Sang On Tiy (Sheng An Tai), was the result of the combination of the last part of the three partners' names – Wing Sang, Wing On and Wing Tiy – indicating the close co-operation of the three large fruit stores in Sydney. The company had some 350 acres of cultivated banana plantation, and managed to supply the Sydney stores with some 10,000 bunches of bananas fortnightly (Guo 1961:5; Yong 1965–6:28, 1977:49).Young and enterprising Kwok Chin, who had worked with Wing On for some time, was appointed manager of Sang On Tiy.

The Founding of Wing On Department Store

What really motivated Kwok Lock, also known as James Gocklock, and Kwok Chin, known as Philip Gockchin, to found a department store may never be fully understood. Some overseas entrepreneurs such as Zhang Bishi, Zhang Yunan and Chen Yixi were influenced by late Qing nationalism which compelled them to contribute to the economic modernization of China (Godley 1981; Liu et al. 1982:304–40; Yen 1982:217–32, 1984:119–35)˙ But no trace of this kind of nationalism can be found in Kwok Chin's autobiography, even though it is reasonable to suggest that the Kwok brothers must have heard of these men and their exploits in China. In terms of wealth, the Kwok brothers were no match for the famous entrepreneurs who founded large enterprises such as railways in South China.

What motivated the Kwok brothers to move to Hong Kong seems to have been its location between eastern and western worlds. As Wellington Chan points out in the next chapter, a large-scale Chinese emporium in Sydney would hardly have been able to capture the necessary patronage among white Australians. On the other hand, a modern department store would have a better chance of success in Hong Kong than in Chinese cities which had experienced less economic and social development and been less exposed to foreign influences. Furthermore, Hong Kong was close to the home district of the Kwok brothers, and Cantonese was the *lingua franca* of the population.

Ma Yingbiao, who came from a village near that of the Kwok family, had opened the first modern Chinese department store in Hong Kong in 1900 (Xianshi gongsi 1924[?]:1–2). Given the close ethnic networks between the Xiangshanese in Hong Kong and Sydney, Ma Yingbiao's hard-earned success must have been known to the Kwok brothers. Neither the founders of Wing On nor their descendants are prepared to acknowledge openly their imitation of Sincere, but privately some Wing On leaders admit that the brothers were influenced by Ma Yingbiao.[2]

Whatever the motives and influences, the Kwok brothers' decision to open a department store in Hong Kong was to change their lives. Based on their networks in the banana trade and the import-export trade, they formed a partnership as the major partners while minor partners included Du Zewen (David Jackman), Guo Xianwen and Liang Huannan. Between them they raised the sum of HK$160,000.[3] Kwok Chin, who had some knowledge of the English language as well as business acumen, returned to Hong Kong in 1907 and soon found suitable premises at 167 Queen's Road, Central. A five-year lease was signed. The name of the fruit store, Wing On – literally meaning eternal peace – was chosen for the new enterprise, and the store was officially opened on 28 August 1907 (Guo 1961:6).

The Early Years

With a capital of only HK$160,000 Wing On had a modest start. By the time rentals and the wages of the more than ten employees had been paid, the level of recurrent capital was low. The traditional way of raising capital through partnership was clearly not sufficient for an enterprise like a department store. Fortunately, the Kwok brothers had learned how to use bank facilities in Sydney, and they quickly extended their social tentacles to the high society of Hong Kong where they got to know Robert Ho Tung, a powerful comprador and wealthy merchant (Ho 1989:11). With his support, the brothers obtained their first large loan of HK$600,000 from the Hongkong and Shanghai Banking Corporation – a loan of almost four times their initial capital. The loan was repaid promptly according to agreement. Once it had established a good reputation for itself in financial circles, Wing On had no difficulty in obtaining subsequent loans from the Hongkong and Shanghai Bank or other financial institutions (Guo 1961:6).

As a modern department store, Wing On practised 'fixed price' policy, contrary to the traditional Chinese practice of hard bargaining. But since neither Kwok Chin's autobiography nor Wing On's Twenty Fifth Anniversary Magazine makes any special remarks about this in their description of the early years, it seems that Chinese shoppers in Hong Kong had already grown accustomed to this practice which had first been introduced by Sincere (Xianshi gongsi 1924[?]:1). Neither did Wing On employ any women shop assistants – something which seven years earlier had proved so controversial for Sincere (Xianshi gongsi 1924[?]:1–2). Wing On was in a position to benefit from the new practices with which the first department store had had to struggle.

Two years after Wing On had opened, Kwok Lock came to Hong Kong from Sydney and became chairman of the company while Kwok Chin retained his position as general manager. Another partner, Du Zewen was made deputy general manager (Guo 1961:6). Together the three formed a strong team. Kwok Lock had accumulated immense experience in Sydney – he was a charismatic leader with business acumen, warm and honest,[4] and a good public relations man. His brother Kwok Chin was more quiet, but good at administration and planning. Also an experienced businessman from his time in Australia, Du Zewen was a good and efficient administrator. He assisted Kwok Chin in managing the company and this three-man team obviously worked well and complemented each other's personalities and skills.

The Structure of the Company

Wing On was not a traditional Chinese company, but neither was it completely westernized. It combined traditional Chinese and modern western elements in a hybrid structure. Both Kwok Lock and Kwok Chin had keenly observed and borrowed from western business practices in Sydney, and Kwok Chin in particular had acquired some knowledge about the west while working in Honolulu. But neither of them had received any formal western education, nor had they worked in a western enterprise as, for instance, Chinese compradors did.

Wing On started as a traditional Chinese partnership where each partner contributed a sum of capital and helped in the business. With just over ten employees, the store appears to have had a simple two-tier structure of management and general staff. As in a traditional Chinese firm (Chan 1982:219–22), there was a strong close link between ownership and management. The traditional method of expansion through taking in more partners was employed until 1912, when the capital base was increased to HK$600,000 (Liu 1932:2). Around this time, the traditional way of raising capital proved inadequate, and in 1916 the company was changed to a public liability company with a capital of HK$2 million. But the control of the company still remained in the hands of the Kwok brothers and their fellow Xiangshanese partners.

By 1932, when the company celebrated its twenty-fifth anniversary, it had become a large conglomerate with branches in Hong Kong, Shanghai, Guangdong, Southeast Asia, Australia and the United States. The parent company in Hong Kong had adopted a three-tier structure, where a board of directors, elected by shareholders, was headed by a chairman. This position was held by Kwok Lock for at least the first twenty-five years (Xianggang Yong'an youxian gongsi 1932:12–6). In this modern company, the board was responsible for making major decisions and produced an annual report for the shareholders, signed by the chairman.

Under the Board of Directors were the management and the general staff. The management was headed by a general manager and a deputy general manager. In 1932, the management of the parent company in Hong Kong consisted of a General Office, Cashiers' Office, Purchasing Office, General Accounting Office, Bills and Cost Accounting Office, Shares Office, and Estates Office. For many years, Kwok Chin was the general manager while Du Zewen held the position of deputy general manager. The overlapping between ownership and managerial responsibility may not seem desirable today, but in Hong Kong before the Second World War, it gave the managers additional authority. As many employees in overseas Chinese communities had little concept of public ownership (Redding 1990:158–9), the employees of Wing On continued to view the company as the Kwok family's enterprise.

The general staff was attached to various sub-departments under the control of a head. By 1932, there were fifty sub-departments covering a wide range of commodities, including furniture, China-ware, electrical supplies, jewellery, hardware, groceries, men's and ladies' wear, money exchange, medicines, music, optical goods, perfumery, photo supplies, blankets, buttons, handbags and umbrellas, handkerchiefs, towels, as well as Chinese and European shoes (Liu 1932:4–5).

The company's attitude to its staff can be said to have been paternalistic. In the eyes of the Kwok brothers, the company was like a large family. They felt morally obligated to look after the interests of the employees, and in return, the employees were expected to do their utmost for the good of the company. The Kwok brothers were strong believers in character building through moral and intellectual education. In his autobiography, Kwok Chin spelled out that employees should be inculcated with the traditional Chinese values of hard work, thrift, loyalty, sincerity, uprightness and trustworthiness; and that senior staff should set an example for their subordinates to follow (Guo 1961:27–8). He emphasized merit as the only principle for appointment and promotion in the company. This, of course, was not a traditional Chinese value, but a modern principle for running a large business organization which Kwok Chin saw fit to adopt for Wing On.

The company set up a Department of Moral Education (Deyu bu) which invited prominent speakers from Hong Kong and overseas for its weekly lectures, and a Department of Intellectual Cultivation (Zhiyu bu) which organized night classes in English and set up newspaper reading rooms. For those employees who had no training in English, night classes provided them with an opportunity to learn the language, which was becoming increasingly important in the colony (Liu 1932:5). In addition, the Department of Intellectual Cultivation also founded a drama troupe and music ensemble for the recreation of employees. Wing On further founded a Department of Physical Education which promoted Chinese martial arts, football and swimming. The combination of virtues and physical health was to create perfect employees who could contribute to the success of the company. As swimming became an increasingly popular outdoor sport in Hong Kong, the company formed a swimming club and erected a swimming shed in North Point for employees and their families. Wing On even provided a free car service after business hours from the store to the North Point swimming shed (Liu 1932:6).

Wing On Opens in Shanghai

Wing On would probably have been relatively insignificant in the economic history of China had it not opened a store in Shanghai. The magazine commemorating the twenty-fifth anniversary of the founding of Wing On states that 'Shanghai is one of the four largest markets in China. Its location is central. It is the financial centre of China where Chinese and foreign merchants concentrated. To follow the trend, the company founded a branch in Shanghai in 1917' (Liu 1932:8). Since the end of the nineteenth century, Shanghai had been China's foreign trade entrepôt and financial centre (Liu 1985:222–30; Tang 1989:359–83; Shanghai shehui jingji kexueyuan yenjiuso 1989:155–203), with a concentration of wealthy merchants who had developed a taste for and power to purchase foreign goods. The import of high quality perfumes and cosmetics into Shanghai, for instance, increased from 50,405 taels in 1894 to 319,822 taels in 1911, a six-fold increase in volume. Similarly, the value of import of luxurious carpets, table cloths and bedroom items rose from about 200,000 taels in 1904 to about 1 million taels in 1911 (Shanghai baihuo gongsi et al. 1988:100). Furthermore, during the First World War the position of western businesses in China was greatly weakened and Chinese capitalists had fine opportunities in the treaty ports (Levy and Shih 1949). Schumpeterian entrepreneurs that they were, the Kwok brothers must have been quick to realize Shanghai's potential market.

Again, Ma Yingbiao was the first to decide to set up a Chinese department store in Shanghai in 1914 (Xianshi gongsi 1924[?]:3), and his project must have inspired the Kwok brothers. The following year, they began their preparations for opening a store in Shanghai. The successful expansion of partnership in 1912 gave the Kwok brothers confidence in raising capital, and the transformation to a public company in 1916 further strengthened their confidence in floating capital. The brothers invested HK$670,000 worth of shares, while the bulk of the capital was raised among overseas Chinese (Zhu 1988:211). This was not without problems, but with the help of their business associates in Hong Kong and Sydney such as Du Zewen, Sun Zhixing, Li Yanxiang, Lin Zesheng, Yang Jinhua, and Ouyang Minqing, they managed to raise the target sum of HK$2.5 million (Guo 1961:8, Shanghai baihuo gongsi et al.1988:104). With most of the capital assured, Kwok Chin and his younger brother Kwok Yik Fai left for Shanghai in July 1917 to acquire a suitable site for the proposed store. In October Kwok Chin signed a 30-year lease with a rich British real estate merchant at 50,000 silver taels per year for an 8.732-acre block of land in Nanjing Road opposite Sincere. Kwok Lock promptly went to Shanghai to take charge of the construction, and a modern six-storey building was completed more than one year later. The appearance of the Wing On building was similar to that of Sincere, but its interior design was superior, and it was more spacious and brighter and had more rooms for customers to move around in. Apart from selling goods, the Shanghai store also housed a hotel, restaurants, an amusement park and a money savings business (Shanghai baihuo gongsi et al. 1988:104–5).

As the opening approached, experienced senior staff was sent to Shanghai. A director of the Hong Kong company and a close business associate of the Kwok brothers, Yang Huiting, was appointed general manager while another experienced businessman, Ma Zuxing, assumed the position of deputy general manager (Guo 1961:9). The head office gathered the best and most up-to-date commodities and despatched them to Shanghai for the grand opening. Large eye-catching advertisements appeared continuously in Shanghai's Chinese newspapers for the fortnight preceding the opening. On 5 September 1918, Wing On in Shanghai was officially opened for business, and the building was packed with invited dignitaries and well-wishers. A great success, the grand opening promoted the store as a top class Chinese emporium with quality goods and fair prices. The stock which was expected to be sold in the course of the following months was cleared within three weeks (Zhu 1988:209).

The success of the Shanghai branch can be measured in terms of rising turnover and net profit. In 1918, when Wing On had been in operation for only four months, its turnover was 1.58 million silver dollars with a small net profit of $15,000. By the following year, the net profit had risen steeply to $620,000 with a massive turnover of $4.556 million for that year. In 1921 the annual turnover was $6.999 million, in 1923 $8.153 million and by 1925 it had reached the remarkable figure of $9.78 million, more than twice the turnover of the first year of full operation. The net profit also rose rapidly from $620,000 in 1919 to $724,000 in 1921, $1.016 million in 1923 and $1.103 million in 1925. The growth of Wing On reached its peak in 1931 with an annual turnover of $13.637 million and net profit of $2.475 million (Shanghai baihuo gongsi et al. 1988:151–2). By this time, Wing On had already emerged as the leader among the four large Chinese emporiums in Shanghai, namely, Wing On, Sincere, Sun Sun and Dah Sun.

Central policies continued to be decided by the board of directors in the head office in Hong Kong. In view of its importance, the Shanghai branch had a chairman, and under him were the general manager and deputy general manager. The chair was first held by Kwok Lock himself who was also the chairman of the board of directors at the head office. The chairmanship was later passed on to Kwok Bew, the cousin of the Kwok brothers who had also lived in Sydney (Guo 1961:9, Shanghai baihuo gongsi et al. 1988:175). The organization of the Shanghai branch was modelled after the head office in Hong Kong. The large company was divided into the administrative and trading arms under the control of the general manager and his deputy. The two arms were subdivided into departments with a clear specialization of functions, and there was a clear line of authority from top to bottom, as in a modern western company.

Marketing and Business Strategies

As an emporium selling commodities from all over the world, Wing On's policy was to have direct access to the manufacturers. In order to bypass foreign trading agencies, Wing On sent its people abroad to secure imports of selected goods which had great potential in the Chinese market, and sole agency rights guaranteed the company a high profit margin. In some cases special purchasing agents were appointed overseas (Shanghai baihuo gongsi et al. 1988:128–30). In his autobiography, Kwok Chin (Guo 1961:28) proudly revealed Wing On's purchasing strategy: 'you buy when the price of goods is up, not when the price of goods is down'.

Marketing was crucial to the success of Wing On. The Kwok brothers had observed how customers were treated in Australia, very unlike the traditional Chinese passive and unfriendly attitude towards customers. The Kwok brothers were determined to change that attitude among Wing On's staff, and in his autobiography Kwok Chin (Guo 1961:25–6) spelt out what efforts had gone into this. He had observed that the attitude of the shop assistants in Shanghai was better than that in Hong Kong, but worse than that of Japanese shop assistants. This, he explained, was due to the character of the Chinese and to lack of training. Thus Wing On shop assistants were taught to treat customers as guests who brought business to the company and on whose patronage their jobs depended. Customers were met with courteous greetings such as 'good morning' or 'good afternoon', and the concept that customers are always right was inculcated in the minds of the Wing On staff. Even when no sale was made, customers were thanked for coming.

One effective marketing strategy was to give customers credit. Of course, there is nothing modern about credit in itself, that also existed in traditional Chinese businesses. But Wing On developed a credit assessment system, and since most of the customers of Wing On in Shanghai belonged to the upper-middle and upper classes, the risk of debts was relatively small. Credit was introduced already in 1918, and within five years, the number of credit customers had grown to more than 4,000 (Zhu 1988:211–2). Chinese and foreign creditors were treated in accordance with their customs, so that the credits of foreigners were settled monthly, while those of the Chinese were settled three times a year – before the Dragon Boat Festival (usually in June), before the Moon festival (usually in September) and before Chinese New Year (in January or February). The success of credit sales was clearly reflected in their proportion to the total turnover of the company. In 1935, the income from credit sales was CNC (Chinese National Currency) 1.278 million, or about 14 per cent of total turnover. By 1939, the income from credit sales had increased to CNC 4.508 million, or 25 per cent of total turnover (Shanghai baihuo gongsi et al. 1988:135–6).

Another marketing strategy was the introduction of gift vouchers (*liquan*). The origin of these gift vouchers was probably western, but they were already sold in the parent company in Hong Kong even before the Shanghai branch opened. Both because of Wing On's prestige and because of the wide range of goods available there, gift vouchers soon became very popular. Designed to look like bank notes, they had values of CNC 1, 2, 5, 10 and 50. In 1935, their sale was worth CNC 458,000, in 1938 CNC 600,000, before increasing dramatically to CNC 1.126 million in 1939 and CNC 2.639 million in 1940 (Shanghai baihuo gongsi et al. 1988:137–8). Gift vouchers invariably increased the volume of turnover, broadened the social base from which customers were drawn and facilitated marketing planning, while the company was simultaneously able to take advantage of cash advances.

In addition, Wing On started a mail order and home delivery service around 1920. As the store's reputation had travelled beyond the boundaries of Shanghai, and its goods were advertised in Chinese newspapers in other major cities, orders came in from places as far away as Shenyang and Andong in the northeast, Xian and Dongguan in the northwest, Chengdu in the west and Fuzhou in the south. The home delivery business was mainly completed through telephone orders which suited the Shanghai rich. As most of these rich Chinese did not worry about cost, the convenience of home delivery helped develop their appetite for more goods (Shanghai baihuo gongsi et al. 1988:138).

But the success story of Wing On cannot be complete without mention of the Kwok brothers' ingenious use of overseas Chinese capital. With their knowledge of Chinese communities in Sydney, Honolulu and Hong Kong, they recognized the importance of savings made by those people who had toiled for many years abroad in order to pay for property, the construction of a house or simply regular family expenditures back home. Most overseas Chinese at that time did not trust modern banks or post offices, but rather someone whom they felt they knew of. The brothers decided to set up a money savings service for these small individual savings. In the early stage in Hong Kong, depositors were mainly local Xiangshanese as well as Xiangshanese immigrants in Australia and the United States. Their deposits were a sign of trust in Wing On which also offered the service of remitting money back home. Wing On paid little or no interest on the deposits, but at that time, most overseas Chinese did not know about interest rates, and went to Wing On mainly for the safety of their money. The management of early deposits came under the cashier's office, but when the number of depositors increased, a separate Department of Savings and Remittance was established.[5] In Shanghai a separate Finance Department was set up in 1921, but unlike the situation in Hong Kong, the depositors were no longer exclusively Xiangshanese. Many were Cantonese, some from the colonies of Hong Kong and Macau, who felt a local attachment to Wing On and were prepared to deposit their savings with the company (Shanghai baihuo gongsi et al. 1988:163–4). The Finance Department was divided into Savings and Commercial Affairs, where the former dealt with ordinary savings while the latter handled fixed deposits and other types of commercial accounts. By 1929, the department was so successful that it acquired semi-independent status within the company. It held reserves of 1 million silver dollars, and set up a major sub-branch in the Hongkou area where business grew rapidly. At its peak in 1931, funds deposited with the Finance Department reached $6.4 million, and were used as operating capital. When in 1929 deposits at the Hongkou branch amounted to $1.43 million, all but $10,000 was injected into the company's liquid capital while the remainder was kept in the Finance Department. In 1930, deposits in the Hongkou branch increased to $1.999 million, and only $37,000 was kept in the Department (Shanghai baihuo gongsi et al. 1988:164–6).

The mobilization of the savings of overseas Chinese was an important innovation by the Kwok brothers and was facilitated by their ability to employ ethnic ties for economic purposes. They first won the confidence and trust of their fellow Xiangshanese, and later widened their base to include Guangdong province as a whole.

Both brothers were active in the community as well. They helped the Xiangshanese Chamber of Commerce (later the Zhongshanese Chamber of Commerce) in Hong Kong to acquire a club house, and Kwok Chin was at one stage its president or treasurer (Liu 1932:6; Guo 1961:22). Kwok Chin was also the president of the Pan Overseas Xiangshanese Relief Association (Zhongshan haiwai tongxiang jinan zonghui). For the development of Xiangshan, the brothers donated a large sum to build schools and also to construct a road (Guo 1961:22–3). They were also generous in donations for local schools, hospitals, and charity organizations in Hong Kong. Kwok Chin was particularly active as director of Po Leung Kuk (Baoliang ju), a charitable organization known for its protection of women and children, as well as deputy director of the prominent Tung Wah (Donghua) Hospital of Hong Kong (Sinn 1989), and president of the Hong Kong Chinese Chamber of Commerce (Xianggang huasheng zonghui). He was also elected to various boards of management of several Chinese schools in Hong Kong (Guo 1961:22). The Kwok brothers' involvement in community work in Hong Kong and their concern for the welfare of their home village, though time consuming, brought them fame and status. This in turn gained Wing On the continued patronage of Xiangshanese as well as of the general public. However, the brothers would hardly fit the romantic description of these so-called 'community-centred entrepreneurs' who sacrificed their self-interest for the sake of the community (cf. Fruin 1982:168–9). They were self-aggrandizing rather than self-sacrificing, and their enterprise undoubtedly benefited from their involvement in the community.

Diversification

The Kwok brothers seem to have realized the importance of business diversification early on. Their first step was to move into real estate. Kwok Chin in particular felt that the acquisition of valuable real estate in Hong Kong would be to the advantage of Wing On. The first shop in Hong Kong had proved too small for future development, and after only two years Wing On moved to new premises in Des Voeux Road, Central, rented for five years with the option of extending for another fifteen years (Guo 1961:6). Instead of opening additional stores in other parts of Hong Kong, the company started buying up property around the rented premises. It acquired a row of shops from 207 to 235 Des Voeux Road, and another row from 104 to 118 Connaught Road, Central, as well as a property in Connaught West where the company's godown was built. Wing On constructed the Great Eastern Hotel on its own land, and the company owned more than 30 shops with a total area of more than 40,000 square feet (Liu 1932:3). The fact that Wing On had to set up a separate Estates Office indicates the growing importance of real estate in Hong Kong and also in Guangzhou. By 1934, the income accrued from the properties in those two cities reached a figure of more than HK$5.5 million, representing about a quarter of the total income of the year (Xianggang Yong'an youxian gongsi 1934:3).

But more important in Wing On's diversification strategy were the moves into finance and manufacturing. Neither of the brothers had any special training in finance, but perhaps their successful mobilization of overseas Chinese capital had given them an insight into this area. Their first foray into the financial world was the founding in 1915 of the Wing On Insurance company specializing in fire and shipping insurance. With a world war in progress, they had obviously expected that Chinese trading ships would have engaged insurance cover. But they turned out to be wrong, and with its limited capital of HK$610,000, Wing On Insurance had difficulty in competing with large western insurance companies. But once again with the help of their business associates and friends, the company succeeded in increasing its capital and acquiring agents in most major cities in China.

The Kwok brothers also went into life insurance which had been growing in popularity in the west after the First World War. Life insurance companies already existed in Hong Kong and the coastal cities of China, but most of them were western-owned. In 1925, Wing On Life Insurance was founded in Hong Kong with a paid up capital of just over HK$1.5 million (Wing On 1975:6). But the company encountered problems due to a lack of confidence in a Chinese-owned insurance company. The efforts of the staff kept the company going for more than a decade, and it gained substantial support after 1938, but then almost collapsed during the Japanese occupation. In the post-war period, the life insurance company grew again and expanded into major cities throughout Southeast Asia (Guo 1961:15–6).

The climax of the Kwok brothers' financial ventures was reached on 19 September 1931 when the Wing On Bank was opened in Hong Kong. Its registered capital was HK$5 million and the bank also registered with the new Guomindang government in Nanjing so that it could operate in Central and South China. It operated like other banks, handling business transactions, mortgages, loans, savings and remittances. It also set up safe deposit boxes for customers which soon gained popularity with wealthy local Chinese. Building on the reputation of Wing On, the new bank had a good start and within two years had attracted more than HK$2 million in deposits. In 1936, it purchased its own building, and the following year established a branch in Yaumatei for customers in the Kowloon area. The bank underwent a very difficult period during the Japanese occupation, but quickly resolved its problems after the Second World War, and deposits with the bank increased rapidly to over HK$30 million (Guo 1961:17–8).

Another major area of Wing On's diversification was manufacturing. Again, it was quite remarkable that the Kwok brothers should go into an area of business about which they knew very little, but the First

World War provided them with a special opportunity when a western owned knitwear factory in Hong Kong became available to them on favourable conditions in 1919. The factory produced underwear such as the popular Eagle brand singlet. Renaming the factory Weixin, literally meaning 'reform', the brothers took over all the machinery and produced a variety of underwear for both domestic and foreign markets (Liu 1932:11).

But the biggest manufacturing enterprise that the Kwok brothers undertook was the establishment of the Wing On Textile Manufacturing Company in Shanghai in 1921 (Guo 1961:10). The idea of undertaking large-scale textile manufacturing had grown out of Kwok's visit to Shanghai in early 1921 – the year of continuing intensification of anti-Japanese feelings in Shanghai and other major coastal cities in the wake of the May Fourth movement when Japanese goods were burnt as an expression of hatred against Japanese economic and political aggression in China. Such attempts to roll back Japanese economic imperialism in China acted as an encouragement to the Chinese manufacturing industries, and Kwok Chin's visit to Shanghai was timely. He must have been impressed by the enthusiasm of the burgeoning Chinese nationalism and the prospect of capturing a vast growing market in the textile industry. In explaining why he founded this textile company in Shanghai, Kwok Chin (Guo 1961:10) pointed out in his autobiography that backward Chinese manufacturing had until then placed economic opportunities in the hands of foreigners. Of course, it also fitted in with the Kwoks' overall strategy of controlling supplies directly. The capital for the company was first authorized at 3 million silver dollars, but was shortly increased to $5 million and then $6 million in order to meet the strong and enthusiastic demand for shares (Liu 1932:9).

Kwok Lock was chairman of the Board of Directors of the Wing On Textile Manufacturing Company, while a younger brother – Kwok Ho Far (Guo Hehui) – was appointed general manager, deputized by another experienced businessman, Leung Chong. The selection of sites and the construction of the textile factory took about one and a half years to complete. The first mill was established in Yangshupu, and the company began its production in the winter of 1922. With the rise of Chinese economic nationalism and with Wing On's fine reputation, the products, including yarn and cloth, received tremendous support among Chinese consumers both at home and abroad. The company went on to build its second mill at Wusong and a third mill at Markham Road, Shanghai. By 1931, the company had doubled its capital base to 12 million silver dollars by capitalizing the reserve for further expansion. In the following year, when the manufacturing company entered its tenth year of existence, its three mills covered about 3.63 acres, employed more than 14,000 workers and staff, and possessed 2,000 weaving machines with 240,000 spindles. The company produced a wide range of cotton piece goods, including two popular brands called 'Golden Wall' and 'Golden Coin' (Liu 1932:9; Guo 1961:10–11).

Other areas of diversification undertaken by the Kwok brothers included the Great Eastern Hotel in Hong Kong, restaurants, a godown and an amusement park on top of the Wing On Building in Shanghai. These were sideline businesses developed to support the department stores by attracting customers, while the godown in Hong Kong solved the problem of storage in the relatively modest premises of the main store.

The head office in Hong Kong stayed in charge of Wing On's many subsidiary companies. With this setup, the brothers could easily redistribute capital from the emporiums to other businesses, a necessity not least because of the political turmoil at the time. In 1930–1, for example, Shanghai Wing On Department Store invested 600,000 silver dollars in the Wing On Textile Manufacturing Company, $310,000 in the Wing On Bank in Hong Kong, $425,000 in the Wing On Fire and Shipping Insurance Company, $300,000 in the Wing On Life Insurance Company in Hong Kong, and another sum of $202,000 in the general funds of the Wing On parent company in Hong Kong (Shanghai baihuo gongsi et al. 1988:161).

Conclusion

During an interview in Hong Kong, one of Kwok Chin's grandsons recalled that in his old age, his grandfather frequented the emporium, watching customers coming and going, and that he enjoyed immensely the flourishing of business in the emporium.[6] This case study leaves the Kwok brothers at the end of the bustling interwar years well before such a scene can have taken place. But the capitalistic attitude and the joy of business that it bespeaks are reflected in the Kwok brothers' constant search for opportunities for business expansion – from the fruit store in Sydney with connections to the banana trade, to the department store in Hong Kong with a sideline in real estate, and further on to the grand opening in Shanghai of what was to become the leader of the 'big four' Chinese department stores, along with proliferating diversification into the money savings business, banking, insurance, manufacturing and more. Operating during several waves of Chinese nationalism, the brothers were aware of the national movements but do not seem to have been driven by them. For instance, when they decided to start textile manufacturing in Shanghai in 1921 in a climate of military and political unrest, it was a calculated risk.

As J.W. Gough (1969:17) has rightly pointed out: 'To call [the entrepreneur] an "intermediary" between capital and labour suggests the salaried official, the modern "personnel manager" rather than the genuine entrepreneur'. The Kwok brothers were not just intermediaries between capital and labour, but rather creators and perpetuators of a modern enterprise. Their foresight and business acumen did not come from formal education, but from their acute observation and ability to turn something new to their advantage. They possessed Schumpeterian ideals, such as acquisitiveness, innovativeness and a willingness to take risks. They successfully mobilized scattered overseas Chinese capital, and as managers they combined a traditional paternalistic attitude with a modern understanding of the importance of staff education and training.

Notes

1 Throughout this chapter names are used in their original transliteration as for Kwok Lock and Kwok Chin, rather than the pinyin Guo Le and Guo Quan.
2 Interview with Dr. Russel Kwok, Hong Kong, 1990.
3 This sum is listed by Kwok (Guo 1961:6). A slightly smaller sum of HK$150,000 is mentioned by Liu (1932:1).
4 Zhu (1988:209–10) claims that Kwok Lock once returned £500 to a bank in Australia which had mistakenly overpaid him.
5 This section is based on interviews with Mr M. C. Kwok and Dr Russel Kwok, Hong Kong, 1990.
6 Interview with Dr Russel Kwok, Hong Kong, 1990.

3

PERSONAL STYLES, CULTURAL VALUES AND MANAGEMENT

The Sincere and Wing On Companies in Shanghai and Hong Kong, 1900–1941[*]

Wellington K.K. Chan

While retailing a great variety of goods under one roof and single management already existed in China by the late nineteenth century, modern-style department stores on the China coast came into existence only in 1900. Organized by Chinese entrepreneurs who had started their careers in Australia, they consciously borrowed managerial techniques from abroad. Sincere and Wing On, the two premier Chinese department stores, expanded rapidly during these years and, in the process, developed new forms of organization and strategy based on western models as well as on traditional Chinese business practices and cultural values. When political and economic turmoil during the 1920s and 1930s slowed the growth of these companies, Wing On emerged as more successful than Sincere. Wing On's path diverged from that of its competitor because its stronger management team was better at blending individual personality, western organization and Chinese cultural values.

Late Nineteenth Century Retailing East and West on the China Coast

The opening of the Sincere Company in 1900 and the Wing On Company in 1907 in Hong Kong, followed by their expansion into Shanghai and Guangzhou during the 1910s, ushered in a new type of marketing to consumers living in the urban areas of coastal China. Commodities such as food, clothing, appliances and furnishings, as

* This chapter is a revised version of a paper by the same title first published in *Business History Review* 70 (Summer) 1996.

well as luxury items such as cosmetics and jewellery, were elegantly displayed by different sales departments according to categories. Under one roof stretching over several acres of floor space, trained and courteous salespeople served their customers with vigorously promoted and uniformly priced goods. Such an innovative way of retailing, evolving from modest *magasins de nouveautés* and dry goods stores, had been first introduced in the west by Aristide Boucicaut's Bon Marché in Paris, A. T. Stewart's Marble Palace in New York and William Whiteley's stores in London during the mid-nineteenth century (Barth 1980:110–47).[1] Its adaptation in China was not unexpected, because the social, economic and technological forces that transformed the nature of urban life in the west and consequently gave rise to modern department stores also changed China's coastal cities. By the early 1900s, there were at least four thriving department stores owned and operated by the English in Shanghai's International Settlement: Whiteaway, Laidlaw (opened in 1904, probably the latest and largest), Hall & Holtz, Lane Crawford & Co., and Weeks & Co. (Clifford 1991:62).

These western establishments on the China Coast served primarily, if not exclusively, the growing number of foreign residents; they had little or no direct impact on the evolution of the Chinese retail business. Up to the 1840s, in urban centers like Shanghai and Guangzhou, small shops staffed by family members (miscellaneous goods shops – *zahuo dian*) sold items ranging from cooking oil, salt, sugar, soy, vinegar, to notions, cosmetics, fans, paper goods, lanterns and candle wicks. Cosmetics, perfumes, notions, especially for embroidery work, combs and brushes and the like, were often also sold by special peddlers, the *huolang*. They would hawk their wares from house to house, serving as a form of home delivery for ladies whose outside shopping was severely limited by cultural traditions. There was another type of specialty establishment, the metropolitan goods shops (*jinghuo dian*), which were better capitalized and catered to an upscale clientele. Their 'jing' goods were elegant handicrafts, usually from Suzhou or Hangzhou, as well as jewellery, snuff boxes, accoutrements for official robes, and expensive gifts. Then there were the foreign goods shops (*yanghuo dian*) selling imported items. Because they were often owned and run by merchants from Guangdong or Fujian, these shops were also known as Cantonese goods shops (*guanghuo dian*) (Shanghai baihuo gongsi et al. 1988:9–25).

Starting with the 1850s, however, 'guanghuo' not only stood for Cantonese goods shops, but also for stores that sold goods based on imported western models but produced by Cantonese craftsmen. Thus, appearing on the shelves of guanghuo dian would be such 'new' domestically produced items as 'guang'-style locks, 'guang'-style lamps, and 'guang'-style hair brushes. Many of these shops also grew in size: family owned or partnerships, they hired managers and clerks to run them. From the 1870s, even larger establishments using a new composite term *yangguang zahuo dian* came about, selling an even wider range of goods: upscale handicrafts, simple and inexpensive everyday goods, as well as fancy imports and improved domestic goods. Finally, by the early 1900s, these establishments became known as Chinese-style department stores (baihuo gongsi) (Shanghai baihuo gongsi et al. 1988:9–25, Lo and Deng 1969).

Neither Chinese-style retail establishments nor the foreigner-run department stores in Shanghai and Hong Kong became the model for Sincere and Wing On at their inception in Hong Kong. There were, however, several intriguing connections among them. The import and adaptation of western products and their skillful modification by Cantonese craftsmen, and the trend towards larger stores selling a greater variety of goods under one roof, were all traditions which propelled the founders of Sincere and Wing On. This tradition eventually allowed them to organize new business structures and to grow spectacularly during the 1910s and 1920s. It also partially explains why these two modern department stores, as well as the Sun Sun and the Dah Sun companies (collectively known during Republican China as the Four Big Department Stores), were all founded by Cantonese merchants. Since the eighteenth century, the Cantonese had the greatest exposure to western influence and just as some Cantonese who stayed home were being affected by western ways, other Cantonese went abroad and decided to bring home western models of doing business, adjusting them to China. Thus, most of the original founders of the four big department stores – the Mas, the Guos, the Cais, the Lis, the Lius, and several more – had spent time in Australia, Hawaii or other parts of North America. And both Ma Yingbiao (*Figure 3.1*) and Guo Le (*Figure 3.2*), the two principal founders of Sincere and Wing On, credited Sydney's flagship store, Anthony Hordern & Son, as the model for their own creations (Xianshi gongsi 1924[?]:Records p. 1–2; Guo 1949:1–2).

The phenomenal expansion of both the Sincere and Wing On companies during the early 1920s was, however, slowed by patriotic boycotts, workers' strikes, and civil wars later in the decade. When Japan invaded China in 1931, the challenges and uncertainties only

Figure 3.1 Official portrait of Ma Yingbiao, founder and inspirational leader of the Sincere Company. Ma ran it as managing director until he lost control in 1935, when the board of directors voted him honorary managing director for life.

increased. Although both companies were buffeted by the same forces, Wing On weathered the storm much better than Sincere. By the end of the 1930s, Wing On was bruised and humbled, but the management remained strong and independent with Guo Le and his brother, Guo Quan, as well as several younger family members, still in control. On the other hand, Sincere lost its independence to the bankers and infighting partners. Neither Ma Yingbiao, nor other members of his family, had control of the management after 1935. This chapter will

Philip Gock Chin (Co-founder)   *James Gock Lock. (Co-founder)*
郭　泉（創辦人）　　　　　　　　郭　樂　創辦人

Figure 3.2 Portraits of Guo Quan and Guo Le, the two principal founders of the Wing On Company. The two brothers complemented each other in personality and entrepreneurial talents so well that even though they started their operation in 1907, several years later than Sincere, they outperformed the latter by the early 1920s.

explain these divergent outcomes by examining the management structure of these two companies, and its interaction with the personal styles and cultural values of the principals involved. But first, a brief account of the rise and expansion of Wing On and Sincere in Hong Kong and Shanghai will outline the background of the story.

Rise and Expansion of the Sincere and Wing On Companies: 1900–1921

On 8 January 1900, with only HK$25,000 as capital and the rather hesitant support of eleven partners, Ma Yingbiao opened the Sincere Company's modest two-store front on Hong Kong's Queen's Road, Central, for business. Ma had worked in several businesses in Australia since the 1880s, moving from miner to store clerk to partner in a Sydney wholesale and import firm before deciding to return to Hong

Kong in 1894. Impressed with the success of Anthony Hordern, who had transformed himself from a mere peddler to the owner of Sydney's largest department store, Ma tried to adapt the western department store format to China. At first, Ma's efforts proved unsuccessful, for several of his earlier partners remained skeptical of his new-fangled idea. They preferred that he continue to run several traditional lines of business under a partnership called the Yongsheng Zhuang. It served as an import and export agency as well as a remittance shop for fellow Cantonese living abroad. But Ma persevered until his partners eventually relented.

Once launched, the Sincere department store combined western retailing techniques with Ma's own ideas, rooted in older Chinese tradtions. First, wares were presented in elaborate window settings (using up most of the capital). Second, he did away with bargaining by insisting that there would be only one fixed price for each item. Third, he carefully selected and trained a sales team of some 25 young men and women, all of them recruited from his home county of Zhongshan in Guangdong province. Ma provided them with the rudiments of commercial learning, and drilled into them the need to be unfailingly courteous to customers. Customers, so the new maxim went, were always right. They were to be at work on time and to maintain clean personal appearance. On Sunday mornings they were to attend a Christian religious service conducted by him on company premises in order to ensure they would lead moral and upright lives (Xianshi gongsi 1924[?]:Records p. 1–2).[2]

These new practices were eventually accepted, though not without conflict. One practice, however, had to be terminated: the hiring of female sales clerks. As an innovation introduced in the west by Alexander T. Stewart and William Whiteley among others, these female clerks had successfully attracted women shoppers into the stores and provided many women with a new and dignified source of income. According to the social historian Gunther Barth (1980:128–30, 137–8), the increasing popularity of shopping in department stores among women turned these institutions into veritable cultural and community centers. In China, where women did not work behind sales counters except in small shops run by husband and wife teams, Ma's fashionably dressed 'salesgirls' created a sensation that led to gawking crowds. Angry partners complained that their presence was disrupting sales and bringing the new venture into disrepute. After months of resistance, Ma succumbed to the partners' demands and laid off all the women clerks, including his own wife and sister-in-law. It was not until some 30 years later that they were successfully reintroduced in China's major cities.

The greater crisis that confronted the company during its first year, however, was the impact of a destructive typhoon that blew away the upper floors of the store, and Sincere almost failed but for Ma's persistence. Only in 1904, when the store was completely rebuilt and refurbished, did the company turn profitable. By 1907 its profits had increased so much that reserves exceeded HK$90,000. Buoyed by the success, Ma's partners supported his proposals to raise new capital among themselves and their friends, and to move to larger premises on Des Voeux Road, Central (*Figure 3.3*). They also decided to apply to the Hong Kong government to incorporate as a limited liability company. This was accomplished in 1909. The partnership was dissolved, and the company, with an authorized capital of HK$200,000, registered under Hong Kong's Companies Acts as the Sincere Company, Ltd. From then on, it grew rapidly, opening new branches and expanding into related lines of business. The paid-up capital quadrupled to HK$800,000 by 1913, then increased again two and a half times to HK$2 million by 1916. Almost all new funds came from shareholders' re-investment of dividends, bonuses, the company's undistributed reserves, as well as from other Chinese who had resided at one point or another in Australia and North America. Meanwhile, new branches were opened, first in Guangzhou (1912), then in Shanghai and Singapore (1917), and finally two buying offices in Kobe (1917) and London (1922). Among the branches, the Shanghai operation, with a separate HK$2 million of paid-up capital and a totally new building providing over 10,000 square meters of sales space on four floors, was by far the largest (Sincere n.d.:12–4, 26–7; Xianshi gongsi 1924[?]:Records p. 1–3, 11–3).

Then, in a departure from his Australian model, Ma quickly expanded into related businesses. First, he added roof-top entertainment quarters to the Hong Kong, Guangzhou and Shanghai department store buildings, together with adjoining bars, restaurants and hotels (the Oriental Hotel). By 1915, he integrated backwards as he set up some ten production workshops in Guangzhou, which included machine shops, craft production industries, and food processors. They provided a stable source for his wares, but it could only be a 'partial' backward integration since as a 'universal provider', he wanted to bring the finest of any goods from anywhere in the world to his customers. In these early years, when Chinese factories could turn out only relatively simple western-style products, Ma's production lines were making either inexpensive items or high quality, expensive handicrafts. Some evidence supports the notion that Ma was trying to gather highly skilled

Figure 3.3 Sincere department store building on Des Voeux Road, Central, Hong Kong, shown here in 1925 as the company celebrated its 25th anniversary with a large crowd watching a Chinese-style fireworks display. It was the main company's store in Hong Kong and its corporate headquarters from 1917 to 1968, when the building was torn down and replaced by a modern 27 storey shopping and office building.

craftsmen to produce quality craft items for his department stores, and to work on improvements from borrowed western models in ways quite similar to what traditional guanghuo dian products had accomplished. By 1921, Shanghai's Product Exhibition Hall, sponsored by the Shanghai General Chamber of Commerce to encourage domestic

73

manufacturing, had given Sincere's workshops at least seven awards, including those for ivory carving, cloisonné vases, laquer works, Cantonese-style embroideries and toys (Wu 1936:ch. 5, 1a-b, 16b, 20b, 24b, 31a).

Sincere continued to expand its small-scale manufacturing. In 1917, as it opened its department store in Shanghai, it also installed a small workshop in the area. Five years later, this workshop had grown into numerous manufacturing facilities, churning out machine-made products as well as custom-made jewellery, employing altogether over 300 workers. One particularly successful line was the manufacture of perfumes, marketed under the company's brand names from Hong Kong to Shenyang, Harbin, Hankou, Ji'nan, Tianjin, Beijing and Shanghai. Finally, two insurance companies, the Sincere Insurance and Investment Company, Ltd. (1914) and the Sincere Life Assurance Company, Ltd. (1922) were founded (Xianshi gongsi 1924[?]:Records p. 10–6; Sincere n.d.:13–8).

Meanwhile, in Hong Kong, another returnee from Australia, from a village neighbouring Ma's in Zhongshan county, started another modern department store in 1907 with a larger, but still rather modest, capital of HK$160,000 in 1907. This was the Wing On Company launched by two brothers, Guo Le and Guo Quan, and eleven other partners (*Figure 3.4*). And like Sincere, the partners were old-time business associates who had shared earlier business ventures in Australia and Hawaii, and a few were also kinsmen from their village. Guo Quan, the younger brother and junior partner, had returned to Hong Kong first to make preparations for Wing On's opening. His early experience of having worked for a British law firm and then at the British Consulate in Hawaii probably made it easier for him to find his way through Hong Kong's British colonial administration. Guo Le followed two years later, leaving the Australian business to their two younger brothers, Guo Yihui and Guo Hehui. The brothers' decision to start Wing On in Hong Kong was probably influenced by Ma Yingbiao's earlier success; they were anxious to learn what they could from Ma. They knew each other well, for like Ma, both Guo Le and Guo Quan had spent many years in Australia – Guo Quan in trade, while Guo Le worked in mines and on farms before turning to trade. Guo Le, who was Ma's junior, had at one time also worked for Ma's wholesale fruit store and import business in Sydney before he and Ma became partners. Moreover, the wife of his other younger brother, Guo Yihui, and the wife of Ma Yingbiao were sisters.[3]

In spite of these multi-layered connections – neighboring ancestral homes, one-time employer–employee relationship, and kinship through

Figure 3.4 Wing On department store building on Des Voeux Road, Central, Hong Kong, c. 1930, constructed in the early 1910s as part of Wing On's first major expansion from its modest original store, which was on Queen's Road, Central, only one store-front wide, and all on the street level. Note that like its main competitor, the Sincere department store a few blocks away, part of the bulding was used as a hotel.

a brother's marriage – it is unlikely that Ma was willing to share his experience. We simply do not know; what is known is that both Ma and Guo were highly competitive. Some ten years later, when both were in Shanghai preparing for the opening of their two department stores there, Ma asked Guo Le for a copy of Wing On's architectural drawings showing the layout of the various sales departments. Guo agreed, and Ma was reported to be pleased, telling his assistants that he had nothing to fear, for Wing On's layout was inferior to what he had planned for Sincere. But on Wing On's grand opening, Ma found a different and far better layout, and realized that he had been deceived. Guo Le had purposely given Ma Yingbiao a set of early, somewhat improved drawings, thus affording him a false sense of confidence. Since Sincere opened first, it was too late for him to make any changes.[4]

In Hong Kong, Wing On's success was immediate. In 1909, as its capital jumped to HK$600,000, it followed Sincere's example of changing from a partnership into a privately owned limited liability corporation. Rapid expansion continued so that by 1916 its capital had

75

increased to HK$2 million, largely through re-investment of its earnings. The next several years saw Wing On expanding into branches, subsidiary production facilities, related lines of business like hotels (Great Eastern Hotels) and roof-top gardens – all in a manner very similar to Sincere's. Wing On also organized several affiliates (*lianhuo*), each with its own independent capital that included, like Sincere's, two insurance companies: Wing On Marine and Fire Insurance Company, Ltd. (1915), and Wing On Life Assurance Company, Ltd. (1925). In 1921, it also launched a modern textile mill in Shanghai, the Wing On Textile Company (Guo 1961:preface, p. 10–1, 14–7).

Both Wing On and Sincere also tried to inculcate a sense of belonging and company spirit in their workers. Like Ma, the Guos were converted Christians who set aside Sunday mornings so that all staff could attend mandatory religious service. In addition to attention to their moral and spiritual life, both companies also developed elaborate activities to increase workers' cultural and physical well-being. This was especially true for their junior staff, a majority of whom lived in company dormitories and dined at the companies' mess halls. Each company had elaborate rules governing every aspect of their employees' professional activities, and these regulations were strictly enforced by fines. To engage staff outside of their long working hours, each company ran an evening school that later expanded to include a drama troupe, as well as organized group sports and calisthenics. In addition, there was also a trust fund to help with the medical needs and burial costs of indigent staff and their families (Xianshi gongsi 1924[?]: Records p. 9; Wing On 1932:section on History). The result seems to have been a rather successful blending of Chinese Confucian benevolent authoritarianism with English Victorian notions of self-help and of accepting responsibility for one's own action.

In 1914, Ma made two special trips to Shanghai, where he became convinced that only Shanghai with its central location, its population of wealthy businessmen, its foreign diplomats and Chinese gentry-officials, could offer Sincere the opportunity to sustain rapid growth and profitability. He raised new capital to open a department store on Shanghai's busiest street, Nanjing Road, that was to be bigger and grander than the original store in Hong Kong (*Figures 3.5* and *3.6*). The Guo brothers again followed in 1915, after sending their own investigation team to study the Shanghai situation (*Figure 3.7*). Then, only eleven months after Sincere's opening, Wing On of Shanghai opened in September 1918 directly opposite the Sincere store. Each had

Figure 3.5 Sincere's tailoring department, Shanghai, c. 1925. Note the juxtaposition of clerks in formal Chinese gowns behind the counters, and the two officers in fashionable western suits in front.

a paid-up capital of HK$2 million, and these ventures were considered the largest subscription of capital up to that time for commercial retail business, though neither Sincere nor Wing On appear to have had much of a problem raising it. Some 75 per cent of the capital in each case came from several thousands of overseas Chinese who placed their faith in Ma, the Guo brothers, and the two companies they managed.

Then, in early 1919, the Sincere Company in Hong Kong formed an amalgamation of all the HK$7 million capital resources of the group under its own board of directors, leaving each of the affiliates and subsidiaries with advisory boards (*canshi bu*) made up of local directors, and making it possible for any of the corporate units to be supported by the group's overall capital resources (Sincere n.d.:14–5). A similar pooling of resources was undertaken by Wing On in the early 1920s, although it adopted a different structure. Thus, even though the afffiliates retained their own boards of directors, the Wing On Company in Hong Kong, as senior member and usually with the largest cash reserves, retained centralized authority by owning about 20 percent of the stock in each affiliate, and by having several of its own key board

Figure 3.6 Sincere department store building, Shanghai, 1924. This is an artist's rendering of the building in western architectural style, on Shanghai's Nanjing Road. Note that the mid-section served as a hotel while the roof was turned into an entertainment garden.

members sit on the other boards. By interlocking the various boards in this way, the Guo brothers, who personally owned 5.6 percent of the Shanghai company's stocks, and probably about 20 percent of the Hong Kong company's stock, were thus able to control the entire corporate group's business, and could move its total capital resources from unit to unit as the need arose (Shanghai Yong'an gongsi 1981:11, 71–4).

Two Turbulent Decades: 1921–1941

The fast-paced growth and diversification of both Sincere and Wing On up to 1921 gave way to more mature developments as the companies confronted new political challenges in the 1920s and 1930s. Sales and profitability of the department stores in both Hong Kong and Shanghai continued to grow handsomely into the late 1920s. However, the Guangzhou operations started to do poorly beginning from about 1920,

Figure 3.7 Wing On department store building on Shanghai's Nanjing Road. This picture was taken soon after the building was completed in 1918, almost one year after its main competitor the Sincere department store's building opened its doors just across the street. The size and layout of the shopping floors were even grander than Sincere's; their presence transformed Shanghai's Nanjing Road into China's shopping mecca.

as military strife amongst several provincial warlords began to destabilize the region. These events seem to mark the beginning of the decline of Sincere relative to Wing On, for Wing On did not invest as heavily as Sincere in Guangzhou. Given the cause of Sincere's troubles, the Guo brothers probably congratulated themselves for having chosen to limit Wing On's main bases of operation to just Hong Kong and Shanghai's International Settlement, allowing them to register their companies under British law and operate their business in foreign-controlled territories. What they did not foresee was that foreign protection would not continue to provide a haven against the increasingly strident voices of students and workers, who would soon demand social justice and better work benefits, and lead violent demonstrations and boycotts attacking western imperialists and their imported goods.

Indeed, as if to presage what was to come, students and workers in Shanghai responded quickly to the historic May Fourth demonstration in Beijing by leading their first city-wide sympathy strike from 5 June through 12 June in 1919. When both Wing On and Sincere, with the encouragement of the British Consulate, tried to keep their doors open, they were confronted for the first time by their workers who forced management to respect the strike (Wei 1987:212). In 1925, boycotts of British made products caused major problems for both companies since these goods were their most important imports. A compromise solution allowed the two companies to keep their existing stock after pledging not to buy any more British goods. But the situation was worse in Hong Kong as the seamen's strike there lasted a full year, from the summer of 1925 through September of 1926. Then in January 1927, as the Guomindang's Northern Expedition forces marched toward Shanghai, workers under communist party leadership formed unions and made a series of demands for better working conditions and better benefits. The management of both Sincere and Wing On fought against them bitterly, but in the end, even after the success of Chiang Kaishek's counter coup in April, during which the two unions were forced to disband and their worker leaders dismissed, workers at both Sincere and Wing On retained most of their gains. Moreover, the Guomindang leadership quickly compounded their losses by demanding that each company buy CNC500,000 of its government bonds (Sincere n.d.:20; Xianshi gongsi 1924[?]:section on Records p. 11; Coble 1980; Shanghai Yong'an gongsi 1981:109–19).[5]

While these problems of the 1920s cut into the companies' profits, they did not stop them from growing, for the underlying urban economy remained strong. The crises during the 1930s, however, were far more serious. In early 1932, the Chinese controlled areas of Shanghai came under Japanese naval bombardment; Wing On lost several properties to fire, and its woodmaking factory in Zhabei was razed to the ground. A depressed economy during the early 1930s further lowered their retail sales, while Wing On's textile mill came under heavy pressure from a combination of much deflated prices and dumping practices by competing Japanese-owned mills. For several months during 1932 and 1933, the Wing On mill would have gone under had it not been for the Guo brothers' move of HK $7 million of cash reserves from Wing On in Hong Kong to the mill in Shanghai. It was a high stake gamble. While it helped prevent the mill's fall, it almost cost the company its entire operations in Hong Kong because in 1935 the Hong Kong financial market suffered a serious crisis, causing runs to hit several local banks, including the two banks belonging to Wing On and Sincere, which in turn threatened to engulf their respective department store operations. What saved Wing On in Hong

Kong was Guo Quan's constant pressure on his brother Guo Le, who was in Shanghai, to sell off the excess stock of the mill at below cost to raise sufficient cash to rush to Hong Kong to regain depositors' confidence there. It was a close call, but it proved the effectiveness of the policy of pooling all capital resources, while allowing affiliates to retain their separate boards (Shanghai Yong'an gongsi 1981:125–8).

Meanwhile, the same financial crisis in Hong Kong had a far more disastrous impact on Sincere, which had already been weakened by poor sales and an earlier run-in with the military strongman and governor of Guangdong, Chen Jitang. In 1932, exploiting the anti-Japanese sentiments at the time and planning to turn the Guangzhou store over to joint official and private partnership, Chen sent a search team to the company warehouse to look for hidden Japanese-made goods – items which Sincere had pulled off the shelves in order to respect the renewed boycott against Japanese goods. On finding the goods, Chen confiscated them and imposed a heavy CNC200,000 fine on the company. This was part of an elaborate plot by Chen's military government to gain control of the company. In 1935, as Chen was about to issue an order forcing the company to accept a government loan, Chen himself was forced out of his post as governor. The series of mishaps in both Guangzhou and Hong Kong, each placing additional burdens on the company's reserves and liquidity, was just too much for Sincere to overcome. The board of directors turned to the Hongkong & Shanghai Bank for a HK$4 million loan. Ma Yingbiao opposed this move, especially because of the bank's conditions: to take over all company assets as collateral, thereby gaining full access to company books, and to have prior approval rights over any major policy changes by management. He lost the struggle, however, accepted the proforma and powerless title of honorary managing director, and neither he nor any other member of his family ever regained control of the company. Chen Lizhen, the new chairman and managing director who had formerly been a manager, precipitated Ma's ouster. Such a blow must have wounded him deeply, for Chen was also the brother of Chen Xiaoxia, who was Ma's early partner, supporter and fellow returnee from Australia. But the new managing director lasted only a year. The board was in dissension, while the real authority for managing Sincere was in the hands of the Hongkong & Shanghai Bank (Xiao 1972:137–8).

One more blow soon followed. On 13 August 1937, after Japan's full assault on China, a stray bomb from a Japanese air raid on the Chinese section of Shanghai fell on Nanjing Road and blasted off a part of Sincere's building. Some fifteen staff members were killed, with hundreds more injured. The blast also shattered all the glass windows on Wing On's lower floors. While Wing On suffered no loss of life, each company sustained about CNC400,000 in property damage. Since the Nanjing Road area was within the International Settlement and therefore off limits to the Japanese bombers, and since the property damaged belonged to companies registered under British law in Hong Kong, Wing On sought compensation through the British Consulate in Shanghai. Yet not even the British authorities supported the claim (Shanghai Yong'an gongsi 1981:147–9)[6] and both companies had to absorb their losses. But in a strange turn of fate, between 1937 and 1941 both companies in Shanghai returned to profitability: the loans from foreign banks were paid back in much depreciated currency, and wealthy Chinese refugees from the lower Yangzi area, anxious not to be caught in the cross-fire of the Sino-Japanese conflict, again swarmed Shanghai's International Settlement and the French Concession. Their conspicuous consumption helped create a kind of eerie short boom during those years, until Pearl Harbor and the Japanese occupation of Shanghai and Hong Kong forced the companies to either collaborate or close down (Shanghai Yong'an gongsi 1981:149–59).

Sincere and Wing On: Similar Structures and Western Influence *vs.* Different Values and Personalities

Sincere and Wing On had much in common during their formative years, for the three principal founders who shaped them – Ma Yingbiao for Sincere, Guo Le and Guo Quan for Wing On – shared many qualities. They were all bold visionaries, willing to take risks, and able to sell new products and build innovative organizations. They could transfer the essence of what others had done in different cultural settings and adapt it to their own world.

Having overcome hardship and deprivation to become successful entrepreneurs in Australia, both the Guo brothers and Ma used their experience and exposure to new ideas upon their return to China. They adopted Hordern & Son's way of displaying their wares, practiced the fixed price system, and gave careful attention to the training of their staff and officers. Ma Yingbiao, in particular, had a vision of how to make these new ways of marketing work in China. He and the Guo brothers also modified their western model in at least two ways – by taking a holistic approach in the treatment of staff, and by promoting rapid growth and financial stability through wide-ranging diversification of their business enterprises, even as the main

82

line of business in department store retailing had barely been established.

Their concerns and empathy for their staff might have derived from their deeply-held Christian faith and their own early struggle in Australia. But the principal impulse was embedded in Chinese cultural values and traditions that taught that a good and strong leader is not simply a paternalistic or benevolently authoritarian, but also loyal and personally accessible to his staff and junior partners. These qualities, required of effective leaders and expected by subordinates, allowed networking based on a proper sense of hierarchy, kinship and regional loyalties. Networking, in turn, created trust and assured the smooth and effective running of operations, especially in the absence of well established legal, governmental and institutional structures (Redding 1991).

Their early diversification into several lines of businesses – hotels, entertainment, roof-top gardens, crafts, manufacturing, and insurance – might seem puzzling at first, but these moves came from the founders' own entrepreneurial background. Their fruit wholesale businesses in Sydney had also engaged in several lines of business. For instance, in addition to fruit, the Guo brothers operated as export and import traders, ran a remittance department, and joined a partnership which set up collecting stations on Fiji to collect bananas and later owned and managed several plantations on that island as well as in Queensland (Chan 1994).

Moreover, the early diversification allowed the two companies to receive additional sources of income as receipts from the hotels and entertainment gardens were added to their working capital and profits. One important subsidiary line of business which has not been discussed so far was the companies' savings or 'banking' departments (*yinye bu*). These departments accepted monetary deposits from clients who were almost exclusively from Australia, Hawaii and North America. These deposits, in turn, provided a major part of the firms' working capital. The departments also functioned as remittance banks to receive deposits for clients' families and friends in Zhongshan county and elsewhere. As noted above, even before setting up the Sincere Company in 1900, Ma Yingbiao had already spent six years in Hong Kong where he owned and managed the Yongsheng Zhuang which, among other lines of business, operated a traditional remittance service, called *piju* ('batch-despatching' office). Likewise with the Guos, who used their own business in Sydney, a separate fruit wholesaler, importer and exporter named Yong'an Guolan, to operate a similar kind of remittance service by linking up with a native bank (*qianzhuang*) in the county seat of Zhongshan county.[7]

This experience in running small traditional businesses for the Chinese community in Australia did not deter them from switching to modern business management when they decided to operate bigger department stores in Hong Kong and Shanghai. Both the Guo brothers and Ma had been exposed to large-scale business organizations and practice while in Sydney, and even though they had no experience of actually running such businesses, they appreciated their efficiency and power. Guo Quan's autobiography includes a chapter on 'Speaking of Experience' in which he compares western and Chinese practices in the retail business and shows how the western ways were far stronger because of their systematic organization and careful attention to market trends and to employees' education and training. On the other hand, he observes that the Chinese ways were a great deal weaker because so much of the retail business was carried out by peddlers or by small operators who lacked organization and paid no attention to service (Guo 1961:24–30).

Guo's admiration for the 'western ways' probably reflects lessons he first learnt during his frequent visits to Sydney's Hordern & Son department store to learn how and what types of goods were displayed, how sales were conducted, and what services were performed for customers in a department store. He and his brother did not choose to establish a modern business in Australia because they realized that they had no chance of being accepted by the majority of white Australians. But to introduce this model to a Chinese community was an attractive and feasible alternative. This was a rather remarkable proposition, for in these early years of the twentieth century, Ma and the Guo brothers were among the very first to recognize the importance of adopting modern organizational structure and business strategy, and putting them into practice. This went well beyond the acceptance of western technology that some Chinese businessmen had already articulated.

Thus both Sincere and Wing On underwent a similar evolution of corporate structure. First, as rather traditional partnerships, then as incorporated private companies, and finally as public companies raising new capital through public subscription. Each had a board of directors at the top, which seldom met except for the annual meeting. Its chairman had little power, while the managing director served as the all-powerful chief executive, with the chief manager and deputy manager reporting directly to him and carrying out his orders. Under the manager were several divisions that were divided somewhat differently at Sincere and Wing On, but which covered the same critical areas of general administration (including personnel), secretarial services, accounting, sales and merchandising (Xianshi gongsi 1924[?]:section on Records p. 8–9, 12–3; Xianggang Yong'an gongsi 1932:section on History p. 4–6; Shanghai Yong'an gongsi 1981:8, 85).

The largest division in both companies was the sales division. Sincere had nineteen departments when it first opened, but expanded quickly until there were between 45 and 55 in each of the companies. For Wing On, every two or three departments formed a cluster, headed by another tier of supervisors. Sincere seems to have had fewer clusters, with one supervisor for each of the four to seven floors of retail space. In Shanghai, where Guo Le served as resident managing director, he would conduct regular weekly meetings with both the supervisors and the department heads. With the supervisors, he would gather information and identify concerns, he would encourage discussion on pending issues, solicit their advice and weigh alternative proposals before making his decision. The other weekly meetings with department heads provided him with further information. Issues would be raised, but there would be little or no discussion. Guo Le or his manager used these meetings to inform the department heads of decisions already made, usually at the supervisors' meetings, so that they could carry out the orders (Shanghai Yong'an gongsi 1981:87). In Hong Kong, Guo Quan and Ma Yingbiao conducted similar meetings with their staff. Acccording to Guo Dihuo, a nephew and U.S.-trained textile engineer, Guo Le was always trying to learn more about the principles of modern management. He thought that the Wing On textile mills, where he became deputy manager, ran a more modern operation than their rival and China's largest textile mills, the Mouxin Mills headed by two brothers from the Rong family, and that during the 1920s and 1930s, only the industrialist Liu Hongsheng was equally attentive to modern management.[8]

But despite these structural similarities, Wing On and Sincere developed into rather different institutions. A major reason for this was that Ma and the Guo brothers had very different personalities and attitudes. This became quite evident after conducting several interviews with retired workers from both companies as well as with relatives of Ma and the Guos. Wing On workers remember Guo Le and Guo Quan as being fair but also very firm. Both would inspect the retailing floors frequently and unannounced, and would not suffer fools easily. Guo Le, who stayed in Shanghai during most of the 1920s and 1930s, kept a suite in the company's hotel next to the shopping area so that he could walk the floors in the evenings, occasionally losing his temper if he found something amiss. At the beginning, Guo Le brought about 50 fellow Cantonese to Shanghai to fill most of the supervisory posts; their predominance lessened over time but never disappeared. He also insisted that they learn the local customs and dialect, and enforced company rules equally on everyone. Guo Quan, on the other hand, was meticulously thorough, self-disciplined and calm. He was a creature of habit, and led a highly ordered life. He consistently practised what he strongly believed, that everything and every person had a proper place and stood in a definite relation to one another.[9]

The two brothers worked flawlessly as a team. Guo Le was dynamic and boldly innovative; Guo Quan was reserved, but also most skillful at improvisations. While the older brother explored new frontiers, the younger one maintained a smooth running operation for a rapidly growing organization. One of their observant business associates states it this way:

> Their personalities were different, yet complementary. Gock Lock [i.e. Guo Le] was tough, hard-driving, a man of undisputed talent as an enterprising businessman. Gock Chin [i.e. Guo Quan] was soft-spoken, calm; a brilliant administrator. Gock Lock adventured and discovered startling ideas; Gock Chin made these ideas work.
>
> (Wing On 1975:18)

On the other hand, a former Sincere employee remembers Ma Yingbiao for being full of camaraderie and spontaneity: 'He was always very gentle with his staff'. Ma also walked the floors, but was often forgetful or too flexible to impose penalties for infringement of rules. This image of a rather bumbling, easygoing personality, however, was not universally accepted by those who worked with him, and he had several bruising battles with his partners and senior staff. For instance, the chief manager of the Sincere Department Store in Shanghai, Liu Xiji, left the company in 1923 to start the rival Sun Sun department store after claiming that Ma would not give him sufficient authority and had treated him unfairly over bonuses and other benefits (Ding 1992:8). Such an open clash foreshadowed later events when Ma was forced out of his managing directorship in 1935, when the impetus also came from a former manager. One retired worker at Wing On commented that whereas members of the Guo family might disagree over what goods to buy or how to resolve some bigger and trickier problem, they would always discuss frankly among themselves, and once a decision was made, the various members would fall into line and present a united front. The image one had of Sincere, he continued, was just the opposite; too many of their managers voiced different opinions, and they fought endlessly.[10] Ma was either unwilling or unable to impose discipline among his senior staff and partners. All these different images reflect the complex and multi-faceted nature of Ma's personality.

Probably, Ma Wenhui, his son and the only family member who had worked quite successfully with him, having risen to chief manager of the Hong Kong department store during the early 1930s, understood him best when he commented that his father 'had lived through several lives'. First, he was a poor struggling miner in Australia, then a revolutionary, who believed in Sun Yatsen's cause and headed a munitions department in Guangzhou. But he soon turned against politics after he quit his post over some squabble with his superiors, and became an entrepreneur with the conviction that only commerce and industry could save China from poverty and foreign aggression. For a time, he also believed in the need for education, contributing generously to the Lingnan College, an American-run Christian college in Guangzhou, and became the first Chinese to sit on its board of trustees. But by 1920, he turned against all forms of formal education, regarding it as stifling to the mind. At the time, Ma Wenhui was still in Lingnan's preparatory school and had not yet entered its freshman class when his father pulled him out of school and told him to go to work as an apprentice in Sincere. To his son's protest, the father responded that he had had only three years of village school education, and that was all he had ever needed. As if to prove his point, his youngest son, Ma Xiaocong, was also taken out of school soon thereafter and put to work.[11] In 1980, shortly before his retirement, he was still working for the company as a sub-manager in the main Hong Kong office.

No other difference in attitudes between Ma Yingbiao and the Guo brothers is more poignant or stark than their opposing views on education. For at about the same time that Ma was denying his own sons college and secondary school education, the Guo brothers were planning to start a large-scale textile mill in Shanghai and moving from retailing, servicing and handicraft workshop manufacturing into modern industrial production. As part of their preparation, they brought in a senior engineer, Luo Ganbo, to be a company director in charge of production, hired a well-known accountant, Pan Xulun, to set up a modern accounting system that included scientific analysis of costs, and they sent four of their sons and nephews, some still studying at Lingnan College, to enroll in British and American technical colleges and universities to become proficient in textile technology.

Their plan paid off, for at least two of them, Guo Linbao, Guo Quan's son, and Guo Dihuo, Guo Yihui's son, returned and became productive, senior officers of the company, and helped the Wing On mill to develop, by the late 1930s, into the second largest textile mill in China (Shanghai Yong'an gongsi 1981:46).[12]

Sincere's existing records do not tell us why Ma did not take the company into textiles or some other modern industrial production. The two companies were seriously competing with one another and Wing On, being the younger company, seemed to be always one or more years behind, so when Wing On launched its textile project in 1921, it was a kind of double first for the company. Ma's failure to respond was not for lack of vision or boldness, or because he was uncertain about raising sufficient capital, but probably due to his ignorance of modern technology and, given his opinion about education, his inability to confront this ignorance.

Cultural Embeddedness and Successful Enterpreneurship: A Conclusion

Recent studies on the role of entrepreneurship outside of North America and Western Europe suggest that Joseph Schumpeter's (1947:151) classic formulation of the entrepreneur as a risk-taking visionary with the ability not only to form 'new combinations', but also to do 'things that are already being done in a new way', needs a major addition to take into account the importance of cultural embeddedness, including such influences as 'social norms and beliefs, psychological motivations for achievement, the legitimacy of entrepreneurship, questions of social "marginality", and the "internal fit"' (Berger 1991). Schumpeter's elegantly simple formula would surely fit both Ma and the Guo brothers nicely. However, the new emphasis on cultural elements helps us understand why Wing On was more successful than Sincere, and why the Guo brothers played a more sustained role in Wing On's successes than Ma did in Sincere's.

The Guos made use of all the cultural supports to the fullest: family solidarity, staff networking, team work between brothers, collaboration, paternalism, localism, and the like. And they balanced them effectively with modern values such as careful attention to technical education, management science and a fair merit system. Ma Yingbiao, too, tried to turn cultural values to his advantage, such as his holistic approach to his staff. But he was unable to collaborate with his staff or partners, and he lacked someone, a brother or a close friend, with whom he could form a complementary team. And finally, he failed to groom his children or someone else from the next generation to succeed him. In the end, in spite of his boldness, energy and vision, he became ineffectual in the Chinese cultural environment, for he seemed unable to successfully balance his traditional cultural values with his modern ideas. And as he failed, Sincere suffered as well. By the early 1930s, as Sincere was about to pass on to a different management, it had lost its early spunk and dynamism – that competitive edge which made its rivalry with Wing On in their golden days of the 1910s and early 1920s so exhilarating and precious.

Notes

1 Barth (1980:110–47) provides a colorful account of the rise of modern department stores in Europe and America in his chapter 4, 'Department Stores'.
2 Interview with Ma Wenfei, son of Ma Yingbiao, Hong Kong, 7 and 9 July 1980.
3 Interview with Ma Wenfei, Hong Kong, 9 July 1980.
4 Interview with Guo Jing, retired employee of Wing On, Shanghai, 26 February 1979.
5 Throughout this period until the mid-1930s, the Hong Kong dollar and the Chinese dollar (*yuan*) were worth about the same.
6 Wing On's response to the British Consulate's rebuff was to change from British to American registration. It provided some company stock to two senior managers of an American firm in Shanghai, Andersen, Meyer & Co., and then invited them to sit on the Wing On board. The Wing On Textile Company, whose mills sat on Chinese territory, was also deeded to the American firm as collateral, so as to prevent Japanese seizure. The American registration, too, lost its efficacy after Pearl Harbor and the American declaration of war against Japan.
7 The names 'Yong'an' and 'Wing On' share the same Chinese characters, the different romanizations being due to their different pronounciations in Mandarin and Cantonese respectively.
8 Interview with Guo Yihuo, Guangzhou, 28 May 1981.
9 Interviews with Charles Mar Fan, Ma Xiaocong, Daniel P.K. Au and Pan Chengrong, with Sincere, Hong Kong Sincere Company head office, 25 June 1980. Interviews with Ma Yubao, Liang Caokui, Ji Gaozhi, Xie Xianglin and Sheng Jiang, with Wing On, Shanghai, 27 and 28 February, and 2 March 1980. Interview with Guo Dihuo, Guangzhou, 28 May 1981.
10 Interview with Xie Xianglin, retired Wing On employee, Shanghai, 28 February 1980; and with Pan Chengrong, former employee of Sincere, Hong Kong, 25 June 1980.
11 Interview with Ma Xiaocong, youngest son of Ma Yingbiao, Hong Kong Sincere Company office, 25 June 1980.
12 Interview with Guo Dihuo, Guangzhou, 28 May 1981.

4

CHINESE STORES IN RURAL AUSTRALIA[*]

Janis Wilton

In 1990, Chinese-born Australian Joe Mah[1] recalled working in the wholesale section of Sincere and Co., Hong Kong, during the 1920s. His uncle had arranged the job, and his uncle organized for his emigration to Australia in 1928. In Australia he joined the staff of another uncle's store in northern New South Wales.[2] Joe Mah was following the network of family and business connections, which had its origins in Zhongshan (Xiangshan), and in Sydney, and which extended to northern New South Wales. The proprietors of stores like Sincere and Co. were originally from Zhongshan, and the money and ideas behind the establishment of those stores came, at least partly, from Chinese-Australian savings and from Chinese-Australian exposure to department stores in Sydney. The links between China and Australia were then maintained through continued investments, employment in stores, visits, and marriages.

Scholarly attention has been paid to the history and nature of Sincere, and of counterparts like Wing On and Wing Sang (Chan 1982; Yen 1991). However, little attention has been paid to the Australian offshoots or cousins of these ventures – those Chinese department stores which were established in Sydney and in rural parts of New South Wales from the 1880s and into the first two decades of the twentieth century.[3] To what extent did they display characteristics similar to the large stores which their returned countrymen established

* The research on which this chapter is based would not have been possible without the cooperation, participation and support of the many Chinese-Australians who have willingly given of their time, memories, personal papers and memorabilia. I thank them while also absolving them of any mistakes or misinterpretations I may have made in piecing together aspects of their histories. I also wish to thank colleagues and friends, Ann-Katrin Eckermann for her constructive and wise comments, and Lai Chi-Kong for his encouragement.

90

in Hong Kong and China? To what extent did they develop characteristics peculiar to their status as Chinese–Australian stores operating in distinctly Australian environments? What was the nature of the links, business or otherwise, between the stores which developed in China and Hong Kong, and those which developed in Australia? What can their histories and characteristics add to our understanding of the nature and development of Asian department stores?

Fragmented answers to these questions lie imbedded in a range of scattered sources in Australia. These include immigration and naturalization files from Australian Archives, some surviving store records, and personal memories and memorabilia. The fragments offer leads which can be taken up elsewhere. They also indicate that an account of the stores constructed from the perspectives of the individuals and families who established, maintained, and developed them illustrates that Chinese values and practices were adapted to the specific local contexts. They further demonstrate that the success of the enterprises depended on negotiating a balance between Chinese traditions, western practices and the tenuous status of the Chinese in Australia.

Chinese Stores in Northern New South Wales

Here a case study approach is adopted. The core method of research has been oral history interviews with members and descendants of the families who played central roles in establishing and expanding department stores in a particular part of rural northern New South Wales (see *Figure 4.1*) (Wilton 1989). These stores had their origins in the tin mining booms which hit the region in the late nineteenth century, bringing an increase in population, including many Chinese. As on other gold and tin fields, the Chinese established occupations and services to meet the particular social and cultural needs of their communities, including the establishment of small shops selling Chinese ingredients and products, some of which gradually found customers among non-Chinese miners and local residents. Ernest Sue Fong described this process in recalling how his father, George Sue Fong, became a storekeeper in Emmaville, a tin mining town to the north of Glen Innes:

> Dad used to work the tin during the day, and at night he made his house into a little shop, selling vegetables from his garden out the back, mainly to other Chinese.

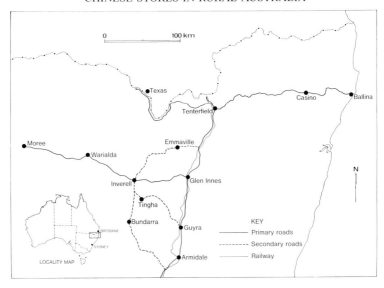

Figure 4.1 Northeastern New South Wales.

From the house, Dad moved into a small shop and he began working in the shop full-time. It was a mixed business and slowly it grew. By 1926, when it was at its height, there were about ten employees working there and the customers were no longer mainly Chinese because most of the Chinese had gone away by then. The business became known as Sue Fong and Sons.[4]

(Wilton 1988)

As the tin was mined out, most Chinese moved on to other parts of Australia or back to China. Some, however, stayed. Of those who stayed, an increasing number followed George Sue Fong's pattern and opened stores. By the late 1880s, the stores were no longer concentrated in the tin mining towns themselves, but were being opened in neighbouring larger towns like Inverell and Glen Innes. Among these stores were two which are still operating as Chinese Australian enterprises – Kwong Sing and Co. in Glen Innes and Hong Yuen Pty. Ltd. in Inverell.

Setting Up Business: Partnerships

Kwong Sing was established in 1886, Hong Yuen in 1889. Family memories and records reiterate that both stores were established as partnerships with three or more partners, although details of who all these partners were and the nature of their backgrounds are unclear. Some indication of the range of possibilities comes from records of other stores in the region. In 1903, for example, W. Warley and Co. was opened in Glen Innes. There were nineteen registered owners at the time, all Chinese. Five were described variously as storekeeper, manager (2) and assistant (2) at Warley, Glen Innes. Twelve had addresses in the then 'Chinatown' area of Sydney, and had their occupations listed as storeman (2), foreman, manager (2), school student (3), market seller and buyer, workman, market seller, and fruit seller. The two remaining partners were both described as managers, one from Guangzhou and one from Hong Kong.[5] Some of the initial partners were clearly members of the same family; others were already working in Glen Innes and were willing to invest a little in a new enterprise; and yet others, particularly the managers in Sydney, Hong Kong and Guangzhou, were providing capital backing, either for a new venture or for family members. The pattern is repeated. Documentary and oral evidence constantly reconfirms that Chinese stores in this northern part of New South Wales invariably began as partnerships with many partners, not all of whom were directly in the employ of the newly established business and not all of whom were necessarily members of the same family or village.

There are a number of possible explanations for the existence and nature of these partnerships. Some of the explanations link to the practices of traditional and emerging Chinese firms in China and Hong Kong; others relate to the specific circumstances of Chinese immigrants in Australia.

In analyses of the traditional Chinese firm, attention has been paid to the role of partnerships. Chan (1982: 220, 228–32) has established that partnerships were one form of ownership and management, with partners having different size shares and at least some, if not all, partners also being directly involved in the business and receiving salaries. Wong (1986: 62–7) has argued that partnerships with non-family members were a common means to initiate businesses. Certainly, an adaptation of these practices saw the establishment of the big department stores like Sincere, Wing On, and Wing Sang in Hong Kong and China (Yen 1991:77–117). Similar characteristics apply to Warley and Co. and, the evidence indicates, to Kwong Sing and Hong Yuen. All three were established through partnerships, with partners having varying size shares, varying investment of human labour in the business, and only some being members of the same family. However, an explanation which stops at an appeal to established and emerging practices in China is inadequate. Other forces were also at work in Australia which made these characteristics a practical, and often the only, means of establishing business.

The immigrant nature of the Chinese presence in Australia had clear repercussions for the nature of the occupations and businesses Chinese entered, and for the means they adopted to establish these businesses. In the first instance, only limited numbers of immediate family members were resident, temporarily or permanently, in Australia, hence the pool of potential family partners was small. Attention consequently turned to other Chinese from the same village or region in China who were living in the same locality in Australia, or who had business interests and assets which could be directed towards small investments in new ventures.

There were also the increasingly discriminatory legislation (Choi 1975:53–4) and attitudes in Australia which forced the Chinese into restricted areas of employment and especially into areas in which they could have the support of compatriots. Small businesses became the most obvious possibility, particularly self-contained enterprises in the laundry and furniture trades. Then, as legislation made Chinese involvement in those trades difficult, small general stores offered an alternative route to employment. These enterprises could be established through many partners each providing small amounts of capital, and could be maintained, at least initially, through employing Chinese workers and managers.

The small investment required of each partner was also attractive because it accommodated the traditional desire of Chinese emigrants to return home. When the time came for individuals to return to China, it was relatively easy to liquidate their share of assets without adversely affecting the business enterprise itself. There was usually another person designated to take up the shares, or to take on the responsibility of managing (and often ultimately owning) a particular store.

Large partnerships also became particularly useful once the Immigration Restriction Act of 1901 was in place. Colloquially known as the 'white Australia policy', this and its accompanying subsequent pieces of legislation were specifically intended to deter, if not prevent, Chinese settlement in Australia. However, exemption clauses were made particularly for Chinese with business interests in Australia. They could claim exemption from the regulations for themselves and for male members of their families who could be brought into the country to assist in their business enterprises (Choi 1975:113–5). The immigration records of the time regularly record Chinese shares or interest in particular enterprises in Australia. Two types of enterprise frequently mentioned were stores and market gardens. Such proven shares in a business in Australia were taken as evidence that applicants were making a worthwhile contribution to the local economy, and could train, employ and support sponsored immigrants.

It becomes apparent that the establishment of Chinese stores like Kwong Sing and Hong Yuen was clearly based on a convergence of the application of traditional and emerging Chinese practices in establishing businesses, as evident in studies of stores like Sincere and Wing On, and the specific circumstances of national and local contexts in Australia. This convergence of factors continued to characterise the history of these stores and is particularly apparent in the development of the stores into family businesses, in the expansion and diversification of the business bases of the stores, in the employment practices adopted, and in the contacts established and maintained with department stores in Hong Kong and China.

Family Businesses

The stores began as small businesses with many partners. As the businesses expanded, ownership contracted and became concentrated with one person who then distributed shares to family members who also became employees of the business. It was a pattern which accords very well with the emergence of the father-entrepreneur identified by Wong (1986) in his study of traditional Chinese firms. For Kwong Sing this father-entrepreneur was Percy Young (Kwan Hong Kee) and for Hong Yuen it was Harry Fay (Louie Mew Fay) (*Figures 4.2* and *4.3*).

Percy Young was born in about 1865 in Yonghao, Shiqi, Zhongshan. At around twenty years of age he followed the path of many other Chinese from the region and emigrated to Australia where, through Chinese (presumably Zhongshan) networks, he spent the next ten years working in a number of different Chinese stores, mostly in rural New South Wales. He also spent some time in China, although he saw better prospects in Australia as he sought naturalization in 1883. In the late 1890s, the network led him to Kwong Sing in Glen Innes, whose main shareholder and manager at the time was Wong Chee (Wong Hoon

Figure 4.2 Percy Young (Kwon Hong Kee), c. 1930 (courtesy of Harvey Young).

Narm). By 1907 Percy Young had become a partner in Kwong Sing, and when Wong Chee visited China in 1908–9, Young became general manager. Then, in 1912, when Wong Chee returned permanently to China, Young purchased a major shareholding in the business. He raised the necessary capital by organising loans from some of the wholesale suppliers in Sydney.

By 1912, Percy Young had sponsored a number of his nephews to begin their Australian lives as assistants in the store and, as the business grew, they acquired shares in it. In 1926, when Percy Young decided to return with his family to China, the management of the store passed to his eldest nephew, Walter Gett, with shares distributed, among others, to Percy Young's sons and to other nephews. When Percy Young returned to Australia and to Glen Innes in 1939, he again purchased a major shareholding in the business, also acquiring shares for his wife and sons. By this time, a number of the other family members involved

Figure 4.3 Harry Fay (Louie Mew Fay) of Hong Yuen, Inverell, c. 1916 (courtesy of Harry Fay II).

with the store had moved out to establish their own stores. This pattern continued until, at the time of Percy Young's death in 1942, the store in Glen Innes was under the ownership and management of members of his immediate family. As a granddaughter recalled:

> By the 1940s essentially different departments were managed by different members of the family. Uncle David and Uncle Norman were in the grocery section, and Uncle Cecil was in the hardware, and our father [Stanley] was always the manager.[6]

Two other sons, Henry and Roger, had established stores elsewhere, as had son-in-law Arthur Yee, and nephews Walter Gett, Frank Fatt, and Harry Yee.[7]

Harry Fay's central role in acquiring Hong Yuen as a family business was very similar. Harry Fay was born in Sydney in 1892. At a young age he returned with his parents and brothers to the family village of Dutou, Shiqi, Zhongshan where he stayed until he was about 18 years old. He then returned to Sydney, first working in the Chinese sectors of the furniture trade and vegetable markets. Fairly quickly, the community network saw him moving north to Kwong Sing in Glen Innes. After a short time there, he accompanied the manager, Wong Chee, to Hong Yuen in Inverell, where Wong Chee was most likely a shareholder. Harry Fay borrowed money, bought shares in the store, and stayed on to work at Hong Yuen. Gradually, he acquired more shares and, by 1916, was described as a managing partner. Over the next two decades he sponsored family members to come to Australia, some of whom not only gained employment in the store but also acquired shares. He also bought out shareholders who were not family members. By 1938, there were seven registered shareholders – Harry Fay, his wife Ruby, his two brothers George Ping Kee and Ernest Lun, his nephews Lawrence Ping Kee and Joe Mah, and fellow Zhongshan compatriot Edward Severn Fong.[8] The ownership of the business had certainly become concentrated in Louie family hands (Wilton 1988). By 1947, the ownership had become even more concentrated. The shareholders, by then, were all members of Harry Fay's immediate family: Harry Fay himself (84,000 shares), the estate of his late wife, Ruby Fay, (10,000), and his two sons-in-law, Thomas Loy (3,000) and Charles Cum (1,000).[9]

This emphasis on family ownership reflected Chinese business practices but it was also reinforced by Australian immigration regulations. Under the immigration legislation, merchants and their assistants were among the Chinese most likely to be granted permission not just to enter Australia but to extend their periods of stay in the country. The saga of Harry Fay's nephew, Lawrence Ping Kee, provides an example. He came to Australia in 1927 under a student permit. In 1933, when the permit was due to expire, Harry Fay applied for a change of status on the grounds that his nephew had now 'reached the stage as fitted to follow commercial pursuits', and that he should be taken into the business. The stated intention was to take him on a trip to China in order to gain knowledge for the business and then, on his return, he would eventually 'shoulder managerial responsibility'. The application was accompanied by references from the Principal of Ping Kee's school and an assurance by Harry Fay that he would pay the required bond. The Department of the Interior's response was to grant Lawrence Ping Kee permission to leave his studies and join Hong Yuen until his departure for China, and to consider his application for re-admission prior to his date of departure. Correspondence reveals that from 1934 there were regular applications for extending Lawrence Ping Kee's certificate of exemption, each time citing his employment with Hong Yuen. Eventually, in 1947, Ping Kee applied for permanent residence. He described the length of his stay in Australia, his time as a student for over six years and his subsequent regular employment with Hong Yuen. In particular, he pointed out that he had transferred from the Inverell to the Moree branch of the store, had been a manager of that store for the preceding seven years, and when a new company was formed under the name Hong Yuen (Moree) Pty. Ltd. in January 1946, had become a Governing Director.[10] It was his status as a contributor to the Australian economy and as a merchant which carried the greatest weight under the immigration legislation. It was a status which eventuated through the sponsorship offered by Harry Fay to family members and through his actions in ensuring that they were given secure positions within the network of stores which emanated from the main store in Inverell.

Expansion

Linked to the family ownership and management of the stores and demonstrating the control and enterprise of father-entrepreneurs like Percy Young and Harry Fay was the expansion of the business interests centred on Kwong Sing and Hong Yuen during the first part of the century. The activities underpinning this expansion also demonstrated characteristics resonant of both traditional Chinese firms and the new style of business attaching to stores like Sincere. As well, it reflected an ability to adapt to the particular local and business concerns confronted in Australia and, especially to the restrictions imposed by Australian immigration legislation.

Expansion of the stores themselves largely took two forms. The expansion of the main stores, and the establishment of a number of branch stores. The expansion of the main stores is well illustrated by the growth in the size of the premises. Hong Yuen, for example, originally occupied a small wooden building on one block of land. A photograph (*Figure 4.4*) dating from about 1900 shows the building reconstructed as a fairly stylish brick edifice, albeit still occupying only one block. Subsequent extensions and additions over the next four decades saw the building grow to occupy the four block frontage seen in a photograph taken in the late 1930s (*Figure 4.5*). Refurbishment and extensions after

Figure 4.4 Hong Yuen, Inverell, c. 1900 (courtesy of Harry Fay II).

the Second World War, including substantial rebuilding after a fire in 1976, resulted in Hong Yuen as it still stands in the 1990s – a shop dominating the northern end of the main street of Inverell (*Figure 4.6*). Kwong Sing followed a similar pattern. From a single wooden store in 1886, a series of additions between 1893 and 1963 saw the building expand to occupy a 44 metre frontage. Wooden sections slowly became brick, and interiors were updated and modernized. Single long counters on either side of the store gave way to more open display areas and increasingly clearly defined departments within the store.

The expansion of Kwong Sing and Hong Yuen may seem small in comparison to that of stores like Sincere or, indeed, to the expansion of department stores in Sydney. However, it is significant relative to the size of the towns concerned. Both Glen Innes and Inverell had populations in the vicinity of 5,000 with an additional 3–4,000 from surrounding rural areas. Kwong Sing and Hong Yuen clearly emerged as department stores in these country towns, and their manager-owners adapted and developed approaches to ensure that the expansion and business could be sustained and that their share of the local market could be secured.

As with Wing On (Yen 1991:96), the completion of new extensions was invariably accompanied by grand openings and local fanfare

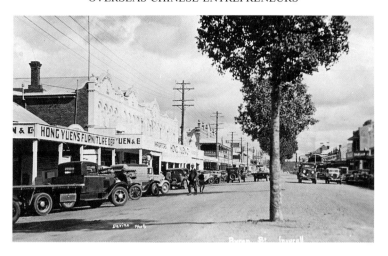

Figure 4.5 Hong Yuen (on left), Inverell, c. 1938 (courtesy of Harry Fay II).

directed at winning and cementing the support of local clientele. When the 1903 extension to Kwong Sing was opened, the local newspaper described the new premises, under the heading 'A fine store', as 'a beautiful massive building fitted up in the latest style' (*Glen Innes Guardian* 1903). A photograph from about 1909 (*Figure 4.7*) gives a sense of the style and facade, including the wooden furniture section which would be the subject of later reconstruction and extension. The new store was opened by the mayor who commended the then manager, Wong Chee, with the following sentiments which clearly echoed a need to establish the acceptability of a Chinese businessman in an Australian country town:

> Mr Chee, as a naturalized British subject, had proved himself to be a man of integrity, of charity, and was known as such throughout the district.
>
> (*Glen Innes Guardian* 1903)

In line with this image of a community-oriented person, the report observed that instead of providing the usual entertainment at the opening, Kwong Sing presented a cheque for purchasing a hose reel for the local fire brigade. The lead-up to the opening also saw regular reports on progress accompanied by reminders of Kwong Sing's reputation and slogan, as 'The noted cheap store', and by the promotion

101

Figure 4.6 Hong Yuen, Inverell, c. 1990.

of a sale of old stock.[11] Similar re-affirmations of the characteristics which were deemed most attractive to local consumers accompanied openings of other extensions. Hence, when Hong Yuen opened new sections to its building in 1925, the slogan of 'Small profits, quick returns' was well publicized (Wiedemann 1981:187).

The profitability and viability of the stores, after all, depended on attracting local non-Chinese customers into the stores. Cheap and competitive prices were a hallmark of advertising, and special 'cut price' sales became a characteristic of the businesses. Abbie Yum, who worked at Hong Yuen during the 1930s, recalled that,

> our sales were something out of this world. Unbelievable. I remember he [Harry Fay] had towels for one shilling, that was one of his specialties. He got in contact with a good towel manufacturer – he would probably buy seconds or discontinued lines and they would come in their thousands. He was a huge buyer. And full page ads in the paper, pamphlets and opening day – the extra opening specials. . . And the crowds that used to gather outside. I remember, everybody ready at 9 o'clock. 'Right,' he'd say, 'open the doors'. And in they'd stream.[12]

Giving credit was also characteristic. Indeed, some local residents claim this as one of the features which most endeared the stores to the local

Figure 4.7 Kwong Sing, Glen Innes, c. 1909 (courtesy of Harvey Young).

customers, especially during the hard times which regularly affected life in rural areas. As one local resident recalled of Hong Yuen:

> I remember the 1918–22 drought when we were all having a very trying time. But Mr Fay stuck to us. He never once turned us down for food for the family and feed for the animals.
>
> (Wilton 1988:21)

Another local resident and an employee of the store similarly asserted that,

> During the Depression Harry Fay got a lot of customers then because he was good to the farmers. He lent lots of money. They'd come with no money and he'd give them things.
>
> (Wilton 1988:21)

Similar evaluations have been offered of the willingness of Kwong Sing and of other Chinese stores in the area to offer credit. It was a willingness provoked, at least partly, by the fact that a good number of customers were farmers and graziers who had to wait for their wool cheques to come in once or twice a year. It was also a practice that accommodated the need for Chinese merchants to offer particularly attractive services in order to win over local non-Chinese customers who, true to the climate of the times, could have been at least a little reticent in shopping at Chinese stores.

The stores also, early on, provided home delivery services and supplied hawkers who would take their goods to the rural districts. At the time, hawkers were an important part of Australian rural life as some of the few visitors families on outlying farms would receive, and the Chinese stores tapped into this need and were able to advertise and market their goods and services in the process. They eventually had delivery trucks with sign writing advertising the stores themselves. A photograph (*Figure 4.8*) from the early 1930s depicts a Hong Yuen hawker's truck loaded up and ready to trek across the rough roads of the surrounding rural district, spare tyre strapped firmly to the front of the car, packages under tarpaulin on top, and advertising on all sides.

The effectiveness of these mechanisms in ensuring the sale of goods and the acceptability and viability of Chinese stores in rural areas is evidenced through the continuing expansion of the main stores themselves, and through the establishment of an increasing number of branch stores and new businesses whose managers and/or owners, most of whom were relatives, began by working in and for the main stores. By 1940, for example, there were branches of Hong Yuen established in Moree, Texas and Warialda. The Moree branch was managed by Harry Fay's older brother, George Ping Kee, and his sons who eventually became the owners of the store. The Warialda branch was established specifically for Harry Fay's son-in-law and daughter, Charles and Eileen Cum. The Texas branch remained with Harry Fay as the proprietor but had a number of managers who were either family

Figure 4.8 Hong Yuen hawker's van, c. 1932 (courtesy of Harry Fay II).

members or had served their apprenticeships at Hong Yuen in Inverell. As well as branch stores, Harry Fay established a number of other small stores in the region including Fay's Cash and Carry and S. Fong Lee, both in Inverell, and another Fay's Cash and Carry in Texas. Like the Hong Yuen branch in Texas, these stores were placed under the management of, and staffed by, family members or other Chinese who had served an apprenticeship with Hong Yuen in Inverell.

The Hong Yuen branch stores were at least initially assisted with credit and supplies from the main store in Inverell. The pattern then diversified. Some of the stores, including the branches in Warialda and Texas, continued to receive at least some of their goods through a common purchasing agreement with the main store, while other offshoots, including the Moree branch and Fay's Cash and Carry in Texas, established their own purchasing contacts and systems. The different strategies were related to the management and ownership of the stores. Those which stayed either directly under Harry Fay's proprietorship or which were managed or owned by members of his immediate family, retained close business links with the main store, while those which became the responsibility of members of the extended family tended towards more independence.

Kwong Sing of Glen Innes was also the birthplace of a number of Chinese stores which were established in northern and north-eastern New South Wales. The pattern, however, was slightly different to Hong Yuen in Inverell in that the new stores which emerged under the management and ownership of Chinese trained at Kwong Sing rarely retained business connections with the main store in Glen Innes, and there is little evidence that assistance was forthcoming with credit. The explanation for this pattern partly rests with the changing management arrangements at the main store. As the ownership of the Glen Innes Kwong Sing store concentrated in the hands of some of Percy Young's immediate family, the income and opportunities generated were not sufficient to support all immediate family members, let alone nephews and their families. They branched out and established new, independent enterprises which, in their turn, were used as the base for sponsoring further relatives from China. In this vein, for example, Percy Young's nephew Frank Fatt and his family established F. Kwong Sing at Casino, another nephew set up Harry Yee and Co. at Ballina, while yet another nephew, Walter Gett, initiated Yow Sing and Co. in Emmaville. Percy Young's brother Roger and his family opened and operated the Busy Bee store in Glen Innes, and his son-in-law Arthur Yee opened Kwong Sing in Bundarra (see *Figure 4.9*).

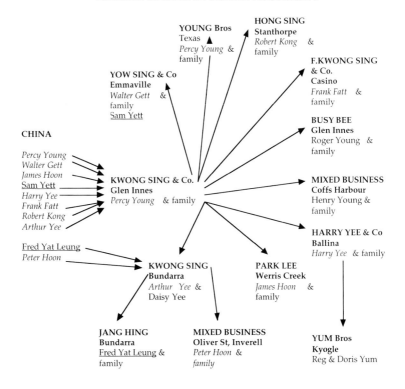

Figure 4.9 Diagram showing Kwan clan sponsorship and the stores established by members of the extended family.

The expansion and multiplication of the stores was also arguably influenced and perhaps partly stimulated by immigration regulations. The legislation dictated that for a firm to sponsor and retain Chinese-born shop assistants under exemption, they had to prove a certain level of import/export business and, from 1934, had to provide a certain level of turnover (Choi 1975:113–4). Some business practices reflected the need to ensure that a specific store could justify employing its overseas-born assistants. This sometimes entailed moving employees from one store to another. It also entailed ensuring that any one store did not seem to be sponsoring an oversupply of Chinese-born assistants.

The shapeshifting required by the regulations is reflected in correspondence to the Department of Interior accompanying Harry Fay's many requests for extensions of Certificates of Exemption in order to allow employees to remain in Australia. In 1932, for example, in response to a request to extend the certificate of Harry Fay's nephew, Joe Mah, the Department of the Interior expressed concern that his then employment in the fruit and confectionery section of the store 'will not be of any great advantage to him in the matter of developing overseas trade on his return to China'. Hence, approval of the extension was granted subject 'to his being transferred to some other branch of your firm in which there are better opportunities of his acquiring a knowledge of overseas trade conditions'.[13] At about the same time, Harry Fay sent a lengthy submission to the Department of the Interior requesting changes in status and extensions of certificates for a number of family members and employees. In this letter, he was careful to detail the extent of his business interests, citing a turnover of about £100,000 Australian for the Inverell store, £52,000 for Moree and £21,000 for Texas with outstanding debts to him 'personally' of about £45,000. He was also careful to detail that, of his approximately 60 permanent employees, 33 were Australians 'while the rest are made up of Australian-born Chinese with only seven Chinese from China'.[14] It was important to emphasize not just the viability and financial success of the stores, but also the extent to which they employed non-Chinese labour and the limited number of overseas-born Chinese among their employees. In a similar vein, in 1938 in applying for extensions of Certificates of Exemption and in requesting permission to sponsor two students, Harry Fay pointed out that on 23 February that year he had formed his business into a limited liability company with capital of £100,000, that he intended to establish a company in China, and that the students he was seeking to sponsor would not 'prejudice the position of any of my present employees'.[15] In 1941, Hong Yuen received a warning from the Department of the Interior, through the Consul-General for China, that the store now had 'assistants under exemption in excess of the number usually allowed for local businesses'. Consequently, further requests for assistants were likely to be viewed unfavourably.[16] Even as late as 1952 when Australia, slowly and reluctantly, was moving towards the dismantling of the 'white Australia policy', directives were still being received to improve overseas trade or transfer employees to 'some firm eligible for their

> We didn't work any set hours but we worked for about 70 hours a
> week. On Saturdays we'd be weighing up and on Sundays bottling
> up – the honey and metho and shellite and benzine. Sometimes
> we'd work Wednesday and Friday nights as well. Upstairs [above
> the shop] there were about five of us living. In the house out the
> back, another seven or so.[18]

The small amount of leisure time available was usually spent with the
other Chinese employees and with their Chinese employers and their
families. It was, at least on the surface, very much the paternalistic and
moralistic tradition identified by Yen (1991:91–2) in his study of the
Wing On company in Shanghai and China. It was the responsibility of
the father-entrepreneur to look after his employees and to treat them as
members of an extended family, inculcating in them traditional Chinese
values of loyalty, hard work, and thrift. Indeed, at Kwong Sing, Percy
Young framed and hung on the wall some Chinese proverbs
demonstrating the values he honoured and that he, presumably,
exhorted his employees to follow. Under the heading, 'Work hard
and save money', they included, for example:

> When men are born they all want to be wealthy, but you have to
> learn to be satisfied with what you have in your daily life.
>   If you are poor it is because you are lazy. Work hard at your
> business and never complain of hardships.[19]

The need to stick together and work hard was also shaped by the social
isolation of the Chinese in these small rural Australian towns. It was an
era when racist policies and attitudes were an accepted trait in Australia
and when foreigners were regarded, at the very best, as exotic and

perhaps difficult to relate to except for business purposes. Harry Fay's eldest son observed that,

> I've learnt the best way to live is not to be outrageous. Remember Pop used to say: 'They'll kiss your feet in the store but ignore you on Central Railway.'

Diversification

As the Chinese stores grew in size and numbers, and as the number of family members, both in Australia and in China, being supported by the enterprises increased, those with capital started to diversify. The father-entrepreneurs sought financial security and growth through seeking different investment opportunities. They sought them at first locally, and then looked beyond the immediate region to Sydney and ultimately to Hong Kong and China.

For example, in 1919 Harry Fay was purchasing shares in mining companies in northern New South Wales, and in the 1930s he had shares in a 60-acre tobacco farm. In Glen Innes, and before his departure for China in 1926, Percy Young invested significant amounts in local real estate, to the extent that a street in the town was named after him. He also bought a number of farms in the surrounding district, and in 1916 bought into a local mining company. His investment in local ventures resumed after his return from China in 1939. His Deceased Estate File, for example, reveals that, at the time of his death, he had a small number of shares in Dunkerly Hat Mills, the Northern Newspaper, and Glen Innes Cooperative Dairy Society Ltd.

Outside the New England region, Harry Fay became joint proprietor of the Nankin Cafe in Sydney. He and his first wife, Ruby, also had shares in Hong Kong and Shanghai based companies like Wing On, Wing Sang, and Sincere and Co.

The diversification reflects, although on a much smaller scale, the business practice also adopted by Sincere, Wing On and by western enterprises – the determination not to depend entirely on the one type of enterprise to ensure present and future viability and growth.

Contacts with China

The investment by Harry and Ruby Fay in shares in Hong Kong and Chinese based companies is no surprise. It emerges from another facet in the history and development of Kwong Sing and Hong Yuen which goes back to the origins of the stores and the proprietorship of Wong

Chee. On his departure from Glen Innes in 1912, Wong Chee became managing director of Sincere and Co. and was involved in the establishment of the Shanghai branch of the store. He obviously kept in contact with his two protégés in Australia, Percy Young and Harry Fay, and may even initially have retained some capital in their respective enterprises. Certainly, the link was sufficiently strong for Harry Fay to visit China in 1916 in order to marry Wong Chee's adopted daughter, Ruby. In 1932, when Ruby and some of the Fay children spent six months in Hong Kong, they paid a visit to Wong Chee in Shanghai which is recorded in a family photograph (*Figure 4.10*). Presumably, it was also through Wong Chee that Harry Fay's younger brother, Ernest Lun, was able to organize a job for their nephew, Joe Mah, in the Hong Kong branch of Sincere and Co. in the mid 1920s. Conversely, it was through Harry Fay and through Ruby Fay's natural brother, William Liu,[20] that Wong Chee's son, Ernest Wong, spent time in Inverell during the 1930s. There is also correspondence from 1939 and 1940 which shows that Harry Fay was using his contacts with the Department of the Interior in an attempt to get permission for Wong Chee's two daughters, Rose and Alice, and their families to come to Australia.[21]

Percy Young also retained his links with his former employer. In 1926 when Young returned to China, he recalled that it was through

Figure 4.10 Percy Young with his sons and nephews, c. 1915 (courtesy of Harvey Young).

Wong Chee that he took up, for a short time, a position as manager of the Tianjin branch of Sincere and Co.[22]

The significance of these links for business terms is hard to judge from the evidence available at the Australian end. There is evidence that contacts in China were instrumental in attempts to set up the overseas trade which Australian legislation required if Chinese under exemption were to remain employed in Chinese stores in Australia. In 1934, for example, Harry Fay wrote to his local politician explaining that his brother-in-law, William Liu, had gone to China to join up with a large company there, and that there were prospects of Harry Fay establishing a business in China and hence that he would need to have well trained people (who obviously could speak Chinese) to send there. The agenda was an argument for retaining and expanding the number of overseas-born Chinese employed in his stores in Australia.[23] Certainly, Harry Fay's reputation as a businessman with contacts and markets in Australia was recognized in Hong Kong. In 1940, for example, a Choy Hon Fan wrote a number of letters to Harry Fay urging him to purchase knives and forks made in Shanghai.[24] It is also apparent that Wing Sang in Hong Kong acted at times as a means to transmit funds for Harry Fay to China, supplied goods to Hong Yuen, and provided an address for people seeking assistance from Harry Fay to get permission to come to Australia. Similarly, and particularly during the late 1930s and the 1940s, Sincere and Co., Hong Kong, was the postal address for a number of Chinese who requested financial assistance from Harry Fay or who sought his assistance in sponsoring them to migrate to Australia. It is also clear that visits to China and Hong Kong were a part of the agendas of the Louie and Kwan clans. While there, the family and business networks ensured meetings with counterparts and relatives working in and for the large department stores and their suppliers. Harry Fay's eldest daughter remembered her family's visit to Shanghai in the early 1930s as a 'wonderful' time filled with visits to luxury homes, singing and playing the piano. She explained that,

> Mum [Ruby Fay] had a lot of other friends – wealthy people who had Wing Sang, the big shop. They had a big mansion . . . She had a lot of friends come every Wednesday[25]

Percy Young's eldest daughter, Daisy Yee, could remember meeting Wong Chee in Shanghai during their visit in the late 1920s,[26] and Percy Young's granddaughter, Valmai Au, recalled that during her visit to Hong Kong in the 1930s 'grandfather used to take us to the shop, probably Sincere. I remember going to the big shop.'[27]

The networks and contacts with stores in Hong Kong and China were maintained and strengthened. However, there is little indication of the extent to which, if at all, the contacts and exchanges involved more than looking after family members and networking to provide employment for relatives and other Chinese from Zhongshan, and for supplying particular goods made in China. It can only be presumed that the contact and visits meant also at least some exchange of information and ideas about the suitability and effectiveness of different business practices.

Conclusion

This focused survey suggests that the characteristics associated with early giants among the Asian department stores like Sincere and Wing On can also be discerned in a small number of Chinese stores in a specific part of rural Australia during the late nineteenth and early twentieth century. Here too, could be found a successful mixing of traditional Chinese business practices with elements of western entrepreneurship. What was different, however, was the impact of specific local conditions. For Chinese stores in northern New South Wales, the problem was not one of winning over a relatively conservative Chinese clientele, but of winning over a suspicious, if not sometimes racist, non-Chinese population and of circumventing discriminatory legislation. The challenge was not one of introducing western models of business into an Asian context, but of accommodating Chinese practices to a western context. The result, however, was much the same – the mixing and adapting of business practices. What is unclear is the extent to which the strategies and business practices adopted were influenced by practices encountered or learnt through sustained contacts with companies like Sincere, and the extent to which they were influenced by the particular Australian environment. After all, the founders of Sincere, Wing On and Wing Sang had acquired their early experiences and knowledge of department stores in Australia. What is clear, however, is that a richer understanding of the nature of the Asian department store, and the networks which developed around specific stores, can be reached by close examination of specific local examples, including examples in Australia.

Notes

1 A note on Chinese names: The spelling and romanization of names reflects that used by the Chinese-Australians whose oral histories provide the core material for this research. Often, the Chinese characters are not known.

2 Interview with Joe Mah, 27 February 1990.
3 Yong (1977) has paid some attention to the Australian ventures. Cushman (1984: 109–110) argued for business histories seen from the perspectives of Chinese–Australian business men themselves as one of the gaps in the historiography of the Chinese in Australia, and as a means to achieving 'a deeper understanding of the strengths and weaknesses of various Chinese business structures'.
4 Interview with Ernest Sue Fong, 14 February 1984 (Wilton 1988:47–54).
5 Certificate of Registration No. 3265, Australian Archives (NSW): SP42/113:04/354.
6 Interview with Valmai Au and Olma Gan, 19 July 1990.
7 This abridged version of Percy Young's story has been pieced together from a variety of sources including the 'Autobiography of Mr. Kwan Hong Kee', 1938, unpublished manuscript, Kwong Sing Papers; *Glen Innes Examiner* 20 October 1903 and 2 June 1942; interviews with Stanley Young; and Percy Young's Deceased Estate File, NSW State Archives.
8 Customs and Excise Office memorandum, 30 November 1938, Australian Archives (NSW): N56/5481.
9 Copy of Form D, Harry Fay to Acting Commonwealth Migration Officer, 30 December 1947, Mar Papers.
10 Lawrence Ping Kee's saga has been pieced together from correspondence files held by a cousin, and from Australian Archives records.
11 For example, *Glen Innes Guardian*, 4 August 1903 and 16 October 1903, and *Glen Innes Examiner*, 28 July 1903, 21 August 1938, and 6 October 1903. This particular opening was presumably particularly spurred by the almost simultaneous opening (and fanfare) by competing Chinese store, W. Warley and Co., and by the then concerted anti-Chinese storekeepers campaign mounted by a group of NSW retail country traders (Yong 1977:73–77)
12 Interview with Abbie Yum, 5 June 1989.
13 Secretary, Department of the Interior, to Messrs Hong Yuen and Co., 25 November 1932.
14 Harry Fay to secretary, Department of the Interior, undated (1933).
15 Harry Fay to Hon. E. J. Harrison, M.P., 19 September 1938, Mar Papers.
16 B. R. Watson for Secretary, Department of Interior, to Consul-General for China, 2 January 1941, Mar Papers.
17 B. C. Wall, Commonwealth Migration Officer to the Proprietor, Hong Yuen, Inverell, 15 February 1952, Mar Papers.
18 Interview with Thomas Loy, 15 February 1984.
19 Kwong Sing Papers.
20 William Liu was a significant figure in Chinese business and community circles of the time (see Wang 1988; Mo and Mo 1991).
21 Correspondence in Mar Papers.
22 Autobiography of Mr Kwan Hong Kee, Kwong Sing Papers.
23 Harry Fay to Hon. E. J. Harrison, M.P., 19 September 1938, Mar Papers.
24 Correspondence in Mar Letters.
25 Interview with Eileen Cum, 18 August 1978.
26 Interview with Daisy Yee, 19 July 1990.
27 Interview with Valmai Au, 19 July 1990.

5

NEW CHINA'S FLAGSHIP EMPORIUM

The Beijing Wangfujing Department Store[*]

Guo Hongchi and Liu Fei

The Beijing Wangfujing Department Store is a large commercial enterprise well-known in China, and is also famous as one of the world's largest retail stores (*Figure 5.1*). It has a staff of about 4,300 and the gross floor area measures 41,185 square meters of which 17,894 square meters are used for operating space. There are 72,000 items on sale, and the circulation of customers averages over 100,000 per day. In terms of sales volume, the Wangfujing Department Store is the fourth largest commercial enterprise in China, with a turnover of 1.8 billion yuan in 1995. This high sales volume makes the Emporium the greatest profit-making retail sales enterprise in China, with a profit of 120 million yuan in 1995 (*Zhongguo shangbao* 1996). Forty years have passed since its establishment, and during this period of time its accumulated sales volume has reached 12 billion yuan. Its tax on profits has reached 1.12 billion yuan which is enough to build 248 new Wangfujing Department Stores! About 1.7 billion customers, both Chinese and foreign, have been received by the Emporium since its founding, which is about 1.4 times the population of China (Beijing Wangfujing Department Store (Group) Ltd. 1995:12). In the numerous customer surveys conducted, the Wangfujing Department Store is considered by consumers to be the best commercial enterprise in China according to an integrated index which takes into consideration factors such as corporate image and customer loyalty. The Emporium is a pearl illuminating retail business in China.

---

* Translated and adapted by Kerrie L. MacPherson, who wishes to thank Yeung Wingyu and the authors for all their help in the preparation of this translation.

Figure 5.1 Outdoor scene of Wangfujing Department Store.

Socio-Economic Background of the Birth of the Flagship Emporium

Commerce in Beijing in the first years of the People's Republic of China (PRC)

Long before the founding of the PRC, four retail business zones, namely Xidan, Qianmen, Dongsi and Wangfujing, developed in Beijing. The Xidan shopping area consisted chiefly of specialized shops in the old Xidan Bazaar, which dealt in daily products, clothes, shoes, hats, cigarettes, wines and food. The zone was also famous for numerous small restaurants, snack shops and venues for musical and acrobatic performances. The Qianmen shopping area specialized in selling Chinese medicine, silk fabrics, knitting wool, shoes, hats, and cakes. This area was characterized by small shops and old shops.

Among the four, the Wangfujing shopping zone was endowed with the greatest geographical advantages. The Imperial Forbidden City was at its west, and to the south was the Dongjiaomin Lane where the Legation Quarters of foreign powers were once located. Therefore, foreigners operated banks, trading companies, restaurants and branch offices in Wangfujing. Shops were also established there to specialize in the sale of luxury commodities including antiques, jewellery, clocks, watches, leather, cameras, and clothing. The Wangfujing Street as a shopping zone was thus made known to the world mainly through the promotion of foreign trading companies. However, the Wangfujing shopping street was in decline on the eve of Beijing's 'liberation' in 1949 due to economic dislocation, shortage in supplies, and, in turn, hoarding and speculation which greatly pushed up prices.

In January 1949, Beijing (then called Beiping) was 'liberated' peacefully by the Chinese communists. The new central government was determined to consolidate the regime. One of the measures implemented was to maintain the provision of basic necessities to the people by stopping speculation and profiteering. The central government adopted measures to supply commodities by stabilizing market prices, which the government hoped would secure its ability to control the market in the commercial field. In February 1949, the Military Control Committee established the Beijing Trading Corporation which assumed the power to take over commercial enterprises owned by the so-called 'bureaucratic compradores', to activate the interflow of products between the city and the countryside, and to supply goods for daily necessities. From March to December 1949, the Central Government restructured the Corporation into ten new state-owned corporations dealing with such daily products as foods, coal, cotton yarn, leather, eggs, and oil. These companies were responsible for coordinating production plans, purchasing related products, and managing supplies in cities as well as in export work. Through these measures, the government gained control of production and purchase, and in turn controlled the market. In order to secure easy access to necessary goods for the citizens, the newly formed Beijing General Merchandise Corporation formed five retail outlets dealing in daily articles. They were located at Tianqiao, Dongsi, Xidan, Dongjiaomin Lane and Donghuamen Street. Furthermore, the Beijing Retail Company was formed in November 1949, to manage 164 retail outlets dealing in basic goods such as food, coal, oil, and salt (*Beijing shangye sishi nian* 1989:449). Formation of these state-run commercial businesses and retail shops under the new government economic policies marked an end to the market monopoly of the 'bureaucratic compradores' and private enterprises. A socialist commercial system appeared for the first time in the history of Beijing.

The establishment of the state-run retail system

Socialist transformation of the private sector of industry and commerce was introduced by the National Government in 1953. Private retail companies were changed to public-private joint ventures. Petty retailers were required to follow the policy of collectivization. The retail outlets were re-organized. Through retail companies set up by the municipal government, the state-run wholesale businesses were able to control the manufacture, purchase and import of certain principal commodities. The supply of commodities was secured, and in turn inflation was controlled and people's livelihood stabilized.

However, Beijing's retail business was still generally weak. Most of the retail outlets operated on a small scale, occupying limited areas of about 100 to 300 square meters. To strengthen and secure control over the market, the state-run commercial sector needed to undergo considerable expansion, particularly after 1953 when the First Five-Year Plan was inaugurated by the Central People's Government. The numerous large-scale plans for economic construction greatly stimulated the employment rate, and in turn increased the people's income and improved their quality of life. But the small state-run commercial businesses were unable to meet the demands of the accelerating economic development and the demands for improvements in the peoples' quality of life. In order to secure market leadership and to satisfy the growing desire for consumption by the people, the government decided to set up new retail outlets of medium and large size. It was under these socio-economic conditions that the Wangfujing Department Store was constructed.

In 1953, the Beijing People's Government decided to build a large emporium in Wangfujing Street, where the Texaco Corporation had been located. There were three factors contributing to the decision to locate the new emporium there. Firstly, Texaco was a foreign firm, which was expropriated by the new government after the founding of the PRC. Therefore, with no need for investing a huge sum of capital for demolishing the old buildings, the new emporium could be located there. Secondly, Wangfujing Street had long been a shopping center specializing in luxury commodities. The street was a source of new fashion, and it substantially influenced the consumption pattern of the citizens. Building the new emporium there would highlight the leadership of the state sector in the market. Thirdly, Wangfujing Street was close to the newly built Beijing Railway Station which was one of the 'ten great constructions' in the First Five-Year Plan. Since this favorable location gave access to shopping for travellers from various parts of the country, the influence of the Emporium was not limited to the city of Beijing, but encompassed the whole country. In this way, the Emporium indirectly encouraged the establishment of state-run businesses throughout the country, as reflected in the fact that large state-owned emporiums mushroomed in several large cities in China after the founding of the Wangfujing Department Store.

On 28 May 1954, Wu Han, the Vice-Mayor of the Beijing Municipality and a famous historian, presided over the foundation ceremony of the Emporium. The Emporium, built at a cost of 4.5 million yuan, was completed in August 1955 and opened on 5 September. The gross built-up area was 20,362 square meters, and the operating area was 12,503 square meters. The front building had six floors and the rear building had four. The first, second and third floors of the main building were the operating halls. The whole building was designed by Yang Kuanlin, a famous architect in China (Quanguo baihuo hangye xiehui 1991:79). The architectural style of the Emporium gave it a vivacious appearance. Relief sculptures with dignified decorations and a strong sense of national style characterized the building. Facilities such as an audio room, dark room, lounge for parents and children, air conditioning and circulation were installed. All of these made the Emporium at that time an advanced large-scale retail enterprise in Beijing with new and extensive facilities, and the rate of space usage was high.

The Emporium was under the supervision of the Beijing General Merchandise Corporation and was named the 'Wangfujing Department Store, Beijing General Merchandise Corporation', and was commonly called the 'number one store of new China'. During the early phase of business the Emporium stocked about 25,000 items. It had a staff of 884 people, with its chief administrators drawn from the five retail outlets of the Beijing General Merchandise Corporation.

As the first department store built after the founding of the PRC, the Wangfujing Department Store was highly regarded by government leaders, because it was a major government investment and it was the first large-scale state-owned emporium in China. Zhou Enlai, Liu Shaoqi, Zhu De, Deng Xiaoping, Chen Yun, Chen Yi, Peng Zhen, and other state leaders inspected the Emporium on the eve of its opening (Quanguo baihuo hangye xiehui 1991:79). The Minister of Commerce, after inspecting the Emporium, ordered that the best goods in the country must be on the shelves of the Wangfujing Department Store. Thus the Emporium enjoyed certain privileges in procuring goods even when the production of these goods was very limited in quantity. Because of this special government endorsement, the Emporium had open access to commodities throughout the country. While commerce in general was weak, and high-class commodities were always in short supply, the Wangfujing Department Store was exceptionally well promoted and became the best-known commercial enterprise in the country soon after its founding.

As mentioned above, the newly built Wangfujing Department Store was equipped with large, comfortable, modern shopping halls, and the privileges granted by the central government guaranteed the concentration of brand-name goods from every corner of the country, so customers could find goods not shelved in other shops. As a result, the Emporium's reputation grew as an attractive shopping center not only for Beijing's urbanites, but also for visitors coming from all over the country. Visitors rarely missed the chance to shop in the Emporium when visiting Beijing. The opening of this department store even affected the sales volume of other commercial enterprises. A survey showed that eight privately-owned stores in Dongdan and Wangfujing had sharp reductions of an average 64 per cent in sales volume on 25 September, the day the Emporium opened, as compared to their sales volume on 18 September. A similar decrease was also found in other kinds of stores: 37.2 per cent for the public-private joint venture emporiums, 33.32 per cent for fourteen stores in the Qianmen Great Street, and 31.3 per cent for six stores in Xidan (*Beijing shi diyi shangye shiliao huibian* n.d.:296).

A number of medium-sized emporiums with operating areas over 1,000 square meters were built after the founding of the Wangfujing Department Store. By establishing these medium-scale concerns, the state-run retail business secured its leadership in the market, and it secured its monopolistic position in the field of commodity distribution.

History and Development of Business

Change of name

The name of the Wangfujing Department Store has been changed four times over the last 40-odd years. These changes help to explain some aspects of the history and development of the Emporium.

In 1955, the newly opened Emporium was under the Beijing General Merchandise Corporation, and its name was the 'Wangfujing Department Store, Beijing General Merchandise Corporation'. It was under the supervision of the Beijing Daily Products Corporation, and was a model state-run commercial enterprise.

From 1956 to 1957, the pattern of supervising commercial enterprises was reformed as the government intended to exercise more effective control over state enterprises. The First Bureau of Commerce was formed to assume management authority for seven companies specializing in commodities such as daily products, cotton yarn, Chinese herbs, and medicine. In late 1958, the Emporium became a component of the First Bureau of Commerce, and its name was changed to the 'Beijing Wangfujing Department Store'.

During the 'Great Proletarian Cultural Revolution' (1966–1976), the Red Guards launched the 'Destroy the Four Olds Campaign' – that is old ideas, culture, customs, and habits. The name 'Wangfujing', because of its historical connotations, was regarded by the Red Guards as synonymous with 'old things' and they demanded that the name be changed. The Emporium was renamed the 'Beijing Department Store'. During this campaign, the Xidan Emporium and the Dong An Market were also renamed, respectively as the Capital Emporium and Dong Feng Market. The new title 'Beijing Department Store' was officially approved by the Beijing Municipal Government in 1968, and the First Bureau of Commerce still headed the Emporium.

In 1991, the Emporium established a commercial group. In 1993 the Emporium followed the reform of enterprise institutions, and changed from a unitary state-run enterprise into a joint stock enterprise. The Emporium became a limited corporation, and its name was changed to the 'Beijing Wangfujing Department Store (Group) Corporation Limited'. The Emporium also registered the name 'Wangfujing' as a trademark. Therefore, the name 'Wangfujing' has become a symbol of this department store to its customers.

History of the Emporium

Forty years have passed since the opening of the Wangfujing Department Store. Its history can be divided into four phases:

First phase (1955–1965). This was the first decade of the Emporium's history. In this period, the fate of the Emporium was influenced by events such as the Great Leap Forward and the three years of great natural disasters (1960–1962). Commodities were always in very short supply. As a centrally planned economy system was practised as a result of the policy of 'following the Soviet economic system', the national economic plan dominated all economic activities such as production, exchange, distribution and consumption. All basic necessities were governed by the policy 'state monopoly over purchases and sales' (*tonggou tongxiao*).

The Ministry of Commerce undertook institutional reform of the state-run commercial enterprises. Various kinds of procurement stations were established by specialized corporations according to the stations' purchase and supply catchment area. The first-level wholesale stations were responsible for nationwide arrangement and coordination of production plans for commodities, and for the procurement and supply of such commodities covering the whole country. The responsibility of the second-level wholesale stations was similar to that of the first-level stations, but they were regional in nature. Commodities produced in other regions could only be purchased through first-level wholesale stations. As the following *Figure 5.2* shows, the Shanghai Procurement Station of the China General Merchandise Corporation was a first-level wholesale station, while its Jinan Procurement Station was a second-level wholesale station.

After this institutional reform, a clear pattern of market segregation and specialization was formed, which brought the market under the strict control of central planning. Channels of procurement by retailers were highly restricted: retailers could not deal with wholesale business or procure directly from producers, but had to procure from the local second or third-level procurement stations. However, the Wangfujing Department Store, China's flagship store, was highly regarded by the

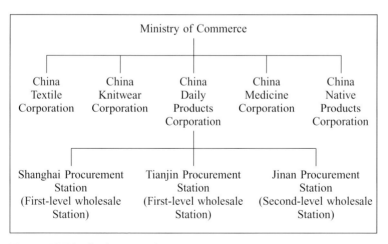

Figure 5.2 Distribution network.

121

government's top leaders, and was granted an exceptional franchise. In contrast to other retail enterprises, the Emporium could procure directly from first-level stations, and could even purchase directly from producers. This was the only exception in the country's commercial system. As a result, the Wangfujing Department Store brought prosperity to the Wangfujing shopping area, and secured its development as a showcase for socialist commerce.

In 1961 and 1962, the country suffered serious natural disasters. Economic development was acutely affected. Reduction of commodity supplies was accompanied by a lack of purchasing power. Thus, the Emporium experienced a considerable reduction in its sales volume and profit rate. The sales volume and profits for the year 1962 were only 46.44 million yuan and 2.7 million yuan respectively. The national economy showed improvement in 1963, marked by an increase in industrial and agricultural production; the operation of the Wangfujing Department Store became more dynamic than ever, and its business grew steadily.

Second phase (1966–1975). This was the second decade of the Emporium, during the 'Great Proletarian Cultural Revolution' that created a chaotic social and political situation. The national economy suffered greatly, social order was in disarray, and the environment for business operations was in a shambles. Various commodities were labelled by the Red Guards as 'problematic' and were banned from sale, particularly those associated with traditional Chinese culture, even including items using historic figures, gods and buddhas, idols of happiness (*fu*), officialdom (*lu*), and longevity (*shou*) as trademarks and brands. Other banned commodities were those using foreign languages or transliterated English in their names, such as whisky brands and clothing. Yet another kind were high-class goods such as cigarettes, wine, cosmetics, and jewellery. Even high-heeled shoes, western-style shirts, playing cards, and mechanical toys were banned. Over 6,583 items, constituting 21 per cent of the commodities on sale, disappeared from the shelves of the Emporium (*Beijing shangye sishi nian* 1989:117).

Another reason for the disruption of business operations was the slump in production and the subsequent shortages of goods. Many commodities were rationed by coupons and certificates. The annual sales volume in that phase averaged about 60 or 70 million yuan. Not until 1973 did the amount increase to over 100 million yuan. In the two decades after the Emporium's founding up until 1975, the sales volume rose by 49.5 per cent.

Third phase (1976–1986). This was the third decade of the Emporium, a period of transformation and economic construction during which China carried out the policy of 'reform and openness' after the arrest of the 'Gang of Four' and the end of the Great Proletarian Cultural Revolution. This marked a phase of development for the Emporium. In line with the national reform policy addressing the break-down of the long-standing system of a centrally planned economy, the new policy proposed a mix between central planning and market readjustments. The new environment in which commerce operated may be vividly described by the phrase *san duo yi shao* (three 'numerous' and one 'less'), that is, numerous channels for circulation, numerous forms of business, numerous economic ownerships, and fewer links in the chain of re-distribution.

Firstly, the number of distribution channels increased when the unitary system of tonggou tongxiao was fundamentally abolished and replaced by other channels such as planned purchase, ordering goods, selective procurement and manufacturers' own responsibility for sales. Commercial enterprises were no longer restricted by the procurement stations in such areas as procurement and sales, but could choose their own channels according to their business needs. Commercial enterprises might procure directly from manufacturers, and manufacturers might also be involved in retailing. Secondly, firms were now allowed to engage in a variety of business, so that wholesale firms might be involved in retailing, and vice versa; factories might deal in wholesaling and retailing; and so on. Thirdly, state-ownership of enterprises was no longer the only kind of enterprise, and commerce might also be effected through collective, individual, and private ownerships. Lastly, the number of links in the distribution chain was reduced, so that commercial enterprises could purchase directly from the factories, passing over wholesalers.

This new environment of 'san duo yi shao' produced a more active market and introduced a mechanism for competition in commerce, which created a sense of crisis amongst the staff of the Emporium. However, the Emporium still occupied a high position in the commercial field as a result of its special endowment: in other words its sound management system, nationwide prestige, good corporate image, excellent location and the advantages of its economies of scale. Thus, the Emporium was free to strengthen its relationship with industrial enterprises and expand its network of procurement throughout the country. Its channels of procurement spread through the 28 provinces or municipalities of the country. It established business relationships with over 2,000 industrial and commercial enterprises. Its involvement in wholesaling was augmented, and thus its economic efficiency was substantially improved. Statistics show that wholesaling constituted only 0.466 per cent of the total sales volume in 1976, but that the figure grew to 4.99 per cent in 1985, a tenfold increase achieved in one decade.[1] As a result of diversification of business, range of products and business forms, a dramatic increase in sales volume and profits was experienced, with sales volume reaching 200 and 300 million yuan in 1980 and 1985 respectively. Compared with 1975, sales volume in 1985 saw an increase of 230 per cent, while profits increased by 204.6 per cent[2] (see also *Table 5.1*).

Fourth phase (1986–1995). This was the fourth decade of the Emporium which was also a phase of development. Before the adoption of the policy of reform and openness in 1978, China practised a highly centralized financial system. The relationship between state and enterprises can be likened to the relationship between a father and his sons; that is, the state dominated the distribution relationship between the two. State-owned enterprises contributed all their profits to the state, and the state was responsible for funding the enterprises. Under this highly centralized mechanism, the state took too much responsibility, making the management system too inflexible. Rights, as well as responsibilities and profits, which should be unified under the management of an enterprise, were segregated into several sectors. As a result of this segregation, enterprises did not have the means or the will to improve.

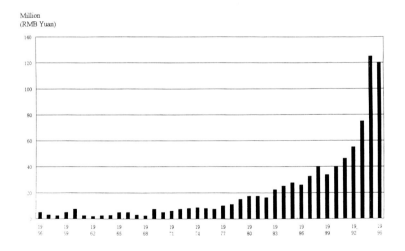

Table 5.1 Operating profits of the Wangfujing Department Store (1956-95).

The Wangfujing Department Store did not benefit from the generation of great profits. Although the Emporium always made major financial contributions to the central government (for example, the amount in 1985 was enough for the government to construct 178 new emporiums), the government neglected the development of the Emporium. Admittedly, some trivial repairs and improvements were made. The central government paid for the fitting of air-conditioning in the Emporium in 1985. Some old cabinets and shelves were replaced, and some of the operation halls were enlarged. However, the state was unable or unwilling to fund substantial repairs of the Emporium's facilities.

During the reform era, in order to invigorate these enterprises, the state tried to introduce reforms to their management system. In 1988, the responsibility system for contracted operating, which emphasized 'two guarantees, one link-up' (*liang bao yi gua*), was introduced. This new system aimed at redefining the profit allocation between the state and the enterprises. Under this system, enterprises had full discretion over the use of their profits except for their fixed contribution to the central government and the reserve fund for enterprise development. Staff wages might also be adjusted according to individual performance. As a result, enterprises enjoyed higher autonomy and initiative in running their businesses, which gave impetus to the development of enterprises. Profiting from this new system, the Wangfujing Department Store achieved a sales volume of 440 million yuan in 1987, and the figure rose to 500 million yuan in 1988.

The readjustment of the profit allocation between state and enterprises fundamentally changed the state's paternal relationship with these businesses. Enterprises became autonomous, self-sustaining, self-restrictive, and had the power to formulate their own development strategies. Substantial change was also observed in investment strategies. Except for legally mandated state taxation, enterprises could make their own plans for investment based on their business needs and financial situation. In the mid-1980s, the Wangfujing Department Store opened new operating halls and it finished massive repairs to its facilities in 1993, the first time in its 38 years of operation that the structure was renovated. This renovation adopted a special style by expressing two kinds of culture, the so-called 'occidental glory and wealth' and the 'oriental simplicity and elegance'. This created a new progressive and modernized image for the Emporium.

The change of investment mechanism made it possible for the Emporium to follow a line of diversification and conglomeration. In September 1991, the Beijing Department Store (Group) was formed. In

1993, it was reorganized as the Beijing Wangfujing Department Store (Group) Corporation Limited when the government introduced the policy of transforming state-owned enterprises into joint stock companies. Its shares were listed on the Shanghai Stock Exchange on 6 May 1994. After listing, the Emporium's capital capacity increased rapidly. Its gross assets were 400 million yuan in 1993, rising to 1.24 billion yuan in 1995, an increase of 210 per cent over the 1993 figure (*Zhongguo zhengquan bao* 1996:4:19).

In 1995, in addition to the Emporium which had three specialized shopping halls grouped into nine departments of commodities, the Beijing Wangfujing Department Store (Group) Corporation Limited had nine proprietary enterprises, and two enterprises co-operating with foreign companies. The range of business included retailing, fashion manufacture, distribution, transport, fast-food, hotel operation, and real estate. Chain stores were opened in cities including Guangzhou, Chengdu, and Nantong and 15 more chain stores were opened in Beijing. In addition, the Emporium gained the power to trade with foreign countries in retailing, generating an import-export business totalling over US$1 million annually.

Today, the Beijing Wangfujing Department Store (Group) Corporation Limited is planning new development strategies. By establishing a chain retail system, the Emporium is weaving a 'Wangfujing' commercial network throughout the country, expanding its operating scale as a means to enhance its competitive capability.

Management Reform of the Emporium

The forty years' history of the Wangfujing Department Store reflects China's transformation from a socialist planned economy system to a socialist market economy system, and from the purely socialist public ownership system to the co-existence of multiple ownership systems. These substantial economic changes presented opportunities for the Emporium to reform and develop continuously, also allowing it to carry out reforms in management.

Change of the leadership mechanism

From its establishment to the mid-1980s, the Emporium was under the leadership of the Chinese Communist Party committee system. All decisions concerning its operation were made under the leadership of the Secretariat. The general manager was subordinate to the Party

Secretariat. In 1986, a reform of enterprises' leadership system was undertaken by the state, and the 'director responsibility system' was adopted. The director assumed a core and leading position in an enterprise, and was made responsible for all the business of that enterprise, thus assuming major initiative in operations.

However, some changes occurred in 1989. The change of political environment in that year reversed the preceding reform of the leadership system. Because of this new policy, the Emporium adopted the 'director responsibility system' under the leadership of the Party Committee as a means to strengthening the role of the Party in guiding the Emporium. In order to harmonize the relationship with the Party Secretariat and make the leadership system work positively in the management and operation of the Emporium, the general manager of the Emporium was concurrently made Party Secretary of the Emporium. This unification of Party and Emporium administration strengthened Party leadership in the Emporium, but did not weaken the decision-making power and leadership of the general manager in terms of business management.

With further expansion in 1993, the Emporium was turned into the Beijing Wangfujing Department Store (Group) Corporation Limited, and a new leadership system was adopted, the 'general manager responsibility system' under the leadership of the board of directors. The general manager thus assumed a core position in the Emporium's operation.

Change of the property rights of the Emporium

As a state-owned enterprise, the Wangfujing Department Store was required to submit all profits to the state, and the Emporium had to petition the state for money for investment. The Emporium was also required to spend a huge sum of money on wages and various staff welfare facilities, whether the Emporium was in surplus or in deficit. This management system was the origin of the Emporium's inertia and the absence of incentives for staff members.

In 1987 the Emporium undertook reforms in its management system and adopted the 'responsibility system of contracted operating'. The state set a quota for its share of the profits of the Emporium. After the quota was satisfied, the rest of the profits was at the disposal of the Emporium. In other words, the more the Emporium earned, the more profit it could retain. In the meantime, the Emporium was allotted a state quota for the various commodity sections and counters, which contracted parts of the quota. If they filled the quota they had contracted, they could draw out part of the revenue as bonus. Therefore, staff could earn more if they worked harder, an incentive that fuelled the development of the Emporium.

Nevertheless, the new management system was far from able to maximize incentives for the Emporium and its staff. The core problem was the question of who had rights to the assets of the Emporium. As the Emporium was as an 'enterprise owned by the whole people', no one knew who represented the state's interests, who represented the enterprise's interests, and in what way the interests of the staff were represented. This problem was fundamentally solved in 1993 when the Emporium undertook substantial reform in its ownership. It was transformed from being a purely state-owned enterprise to a limited joint stock company. The following *Table 5.2* shows the share allocations (*Zhongguo zhengquan bao* 1996:4:23).

The state shares, corporate shares and part of the public shares did not circulate publicly. About 65 million of the shares owned by the public circulated in the market, constituting 35.37 per cent of all shares. The new share structure clearly explicated a substantial change in the ownership of the Emporium, changing it from a purely state-owned enterprise to one co-owned by the state, the Emporium, other enterprises and the general public. A new type of structure for the property ownership of enterprises appeared. Correspondingly, the Emporium was no longer responsible to the state only, but had to be responsible to other enterprises, the board of directors and the thousands of shareholders among the public. The new system placed great pressure on the administrators of the Emporium, who had to rejuvenate the Emporium continuously and maximize the earning power of the Emporium in order to reward its shareholders.

Reform of purchasing management

Under the planned economy system in the 1950s, retail shops could only purchase from local wholesaling units. But because it was the

Allocation	Shares	Percentage
State	77,620,000	42.24
Sponsor Corporation	8,750,000	4.76
Social Corporation	4,620,000	2.52
Public	92,769,000	50.48
Total	183,769.000	100

Table 5.2: Share allocations in the Emporium.

flagship department store of the PRC, the Emporium was assisted through administrative measures of the supervising units in purchasing according to the planned quota system and as a result had a distinctive purchasing system at that time. The Emporium centralized the power to purchase goods from outside Beijing, and the various commodity sales sections of the Emporium were given the power to procure from local sources. This system was beneficial to the Emporium under the planned economy system in that the Emporium could centralize the use of capital and minimize purchasing fees. However, because of the development of a market economy and reform in the system of distribution, the existence of multiple sales methods and multiple channels of distribution required the Emporium to show a quick response to market changes. In order to minimize the number of links in the distribution chain and to enhance adaptability to the market, the Emporium granted the power of purchasing goods from cities outside of Beijing to the various commodity sections, allocating them a fixed expenditure allowance. As a result, the commodity sections gained both the functions of sales and purchasing. Within a fixed amount of capital, the commodity sections could adjust the quantity and variety purchased according to changes in market demand and supply. As the sales volume expanded, the Emporium handed over such purchasing power to the sales counters, so they could adjust procurement according to their daily sales volumes.

After the Wangfujing Department Store became a limited stock company in 1993, it continued to expand its investments. Wangfujing branches were set up in other provinces and cities around the country, and chain stores also operated in Beijing. Expansion of business will continue to make the Emporium reform its system of purchasing and establish a center of commodity distribution and transportation. This will be an important reform of the purchasing management system of the Emporium.

Exploration of New Modes of Operation

During the mid-1980s, the new market environment greatly stimulated the Emporium to compete for new sources of procurement, expand the sales volume, and introduce famous brands, high-quality and luxury commodities. In line with this expansion, the Emporium initiated new operating methods.

Direct sales by factories

Factories producing high-quality, famous and new commodities were invited to set up special sales counters in the Emporium to sell their products directly to the customers. The factories had to adhere to the various regulations and requirements of the Emporium. Matters including the provision of capital, transportation, and sale of commodities were all the responsibility of the factories, but the sales volume and profits were credited to the Emporium. Through this channel, the factories might communicate directly with consumers and make use of the prestige and operating halls of the Emporium to sell their own products. Customers also benefited from this system as they enjoyed more discounts through the factories' direct sales strategy, and it was easier for them to communicate problems concerning the quality of the products to the factories. This device facilitated the management of the Emporium through a reduction in the number of sale assistants, processing fees, warehouse occupation, and capital investment. By the early 1990s, the Emporium had introduced more than 100 factories which occupied over 190 sales counters and supplied about 1,000 items on sale (*Wangfujing* 1993:397). Among these items, over 80 per cent were new products.

Setting up speciality counters

The Emporium assigned its shop assistants to prepare specialty counters in the operating halls, selling commodities which were generally high-quality, new, and special, each counter selling special goods from only one famous factory. The factories supplied the products, and the Emporium undertook to sell them. This method made it easier for the factories to advertise and sell their products, and also benefited the Emporium by centralizing management. In 1992, the Emporium set up such special counters for 44 factories, whose sales volume amounted to about 60 million yuan.

Opening 'shops in the shop'

It has been a long-established custom for Chinese retail enterprises to manage their businesses by categorizing products according to their nature. For example, the first floor (*Figure 5.3*) of the Emporium sold food, daily products, cosmetics, enamel products, and so on. The second floor (*Figure 5.4*) sold fashions, cotton goods, stationery and

Figure 5.3 Shopping hall on the ground floor.

other related items. Accompanied by the increase in the operating floor space, the Emporium made a significant departure from the old custom in management in 1985. 'Shops in the shop' (*dian zhong dian*) were opened on the fourth floor of the Emporium, that is, shops of famous brands set up their own branches there selling luxury goods and well-known commodities (*Figure 5.5*). This method was very popular among large retail enterprises abroad, but was a new departure in China's retail business. For a long period of time after its introduction into China, it was criticized by some people. But the management staff of the Emporium believed that this new operation method would eventually be accepted by customers, and subsequent developments proved them right.

Retail businesses in other countries utilize the open shelf and self-service concepts as the principal methods of operation. These methods minimize conflicts between customers and staff members, and maximize customers' freedom in shopping. In China, the traditional operation method of retail businesses was the adoption of sales counters. This method was closely associated with the enduring shortage of commodities under the planned economy system. Following the policy of reform and openness and the rise of productivity, commodities became more diverse and the market more

131

Figure 5.4 Shopping hall on the second floor.

active. A sound material foundation was created for retail business. Compared to the diversification of commodities, sales methods were more difficult to change. Because it was one of the four large department stores in Beijing, the Wangfujing Department Store had a customer admission rate of over 100,000 per day, a figure rising to 150,000 during festivals. That is to say, the average area per customer was only 0.1 square meters on an operating floor of 12,000 square meters. For such a large customer flow, it was very difficult to reform the traditional sales method when considering the potential theft problem. In spite of this difficulty, the Emporium adopted the open-shelf method in the 'shops in the shop' on the fourth floor in 1985, and self-service was gradually introduced in the selling of commodities such as fashions and electric appliances. Nowadays, restrictive counters, open-shelf, and self-service co-exist as sales methods in the Emporium.

The Emporium's supermarket

Although supermarkets have been a common feature of retailing in foreign countries since the 1960s, in China they were only selectively introduced in some large cities like Beijing in the early 1980s. It was

Figure 5.5 Shop in the shop on the fourth floor.

expected that the convenience to shoppers of a self-service operation, where items could be selected by shoppers and paid for at the same check-out point when they left the supermarket, would be attractive. Furthermore, the operating costs of a supermarket are low due to the smaller number staff needed to service the customers. However, the results were unsatisfactory. The price of commodities was too high, expenditure was great, and the number of customers fell far short of expectations. As a consequence of these diseconomies, great losses were incurred and liquidation resulted. Furthermore, there was no precedent in China for operating a modern supermarket in a large department store. In the 1990s, with the transformation of retailing following the reforms, and with the abolition of old modes of operating, 'supermarkets' once again captured the attention of retailers. In 1995, the Emporium decided to operate its own supermarket in the store. Sales at individual counters was no longer the only method of operation and, as we have discussed above, multiple modes of operation were adopted to suit different commodities, and flexibility in the sales operation was the key to satisfying the needs of customers who wanted a wider choice among the items for purchase.

Establishment of chain shops

The establishment of chain shops represents an organizational reform of the Emporium in terms of both its mode of operation and the expansion of the scale of its retailing. However, the Emporium operates in a restricted geographical area, making it difficult to expand its business. Because of the increasing competition that resulted from substantial development of China's commerce in the 1990s, the profitablity of the Emporium was threatened and it was deemed necessary to reform its mode of operation. In 1994, the Emporium opened a branch store in Chengdu, Sichuan Province, which has set a precedent in China for branch stores in other cities. Subsequently, another branch was opened in Guangzhou, Guangdong Province, and some fifteen branch stores were opened in Beijing, marking the beginning of the chain store business. The Emporium became a prototype in the enterprise business in China.

Diversification and conglomeration

From the time of its establishment, the Wangfujing Department Store was essentially a retail operation, though the expansion of its scope of operation included some wholesale business. In the late 1980s, the Emporium began manufacturing its own brand of fashions. In 1994, the Emporium, that had recently become a limited stock company, was listed on the stock exchange, thus increasing its pool of capital. Besides retailing and wholesaling, the company has expanded its range of business to include distribution, fast-food and hotel business, as well as property dealing, thus developing into a diversified enterprise.

Reform of employment and wage systems, and abolition of the 'iron rice bowl' and 'iron wages'

In 1984, the government implemented reforms in commerce and the service industries. The state granted individual powers to enterprises in six areas: autonomy in management, partial discretion in personnel appointment and dismissal, power of employment, financial manage-ment, power to set up new organizations, and partial discretion on price control. In the past, employment had not been at the discretion of the enterprise, but was under the control of the state's centralized planning system, termed the 'iron rice bowl' system. It is actually a lifelong tenure system in which an employee works for an enterprise until retirement and then receives a pension until death. In the mid-1980s, after the government carried out a reform of the employment system, the Emporium was allowed to hire its employees in the labor market in response to its own needs. Although an enterprise possessed the right of employment, the 'iron rice bowl' system was still retained, but as further reforms were carried out, this system was replaced by contract employment. A contract is signed between the employer and the hired employee, usually for a three-year term of employment, and on expiry of that contract both management and employee have the option to renew the contract. The contract employment system effectively demolished the old system of the 'iron rice bowl'.

Exploration and reform of the wage system was also undertaken by the Emporium. Before the era of reform and openness, an employee's wages were determined by a state-centralized hierarchical wage system called the 'iron wage', where the only criterion in deciding the wage level was the employee's seniority in service. The management of an enterprise could not adjust wages according to an employee's ability and merit of service or based on the sales performance of the enterprise itself. In 1986, however, the Emporium reformed the hierarchical wage system in order to stimulate the working incentive of the staff, and wages were made proportionate to the profits of the Emporium, the first step being to link wage adjustments to staff performance. The 'iron wage' system was thus abolished and replaced by the *dai gang* and *xia gang* systems. 'Dai gang' refers to a punishment meted out through a deduction in wages and bonuses when serious mistakes are committed by the staff, while 'xia gang' refers to a punishment imposed through the suspension of wages and bonuses when staff who have committed serious mistakes do not improve their performance. Later, several more reforms were introduced. For example, wages and bonuses were made proportionate to sales volume, and wages were calculated as the sum of the basic salary plus a specific share of the sales volume. As the economic performance of the Emporium greatly improved, the average wages of its staff members grew to feature amongst the highest paid by large retailing businesses in Beijing.

Enterprise culture

The 'blazing spirit' (*yi tuan huo*) which is the essence of the Wangfujing Department Store's enterprising spirit, is well-known in China's commercial world. It is the core of the enterprise culture of the Emporium, and represents the goal of the company: to wholeheartedly serve the people (*Figure 5.6*).

Figure 5.6 The 'Blazing Spirit' statue of Zhang Binggui in front of the entrance to the Wangfujing Department Store.

This 'blazing spirit' is embodied by Zhang Binggui, a shop assistant in the Emporium, and actually evolved from Zhang's work experience and skill. Zhang Binggui (1918–1987) was a native of Beijing and worked as an apprentice in a shop run by a capitalist before being employed by the Emporium – 'new China's number one store' – in 1955. In the 1950s, due to the deteriorating economic situation and the shortage of goods, customers waited in long queues to purchase the commodities they needed. Working at the counter selling candies, Zhang acquired the skills of prompt measurement of the exact amount of goods ordered by customers (*yi zhua zhun*) and quick quotation of the accurate total sum of money customers needed to pay (*yi kou qing*). These skills enabled Zhang to process transactions quickly and reduced queuing time. During his many years of service at the candy counter, Zhang strove hard to provide excellent service and described the process of transaction as having six parts: inquiry (*wen*), pick-up (*na*), measurement (*cheng*), packaging (*baozhuang*), payment (*jiezhang*), and lastly, collection of money and giving of change (*shou zhao qian*). He perceptively recognized several principles which characterized the provision of good service, for example, the 'five eagernesses' (eagerness to prepare the counter, to serve the people, to conduct quick transactions, to learn, and to persevere); the 'ten watchwords': take the initiative (*zhu dong*), enthusiastic service (*re qing*), patience (*nai xin*), thoughtfulness (*zhou dao*), and sincerity (*cheng ken*); and the 'four impartialities', that is, impartiality towards customers whether they buy or not, whether they buy large or small quantities, whether they are regular or new customers, and whether they are local or foreign visitors. Zhang's skills, patience, and enthusiasm to provide good service earned him the respect and support of his customers.

In the late 1960s, the Emporium designated Zhang Binggui as a model sales assistant. All staff were exhorted to learn from Zhang Binggui's experience in the hope that they would improve their attitudes in serving the customers and enhance the overall quality of service. This lesson was deemed a necessary prerequisite to expanding the Emporium's scope of business and inventing new techniques for serving its customers with sincerity.

In the ensuing years, Zhang Binggui was honoured several times as a state-level model worker, and in 1977 he was described in local newspapers as 'having a blazing spirit in his heart to warm millions of people' (*Hongqi* 1977). This popularized Zhang's contribution in improving the quality of service in the nation's retail trade, and 'learning from Zhang Binggui' inspired a large number of shop assistants who followed in his footsteps. As the trend towards improving customer service reached a high tide, the management of the Emporium realized that the 'yi tuan huo' spirit was an invaluable spiritual asset of the enterprise and a unifying force. They implemented a programme of continuous thought education for their staff, encouraging them to develop this 'blazing spirit', which meant loving their jobs and devoting themselves to serving their customers. As a result, the staff understood that this 'spirit' was the key dynamic internal driving force that would enhance the enterprise's overall performance and ensure its survival in the face of unprecedented competition. In commemoration of Zhang Binggui, who passed away on 17 September 1987, the staff redoubled their efforts to push forward the reform and development of the Emporium. The Emporium benefited by being honoured as an excellent commercial enterprise in the country's service industry.

On 25 September 1987, the Wangfujing Emporium celebrated its thirty-second anniversary. At the commemorative ceremony, the management formally enshrined the 'yi tuan huo' spirit as its supreme principle and guiding force. Thus, Zhang Binggui's excellent service over 30 years of practice and promotion evolved from an isolated model based on one individual's experience to a common spirit shared by the entire enterprise. It expressed the unique culture of the Emporium, and in the decade of the 1990s, the management of the Emporium continues to strive for progress and to develop and extend the 'blazing spirit' throughout the whole of society.

Gradual modernization of management

The immediate effect upon the administrators of the current National Reform policies and openness was the disintegration of their traditional concept of management. They were liberated from the old planned economy system and now had to employ new concepts and theories to challenge their competitors under the new market economy. The experience of competition has convinced the Wangfujing Department Store that modernization of thought is only the first step. Modernization of management skills is even more critical for the enterprise. Backward management diminishes an enterprise's capacity to compete with both foreign and domestic companies, and retail enterprises must leave behind the traditional management methods based on past experience and shift to scientific management. As mentioned above, the Emporium greatly improved the hardware facilities of its operating environment in 1993, and at the same time invested over 10 million yuan in the introduction of a computerized management system.

Reforms in China, which are progressing step by step, have benefited the Wangfujing Department Store. Today, the Emporium is planning new developmental strategies. Entering the twenty-first century, the Emporium will implement even more substantial changes, and will proudly face the outside world.

Notes

1 *Genju Beijing shi baihuo dalou linian jingying qingkuang ziliao jisuan* (Business records based on the historical operating costs of the Beijing Wangfujing Department Store).
2 *Genju Beijing shi baihuo dalou linian jingying qingkuang ziliao jisuan* (Business records based on the historical operating costs of the Beijing Wangfujing Department Store).

Part II

Visions of Modernism and Japanese Department Stores

6

THE BIRTH OF THE JAPANESE DEPARTMENT STORE[*]

Brian Moeran

Like the Parisian department store of the late nineteenth century, the Japanese department store stands today as a monument to the 'bourgeois' middle-class culture on which it has been built and which has over the years underpinned, nourished, and wondered at the goods that it has displayed (to paraphrase the words of Michael Miller [1981:3] on the Bon Marché).

For many years, people all over the world have remarked upon the apparent ease with which Japanese have always seemed to be able to 'adopt' things foreign and 'adapt' them into things Japanese. So with the department store – an idea first borrowed from the United States, developed according to models found there and in Europe, and gradually fashioned into something apparently special enough to attract the attention of a visiting journalist from *The Herald Tribune* in 1935 (Hatsuda 1993:135). There is, of course, a danger of reducing this perceived tendency of 'adoption' and 'adaptation' to yet another orientalist cultural trait that neatly categorizes 'the Japanese' as something 'other' than those living in 'the west', but in its (only partly disciplined) display of goods of all kinds from Europe, America, and other parts of Asia, the Japanese department store has been instrumental in creating in Japan what Ulf Hannerz (1991) would refer to as a 'creole culture' – a culture which has seen its image reflected in that multitude of mirrors and displays found in every store and which has preened itself accordingly.

In Japan the department store emerged in the first decade of the twentieth century as an end product of 'civilization and enlightenment'

---

* The author would like to thank Ōtsu Kunihiro, General Manager of Mitsukoshi Enterprises Co. Ltd., Hong Kong, for his assistance in obtaining copies of many of the illustrations used in this chapter.

(*bunmei kaika*), a phrase that was coined in 1867 by Fukuzawa Yukichi and which formed the ideological backbone of the Meiji regime's resistance to western encroachment. Inspired at the beginning of the twentieth century by the *grands magasins* of Paris, London, Philadelphia and New York, the Japanese department store has been part of the world's first non-western industrializing nation's drive to master a fascinating, new, but nevertheless slightly alien, material world that was not of its own invention. In the goods that it sold, in the services and various forms of entertainment that it provided, and in the values that it projected, the department store reflected the new hybrid culture's identification with appearances and material possessions, reaffirmed and spurred on that culture's dedication to productivity and to catching up with the west, and personified the new modern intelligentsia's aspirations for enrichment, self-fulfilment and gracious living during the period of Taishō democracy (1912–26) (Seidensticker 1983:279). In short, from its very beginnings, the department store was not just 'a city within a city' (Hatsuda 1993:102), but a dream world where western, and thus bourgeois, culture was on display. It celebrated both, revealing what Japan's new hybrid culture stood for, where it had come from, and where with the store's help it might yet go in terms of values and lifestyles (cf. Miller 1983:3–4) – to be transformed into a creole culture that generates its own new structures among other cultures and that is, in turn, wondered at, emulated, adopted and adapted by other people in other lands.

But the Japanese department store did not just perform an important role in the formation of a new hybrid consumer culture through its conscious and conspicuous blending of Japanese and foreign goods. In its early days, it also made an important contribution to Japan's economic development in the face of western capitalism (and later on, as Ueno Chizuko shows in the next chapter, it showed how such development could be rechannelled into new forms of corporate capitalism). For example, the department store put into effect sales techniques learned in Europe and the United States and so revolutionized traditional retailing methods – firstly by displaying goods; secondly, by gathering a wide variety of such goods under a single roof, financing them from a single source of capital, and classifying them by category, or 'department'; thirdly, by coordinating all kinds of sales-related activities – from advertising to home deliveries by way of art and culture exhibitions. Such innovations, in turn, imposed a need for the mass employment of staff,[1] many of whom were women, and so induced new forms of financial and personnel management, involving new flows of capital, commodities and people. As we shall see, these flows were closely connected with the development of (underground) railway transport which permitted staff to commute to work, rather than live in as before, and consumers to flock *en masse* to city centres where the stores were located.

This chapter gives a brief account of the birth and development of the department store in Japan. It focuses in particular on Mitsukoshi Department Store, since Mitsukoshi was in many respects a leader in the kind of innovations alluded to above, but it also takes account of other leading Japanese stores – concerns like Shirokiya, Daimaru, Matsuya and Matsuzakaya – as it traces the development of the department store from its prototype in the form of the *kankōba* emporium or bazaar to the emergence of the world's first railway terminal department store. During the course of this discussion, I shall look at the relationship between stores and their clienteles, on the one hand, and between shopping and entertainment, on the other, as well as at the ways in which the Japanese department store set about marketing its products, its services, and its name as a brand that would be readily recognized and trusted by the consumers that it sought first to attract, then to woo, and finally to conquer. Hopefully, this chapter will thereby complement that written by Ueno Chizuko on the post-war development of Seibu and its detailed strategy of image marketing, as well as link back to discussions of the development of Chinese department stores in Hong Kong and Shanghai earlier on in this book.

The Kankōba Bazaar

On 2 January 1905, Mitsui Gofukuten (Mitsui Dry Goods Store) placed a full page advertisement in the *Jiji Shinpō* and other daily newspapers announcing that it had changed its name to Mitsukoshi and that it would henceforth increase the variety of goods it stocked and sold, and so be like an American 'department store' (this being the actual phrase used). Thus was Japan's first department store publicly announced.[2]

Although, as well shall soon see, the new Mitsukoshi was about to initiate what its managing director, Takahashi Sadao, thought of as a retailing 'revolution' in the display and pricing of goods, there already existed a precursor to the department store in both Tōkyō and Ōsaka. In 1878, the Tōkyō Prefectural Government staged what it called a kankōba, emporium or bazaar, where goods previously collected from all over Japan for inclusion in a government-sponsored Domestic Industrial Exhibition (Naikoku Kangyō Hakurankai), held in Ueno Park between August and November the previous year, were displayed and put on sale to the general public. A large area was selected for the purpose in Eirakuchō, Tōkyō, and a building erected in the style of an Edo period (1603–1868) samurai residence. There, numerous stalls or boutiques were gathered together under a single roof, separated by narrow aisles allowing shoppers to walk through (without their shoes),[3] look at and make their own selections from the items being displayed. It thus differed from the previous year's exposition in that people were not obliged to pay an entry fee, and could buy what was on display. It met with immediate success (leading to the erection of new buildings to cope with the crowds) – partly because the Eirakuchō bazaar was also located in a large park area where visitors could eat and relax, and even watch the occasional performance of a *nō* or *kabuki* play (Hatsuda 1993:9–16).

The Eirakuchō kankōba was modelled on 'bazaars' and 'fairs' in London and New York, as reported to the Tōkyō Prefectural Government by Japanese who had been abroad. Its success allowed it to continue on this site until 1887, and led to other similar kankōba being quickly established in other parts of Tōkyō – first in Kanda and later largely concentrated along the Ginza, now the city's premier shopping street. By 1883, Tōkyō had twelve such bazaars (in Ōsaka they started slightly later, in 1884), which reached their zenith in the 1880s and 90s so that by 1902 there were 27 operating in the city. In 1907, two years after Mitsukoshi's declaration of intent to become a department store, however, their number had gone down to nineteen and they faded into insignificance soon after, to be replaced by the emergent department stores.

There were several factors linking the kankōba to department stores and making them very attractive to Tōkyō's inhabitants at that time. Firstly, the fact that bazaars displayed goods meant that shoppers could purchase things directly without having to go through the traditional *za-uri* buying process of explaining to a salesman what they wanted and have things shown to them one by one until a choice was made. Secondly, the fact that all items were affixed with a price tag meant that shoppers no longer had to bargain, even haggle, over the price of what they wanted to buy. They merely selected an item and paid for it at a cash counter. Thirdly, kankōba facilitated shopping since all kinds of different items – from pots to pipes, by way of mirrors, needles, dolls, deer horn, cosmetics, clothing, clogs, carvings, ivory, antiques, glasses, hats, and stationery – could be found and bought in the same place.

The fact that some bazaars had long opening hours, put on monthly discount sales, and – like the 1899 Imperial Merchandise Pavilion (Teikoku Hakuhinkan) – included such attractions as a barber's shop, tea house, photographer's booth, and even a replica of an Edo pagoda, meant that the kankōba mixed shopping and entertainment to create a new style of consumption. Later developed by department stores, this style of consumption aimed first to attract people to the kankōba, and then to induce them to buy the goods displayed therein. It was distinctive in two important ways in that it allowed people a choice of goods *within* a single bazaar, and a choice *between* different bazaars located in a single area. It was the latter which encouraged people to move *en masse* along the city streets from one consumption site to another and, since many of the kankōba were located in the Ginza area, which helped give rise to the age of Japan's first *flâneurs* and *flâneuses*, whose leisurely enjoyment of the city's streets, shops, merchandise and general atmosphere was soon to be made famous by the new idiom of *ginbura* ('idling in the Ginza').

Japan's First Department Store

Mitsukoshi is part of the Mitsui group of business concerns and traces its origins back to Echigoya, a drapery store founded in both Kyōto and Edo (present day Tōkyō) by Mitsui Takatoshi in 1673 (and featured in a number of woodblock prints during the Edo Period). Right from its very beginning, Echigoya marked its difference from competitors with the slogan 'cash payments and no haggling' (*tanasaki genkin kakine nashi*) (Mitsukoshi 1990:22–3),[4] and by selling goods at a low profit but in large quantities, the store soon flourished. With the end of the feudal era and Japan's emergence into the modern world, however, Echigoya went through a number of name changes and different management policies before undergoing transformation at the hands of a new managing director, Takahashi Sadao, who was transferred there from the Mitsui Bank back in August 1895 and made managing director of what was then called Mitsui Gofukuten.[5]

Takahashi had already been to business school in America, where (in 1881) he had looked at the organization of Wanamaker's in Philadelphia and decided that Japanese retailing should embark upon the same path of modernization. He envisaged a retailing 'revolution' which would affect both the purchasing and sale of goods, methods of accounting, the employment of personnel, and the very nature of consumption itself. More specifically, he advocated that the store purchase its merchandise directly from manufacturing sources, rather than continue to go through wholesalers; that all goods be sold by display rather than by the traditional method of za-uri sales;[6] that the store adopt a western-style accounting system, rather than continue to use the old-fashioned day-by-day ledger (*daifukuchō*) for entering sales; that there be a new system of personnel management and employment of people with good educational qualifications who would receive regular salaries (rather than seasonal rewards) and commute to work (rather than live in); and that advertising and other public relations activities be pursued as a means of creating shopping fashions (which would be enhanced by the introduction of new designs for women's clothes) (Mitsukoshi 1990:32; Hatsuda 1993:63–4).

These innovations were quickly introduced. In November 1895, the second floor of the old store in Nihonbashi (which had hitherto been used to entertain special clients) was converted into a sales area with display cases (*Figure 6.1*). This met with such approval on the part of the store's customers that Takahashi proceeded to convert the whole of the ground floor into a similar display area. When renovations were completed in October 1900, the store's opening day sales were the highest in its history. Passers-by were further encouraged to enter the store and buy things by the introduction of shop windows in 1904, following an employee's visit to New York in March the previous year (Hatsuda 1993:67–8).

Mitsukoshi's success had an immediate effect on other drapery or dry goods stores which rushed to follow their rival's example. Matsuya put in display cases on the second floor of its renovated building in 1901, introduced shop windows in 1904, and then designed the whole of its new building with display floors in 1907. Shirokiya did the same when it rebuilt its premises in 1903; it also took the opportunity to instal two Belgian glass-plated shop windows, one each side of its main entrance. By the beginning of the second decade of the twentieth century, all of Japan's largest department stores had shifted from traditional za-uri to modern display and sales (*Figure 6.2*).

As these transformations in the presentation of goods took place, more and more people – especially families and women with children – began to spend their days in the city's new shopping areas. Clearly, these new retailing methods were instrumental in stimulating interest in commodities and thus in consumption itself, but stores themselves also contributed to this new shopping mood by trying to create fashions to spur on consumption. In the old days, when choosing goods, customers had consulted pattern books to select the particular cloths they

Figure 6.1 Poster for Mitsui Gofukuten showing new upstairs display cases (centre) with downstairs old-style *za-uri* sales area, 1896 (courtesy of Mitsukoshi Department Store).

preferred, and had made use of a fixed range of patterns from which old and young alike had taken their pick, almost regardless of the seasons. From 1895, however, Mitsukoshi began to employ a number of artists to create and draw new designs in order to enable the store to promote particular motifs and colours for particular seasons and social contexts.[7] Takahashi had been prompted to initiate the idea of fashion during a visit to Paris where he noted how new clothes designs were being introduced every year before spreading to other European cities and even as far afield as the United States. He envisaged a similar process taking place in Japan and, taking advantage of the country's favourable economic

Figure 6.2 View of Mitsukoshi Gofukuten, with its new shop windows, 1904 (courtesy of Mitsukoshi Department Store).

climate, introduced the so-called 'dandy pattern' (*date moyō*) for clothes and accessories in 1896. This met with great success, partly because of Takahashi's clever marketing strategy of issuing local Shinbashi geisha with Mitsukoshi-made *kimono* dyed in this style, and of then ensuring that they wore them when dancing at parties they attended.

Probably the most famous fashion of all initiated by Mitsukoshi during this period was that of *Genroku* – a coordinated style that covered not just kimono, but *kazashi* hair pins, shoe wear and bags, as well as men's ties (Yamamoto 1984:108), lacquerware and pottery. Created just after the store's first art exhibition, featuring the works of the Edo period Ogata Kōrin (who lived during the Genroku period [1688–1704]), the Genroku style matched the flamboyant mood of the country following its victory in the Russo-Japanese war of 1904–5 and became a major hit from 1905 to 1908. Orchestrated almost entirely by Takahashi, who himself composed a 'Genroku dance' performed by geisha in the entertainment area in Shinbashi as well as by kabuki actors, this was the first major fashion boom in Japan (*Figure 6.3*). Mitsukoshi's example was, not surprisingly, soon followed by other stores (Hatsuda 1993:74–6).

In order to ensure the success of its fashions, Mitsukoshi made sure to back up its sales campaign with advertising and all kinds of public relations ploys. For example, it launched its own PR magazine

Figure 6.3 A Mitsukoshi poster from 1907, with Shinbashi *geisha* in the *Genroku* style (courtesy of Mitsukoshi Department Store).

(*Hanagoromo*) in January 1899 (renamed *Jikō* in 1903) with articles and illustrations designed to stimulate an interest in fashion *per se*, as well as to attract attention to particular trends being created by Mitsukoshi. Takashimaya, Shirokiya and Matsuya soon followed suit, so that by the end of the first decade of the twentieth century, most stores were publishing their own PR magazines regularly, almost all of them with the express intention of fostering trends and making their readers feel that fashion was somehow crucial to their everyday lives.[8]

PR gimmicks were by no means new to Mitsukoshi which (as Echigoya) had, from the end of the seventeenth century, lent hundreds of customers umbrellas embossed with its store logo as part of its 'service' on rainy days (Yamamoto 1984:104; Mitsukoshi 1993:25). The introduction of shop windows, too, can be seen as a new form of public relations and advertising medium – as can the early provision of toilets, readings rooms and restaurants where people could relax and meet one another in a socially acceptable environment. In 1903, too, Mitsukoshi purchased a French-made delivery van to drive through the streets of Tōkyō with the store's name emblazoned on its sides and deliver purchases to the homes of customers. At a time when cars were few and far between in the city, Mitsukoshi's (and Japan's) first delivery van attracted a lot of public attention and comment.

Use of public relations media was part of stores' overall marketing strategy and here again Mitsukoshi led the field. In March 1906, for example, it developed a direct debit system in conjunction with the Post Office to enable it to accept telephone orders from all over Japan, and in June the same year initiated a gift voucher system. That same month, it also placed an exhibit in a 'railway exposition' (*kisha hakurankai*) which travelled all over the Kansai area around Ōsaka, stopping at all major stations en route for people to visit. Other marketing gimmicks were to be found in the store's advertising. As a means of attracting attention, for example, it purchased a large block of empty space in the middle of one page of the *Jiji Shinpō* Newspaper on 19 December 1906, and included just one short phrase stating that this was where the following day's Mitsukoshi ad could be found (Mitsukoshi 1990:46–7).

Although strategic advertising was not unknown during the Edo period (see Moeran 1996:6–7), department stores were among the earliest advertisers,[9] and soon livened up city life with their striking posters, billboards and illuminations, thereby contributing greatly to the development of Japan's fledgling advertising industry (Yamamoto 1984:103). Among Mitsukoshi's earliest memorable campaigns were the 'famous beauty' (*bijinga*) posters placed first of all in the waiting rooms of Shinbashi, Ueno and (Ōsaka's) Umeda stations in 1899, before being distributed to 39 more stations located throughout the country. These soon attracted their imitators as other stores launched similar campaigns (Yamamoto 1984:196). A few years later, in 1908, Mitsukoshi went so far as to put a poster proclaiming itself 'Japan's Number One' (*Nihon ichi*) at the top of Mount Fuji, the country's highest mountain. The store was responsible, too, for the famous slogan, 'Today the Imperial Theatre; tomorrow Mitsukoshi' (*Kyō wa Teigeki, asu wa*

Mitsukoshi), inviting people to spend alternate days at these two prestigious establishments located in Tōkyō's Nihonbashi area. By 1915, its success in creating both the idea of fashion and the name of Mitsukoshi was almost arrogantly proclaimed in 'Don't talk about fashion without first visiting Mitsukoshi' (*Mitsukoshi o otozure shite ryūkō o kataru nakare*). It was this new attitude towards the consumption of fashions which allowed for the free flow of mass-produced goods made possible by the industrial revolution and which, in turn, stimulated further manufacturing. In this respect, department stores like Mitsukoshi not only sustained mass production but played an important role in the development of industries generally, and thereby helped Japan enter an era of modernity through consumption (Hatsuda 1993:80–1).

Developing New Clienteles

Who, then, was most active in the new style of consumption encouraged by Japan's emergent department stores? During the Edo period, old drapery and dry goods stores like Echigoya, Matsuzakaya (founded in 1611), Shirokiya (1662) and Daimaru (1717) had each developed certain types of clientele which they carried with them into the modern era. This meant that, in its early years, Mitsukoshi and other department stores were not frequented by the kind of (upper) middle-class customers who later came to form their regular customers, and it was not until after the great Kantō earthquake in 1923 that stores became really popular with the lower-middle class urban masses. Thus Mitsukoshi, for example, cultivated the merchant capitalist class and Kyōto aristocracy; Shirokiya former *daimyō* feudal lords and their families; Takashimaya members of the Imperial Household; and Matsuzakaya the Buddhist and Shintō clergy. Only Daimaru had customers from the lower and middle classes and so from its beginnings catered to a fairly general mass clientele (Hatsuda 1993:84).

Each store thus had different characteristics based on its different clientele, and one of the problems facing department – as opposed to dry goods – stores was how to develop new regular customers. Mitsukoshi decided to target those living in Tōkyō's Yamanote uptown residential district, which was rapidly expanding from around mid-Meiji and accounted for half the city's population growth during the whole of the Meiji period (Seidensticker 1983:236). The 'high city' was beginning to house the new upper-middle class elites working in the military, government, academia, banking, and large trading corporations, and so to accumulate, in Edward Seidensticker's words

151

(1983:249), 'the money, the power, and the imagination'. One reason for Mitsukoshi's trying to develop this kind of clientele was, of course, that it was comparatively wealthy; another was that the patrician clientele's social prestige would redound upon the store's own status; yet another, more practical, was that the Yamanote district was linked to downtown areas by the new transportation systems being opened up at that time, thereby breaking down the old barriers between neighbour-hoods that had hitherto existed and so restricted shopping activities to local areas. People taking up residence in the uptown areas of Kōjimachi, Akasaka, Azabu, Shibuya, Ushigome, Hongō and so on were people who commuted to work every day and who, as a result, began to make their purchases in the big stores located near their offices in and around Nihonbashi, at the north end of the Ginza. Just as importantly, these customers were comparatively well off, literate, educated and clearly prepared to take the lead in adopting western styles of living – putting in sewerage systems, for example, as well as gas and electricity supplies, to their homes and enjoying a fairly high level of consumption (Hatsuda 1993:84–5). It was these people who read upper-class, intellectual newspapers like the *Jiji Shinpō* and whom Mitsukoshi thus addressed directly in its numerous advertising campaigns (Yamamoto 1984:106).

In December 1904, a new president was appointed, Hibi Ōsuke (1860–1931), who continued Takahashi's radical changes and took Mitsukoshi into a new age as a department store. As part of the store's strategy of transforming its image from downmarket dry goods store to upmarket department store, Hibi cultivated foreign customers and entertained a number of members of royalty and distinguished government officials from Europe and the United States – including General Tuft and the Prince Connaught.[10] This courting of high society also extended to Japan's own aristocracy and senior officers in the armed services, as Hibi tried to make Mitsukoshi into a place where the upper classes might meet and consort, rather than simply shop.

As part of this general business strategy focusing on corporate image and building up the store's customer base, Hibi also set up a number of discussion or study groups consisting of famous scholars (such as the archaeologist and anthropologist, Tsuboi Shōgorō), artists (like Kuroda Seiki, who introduced Impressionism to Japan), writers (like the famous novelist, Mori Ōgai), and other educators and intellectuals, who would gather from time to time to discuss particular themes selected for inclusion in the store's PR magazine, *Jikō*, which then published the proceedings of their deliberations (on, for example, the exhibits at a Tōkyō art show, the colour of western-style umbrellas, Mitsukoshi's new fashion designs, and so on). Sometimes they were called upon to judge design competitions run by Mitsukoshi; at others to participate in public lectures and round table discussions, but, whatever their activities, Hibi's aim was to create an intellectual 'salon' that would redound to Mitsukoshi's credit. Membership increased over the years and the group was named the 'Jikō Club' in January 1925, when such well-known figures as the folklorist Yanagita Kunio, poet and playwrite Yoshii Isamu, and western-style artist Wada Eisaku were included in the group's membership (Hatsuda 1993:87–90).

In addition, Mitsukoshi established other study groups whose main aim was to focus on customer feedback in an attempt to boost sales (of, for example, products in the children's market), but which also contributed to the Mitsukoshi management's determination to help Japan modernize and catch up with more advanced nations like England and the United States. In this respect, as we have already seen in earlier chapters on Chinese department stores, there was a nationalist sentiment driving the development of the department store. Hibi promulgated such concepts as service and hard work on the part of his staff, as well as the cultivation of long-term relationships between store and customers, because he felt that, by getting Mitsukoshi to help improve the retail industry in this way, the store would encourage the growth of consumption, which would then itself permit the continued manufacturing of improved and standardized goods (Hatsuda 1993:90–2).

Mitsukoshi as Brand

As part of such product improvement and standardization, and as a part of its overall strategy of enhancing the store's status, Mitsukoshi soon began developing its own branded products. In June 1913, it linked up with a Japanese manufacturer, Mitsuwa, to put on sale a soap with the Mitsukoshi logo printed boldly on the package – a ploy that was appreciated by customers who quickly made the desired equation between product, store and quality. As a result, Mitsukoshi soon branded two types of student shoes, and, in 1917, started marketing its own *eau de cologne*, knife sharpening powder, butter, flour, and even refrigerators – all with the Mitsukoshi name. Thereafter, the store introduced foodstuffs, groceries, utensils and tools as brand goods to complement the products that it had been accumulating since its shift from dry goods to department store: bags, vests, shawls, silk parasols, embroidery, folding screens, and other goods that might appeal to foreign customers (in 1902); cosmetics, hats, children's dress (in 1905); western-style clothes (discontinued back in 1888, in 1906); shoes, umbrellas, hair pins, soap, bags, footwear and art objects (in 1907); safes for valuables, tobacco and stationery (in 1908); and interior decorations and furniture (in 1912) (Hatsuda 92–5).

The proliferation of such goods is reflected in the increase in the number of the store's departments during the first three decades of the century. A 1908 floor plan of the main store's three-floor building, for example, includes departments for shoes, tobacco, blankets, hats and accessories, clogs and umbrellas, cottons, woollens, imported cloths, and a 'Gothic'-style restroom, on the ground floor; dyed textiles, plain cloths, decorated cloths, bags, shawls, ribbons, jewellery and precious metals, *obi* sashes, and 'Louis XIV'-style restroom, on the first floor; and art display, display for foreigners, photographer's, and two restaurants, on the second floor. By 1922, when the store had been rebuilt, there were fifty departments ranging over six floors, with new items in the plan including an art gallery, smoking room and hairdresser, plus departments for Japanese-style furniture, western-style furniture, toys, musical instruments, stationery, shoes, cosmetics, foods, children's wear, western clothes, and gift vouchers. Four years later, with further rebuilding as a result of damage in the great Kantō earthquake of 1923, Mitsukoshi boasted 61 departments, including radio, wedding, shawls, hats and *furoshiki* wrapping cloths, while in 1929 it had 98, and was selling baby goods, sewing machines, bicycles, exercise equipment, magazines, arts and crafts, household electrical goods, furs, and watches, all in specialized departments (Mitsukoshi 1990:299–300).

We can see from the above that Mitsukoshi was quick to import and brand foreign goods – partly because they sold well, but also because foreign goods were perceived to be of high quality compared with Japanese goods, and thus provided Mitsukoshi itself with a high quality image through a rubbing-off process.[11] Needless to say, perhaps, it was not just Mitsukoshi which broadened its sales activities in this way. Shirokiya, for example, arranged with a British supplier, Arthur Davey, back in 1888 to supply it with western clothes, and in 1908 was selling ready-made clothes and shoes. In 1910, the store introduced women's overcoats and stationery, and in the following year photographs, foodstuffs, furniture, ceramics, lacquerware, watches, safes and musical instruments. In 1916, it also put on sale a 'Shirokiya-made Wells Fountain Pen' (Hatsuda 1993:96), but Mitsukoshi was definitely the leader in terms of branding and consumers generally thought of the store as being able to provide high quality, prestigious goods. It thus epitomized high-class merchandise and high-class culture and soon came to be seen as a modern retailing department store, rather than the old-fashioned and conservative dry goods store that it had once been.

Part of the process of 'branding', or image making, can be seen in the numerous and ornate building programmes upon which almost all stores embarked from the second decade of the twentieth century. As stores began to stock, display and sell more and more varieties of merchandise, they found themselves being obliged to expand their premises in one way or another. This meant, basically, increasing each store's sales floor area and heightening buildings to accommodate more sales floors. As a concomitant of these needs, stores had to make a move from their old traditional-style Edo period buildings to modern western-style architecture which allowed their stores to rise from two to first three, then four, and later six or seven floors in height. In addition, they often added pinnacles or towers for emphasis and created opulent facades that would attract people's attention and contribute to their own prestige, as well as to the market-value of the store's name.

Mitsukoshi itself was obliged to rebuild when the Tōkyō government decided to widen the main Nihonbashi road on which the store faced as part of its general city renovation plans. In 1907, therefore, the store relocated itself in the same block and built a three-floor renaissance-style building (opened on 1 April the following year). It was this enforced move which allowed Mitsukoshi to expand its selection of miscellaneous goods, foreign imports, art objects, precious metals and so on, and so propelled it forward to becoming a 'proper' department store of the kind found in Europe and America at that time (Mitsukoshi 1990:50).

In 1914, a similar renaissance-style, five-floor main building (with basement and roof garden) was completed in reinforced steel on the same block, and the store's famous lions – directly modelled on those found at the base of Nelson's Column in Trafalgar Square, London – were placed at the main entrance (*Figure 6.4*). When it opened on 1 October, comparisons were inevitably drawn in the press between Mitsukoshi and department stores in America and Europe, since both the interior and exterior of the new store were utterly 'modern'. This particular building included an elevator and Japan's first escalator, which together at once gave people a lot of pride in their country's perceived progress towards modernization. Thus Mitsukoshi found itself being called 'the largest store east of Suez', and 'incomparable to anything east of Suez'. Beside the main entrance, people's attention was attracted to the enormous twelve by eighteen metre open hallway in

Figure 6.4 Exterior view of Mitsukoshi's Renaissance-style main building, 1910 (courtesy of Mitsukoshi Department Store).

the centre of building, flanked by grand staircase and balustrade, and by the ten marble covered columns (decorated at the top with children, flowers and musical instruments) which supported an arched, stained-glass roof (*Figure 6.5*). Said to have been modelled on Wanamaker's and Harrods, the architectural style was rather more like that of the Bon Marché in Paris. Whatever its inspiration, however, the new building certainly placed Mitsukoshi in line with the rest of the world's great department stores, all of which went in for grand designs as part of their image development (Hatsuda 1993:99–102).

Most other stores found themselves in one way or another renovating old buildings and/or constructing new buildings during this period, and in the process introducing architectural novelties that attracted the crowds.[12] Shirokiya, for example, had a revolving door in its main entrance and was the first of Japan's department stores to put in an elevator (in 1911), manned by boys and replete with benches for sitting on. This acted as a magnet for shoppers and as a prestigious symbol of modernity (and capitalism) since at that time the only other elevators found in Japan were in the Bank of Japan and one or two large corporations like Mitsubishi's Third Building. As we have seen, Mitsukoshi soon followed suit with both elevator and escalator, and although the latter was both costly and inefficient, the fact that people

Figure 6.5 Interior view of the main hall of Mitsukoshi's new building, 1910 (courtesy of Mitsukoshi Department Store).

thought it prestigious eventually persuaded the store's management to continue with this system of customer transportation in 1923, when it was rebuilding its store after the great Kantō earthquake (Hatsuda 1993:103–9) (*Figure 6.6*).

So, in general, all stores went in for such luxurious building programmes, with mammoth structures, grandiose designs, elaborate staircases, pinnacles, cupolas and rotundas (cf. Ewen and Ewen

Figure 6.6 Escalator (and escalator boy) in Mitsukoshi Department Store, 1914.

1982:69). This was because: firstly, they helped create an image for the store, which could spread fairly quickly among a large section of the populace (especially in a city in which there were very few buildings higher than two floors at the time); secondly, stores wanted to appeal directly to the new wealthy upper-middle class which, like Mitsukoshi in the Yamanote district, they were cultivating as their new clienteles; thirdly, they also wished to give outward expression and support to the foreign culture and art that they were displaying inside, as an example of what Japan should be emulating; and fourthly, they were attempting to create an overall cosmopolitan harmony between the style of their architecture and the character of the goods that they were displaying and selling.

Sites for Consumption, Sights of Consumption

As Stuart and Elizabeth Ewen have had occasion to point out, early department stores in the United States were not just sites for consumption, but sights of consumption where 'goods were graced in monumental splendour' (Ewen and Ewen 1982:68). Japanese department stores are no exceptions to this rule. In the old days, as one grand new building after another joined the Tōkyō skyline, whole families would gather in the city centre to marvel at their wondrous illuminations, escalators, elevators, revolving doors, even open-air film showings.[13] In this respect, stores were clearly designed to be tourist, as well as shopping, attractions; and thus to be palaces of culture as well as of consumption.

Japanese writers such as Hatsuda Tōru (1993:115) have commented on the fact that Japanese department stores from the start differed from their counterparts in Europe and the United States in the comparatively large number of women who visited them and shopped with their children in tow, rather than leave them in designated play areas while they shopped alone. This meant that Japanese stores had to cater for whole families, rather than simply single women, in its provision of restaurants, restrooms, roof gardens and exhibitions. Thus, from early on, stores started to operate at least one restaurant on their premises, where a wide variety of food was served to all sorts of people, of all ages, at virtually any time of the day. Shirokiya was the first to open a restaurant, serving noodles and *sushi* rice balls, in 1904; this followed its provision of a children's playroom with see-saw and rocking horse in the previous year. Mitsukoshi opened its restaurant in 1907, two and a half years after declaring itself a department store, and served Japanese-style food, as well as western-style cakes, coffee and six kinds of Indian tea (Hatsuda 1993:119).

These restaurants soon became quite large. When rebuilding its store in 1911, Shirokiya included a restaurant seating several hundred people who could select from a menu that included a midday meal, sandwich box, sushi, cakes, fruit and boiled eggs, among other things. Mitsukoshi, too, gradually expanded its operations so that, by 1921, store restaurants seated more than 600 people, with a western-style restaurant with seating for a further 300 people being added in the following year. Special children's menus were offered when the store reopened after the 1923 earthquake, with dishes including such present-day favourites as a 'children's lunch' (*okosama lunch*), chicken rice, hashed rice (*hayashi rice*), and ice cream. By 1933, more than 10,000 people daily were using Mitsukoshi's main store restaurants, with a further 16–17,000 on weekends and holidays (Hatsuda 1993:121–4).

Roof gardens were another area which stores developed for family entertainment and, perhaps not surprisingly, an early text on department store architecture advised practitioners to take into account the fact that people went to stores not just to shop, but to be entertained in one way or another. Mitsukoshi opened its 'Sky Garden' in 1907, replete with pond, fountain, shrubs, and *bonsai* plants. It also installed a telescope, which soon broke owing to mishandling by an enthusiastic crowd, and Panorama Room (probably modelled on something once shown in London in the 1820s). Roof gardens came to be an essential part of every department store's rebuilding programme during the Taishō period, and included hot houses, Shintō shrines, music stands, tea ceremony huts, and pergolas, as well as things seemingly more appropriate, such as plants, flowers, seeds and gardening equipment. Daimaru installed a roller skating rink on the roof of its new Kyōto store in 1912, and after the Kantō earthquake Matsuzakaya created a mini-zoo with lion and tiger, while Matsuya constructed a 'sports land' on the roof of its new ferro-concrete building, complete with another mini-zoo and funfair. Not surprisingly, perhaps, these gardens were seen as city parks by the people who visited them, so that stores themselves came to be regarded not merely as trading organizations, but as places that contributed to the very atmosphere of the city in which they were located (Hatsuda 1993:124–9) (*Figure 6.7*).

As sites for consumption, stores put on bargain sales, art exhibitions and various other displays as a means of attracting customers. From very early on, before 1914, Mitsukoshi was putting on arts and crafts exhibitions, as well as shows with history, photography, regional products and so on as their main theme. Sometimes it was difficult to distinguish between sales and exhibitions, but other stores soon followed suit and, by the mid 1920s, all of them were putting on special displays of one sort or another throughout the year – including special children's exhibitions, classical music concerts, performances by youth bands. Then there were bargain sales, the idea of which is said to have been adopted from European and American stores

Figure 6.7 A Tokyo department store roof garden (from *Changing Japan Seen Through the Camera*, Tōkyō Asahi Shinbunsha, 1933)

(Hatsuda 1993:131). If so, it came very early on in the development of Japan's first department store, for Mitsukoshi records suggest that the country's first bargain sale was in fact held back in April 1905 (Mitsukoshi 1990:44).

Be this as it may, Japanese stores did not make turnover and profit as such their direct and obvious aim. Instead, they tried to sell things by means of spectacles, and it was these *events*, rather than the goods themselves, which were designed to attract people's attention. Thus, for stores like Mitsukoshi, selling consumption soon became 'a matter of

161

seduction and showmanship' (Miller 1981:167), in much the same way that it had done for stores in Europe and the United States (cf. Miller 1981:165–78; Ewen and Ewen 1982:68–70, 193–5). Already in 1908, Mitsukoshi had a stage at the top of its main staircase, together with music room and piano on one floor, and an art gallery which in later years was considerably enlarged. It is true that the Bon Marché had included an art and sculpture gallery in its 1875 building, and that Wanamaker's had a music room in its New York store, and a pipe organ in its Philadelphia store some decades earlier, but in some respects perhaps Japanese stores were generally more active in the promulgation of cultural events. In its 1927 building, the store added a 'Mitsukoshi Hall' which boasted a 160 square metre stage for music and dance performances, with 542 stall and 136 circle seats. It was ventures such as these which made Mitsukoshi, like the Bon Marché, a permanent event, 'part opera, part theatre, part museum' (Miller 1981:168), and which helped the store make consumption respectable as it sold not just goods but a whole new way of life. However, although primarily inspired by what was going on in Europe and the United States (employees were sent regularly to both continents on study trips), Mitsukoshi tried to retain a tension between imported western goods, on the one hand, and Japanese 'tradition', on the other (Hatsuda 1993:155–6), so that it seems to have been primarily concerned with how best to harmonize the two and create a new-style consumer culture that would appeal to the emerging new white collar class in urban Japanese society.

The Railway Department Stores

On 15 April 1929, in a move totally unrelated to the way in which department stores had hitherto developed from drapery and dry goods stores, the Hankyū Railway Company founded a department store in its Ōsaka Umeda station. This was the world's first railway store. It also heralded a whole new style of Japanese department store, known as 'terminal depāto', which now include such other railway-related retail conglomerates as Hanshin and Keihan in the Kansai, and Tōkyu, Tōbu, Odakyū and Seibu in the Kantō regions of Japan.

Hankyū Dentetsu was founded by Kobayashi Ichizō in 1906 as the Minoo Arima Railway.[14] This private company opened a restaurant at its railway terminus in 1920, when its first line between Umeda and Kobe was completed. At the time, this restaurant had attracted attention because it served only western foods like beefsteak, omelette, ham salad, potato croquettes, curry, and so on. Its success encouraged Kobayashi in 1925 to experiment further, first by rehousing the restaurant above a food market on the first and second floors of Hankyū's headquarters building, and then, when foods started to sell well, by putting both restaurant and market on two floors each. By 1927, an average 4,718 people a day were eating there.

The fact that Hankyū was a railway company with no expertise at all in food retailing prompted Kobayashi to pay considerable attention to marketing and in the late 1920s he sent a team of employees to study American methods of retailing. Upon their return, they suggested that a new department store should cater primarily to the needs of the passengers travelling on the Hankyū railway line; and that, to ensure a quick turnover of goods, the store should focus first on foodstuffs, although it could also profitably sell other mass market items like stationery, small household items, medical supplies and so on (Hatsuda 1993:171–2).

Under such circumstances, it is not surprising to learn that, when Hankyū ventured into the department store business, Kobayashi asserted that he wanted to run a department store which had a restaurant at its centre. This was indeed more or less precisely what transpired. In the first year of the store's operations, between November 1929 and April 1930, more than 200,000 people a month ate in the restaurant during the course of shopping at a store which started by devoting itself to the sale of groceries and foods, furniture, toys and other household items, rather than high-class prestigious goods of the kind handled by the old dry goods stores, but which soon boasted sections for sports equipment, fishing, and clothing, together with a hairdresser's salon and even, from 1934, a marriage bureau. Clothing, in particular, was crucial to both sales and prestige and so to the success of a fledgling department store like Hankyū. Yet, by introducing high quality clothes from the beginning of the 1930s, the kinds of goods that it offered customers soon ceased to be *that* different from those displayed by the old department stores that had developed from Edo period drapery shops.

From their inception, railway department stores like Hankyū focused on a mass market, selling mass-produced, good quality merchandise that people used in their everyday lives, at the cheapest possible prices. This mass market was developed through the private railway line operated by the company concerned. Hankyū, for example, quickly developed residential housing areas on land adjacent to its railway lines as a means, firstly, to increase the number of commuter passengers travelling on its trains, and then to attract those same passengers into its department store in Ōsaka. It further encouraged travel by constructing various entertainment areas along its lines. As the Minoo Arima Railway company, for example, Hankyū had already set up a zoo in Minoo (a suburb of Ōsaka) for families to come and visit during weekends and holidays; Kobayashi was also responsible for the founding of the now famous women's revue theatre in Takarazuka (near Nishinomiya, between Ōsaka and Kobe) in 1915. It was these new white collar, middle-class railway passengers who formed the backbone of the new urban lifestyle that was developing in the Kansai area. As a department store, Hankyū did its utmost to appeal to their cosmopolitan tastes – not only by establishing a hairdressing salon and marriage bureau, but by introducing such delicacies as Swiss rolls and chou-cream éclairs (which became immediate hits). As a result of the profits generated from its railway lines, real estate, and retailing activities, Hankyū was soon able to rebuild an eight-floor department store above Umeda station.

Kobayashi's success quickly encouraged Tōkyō private railway companies to follow his lead in providing passengers with station restaurants. The Tōkyō Yokohama Railway line (now Tokyū) opened its first restaurant in Shibuya station on Christmas Day 1927, a kiosk on New Year's Day in 1932, and a seven-floor department store on 1 November 1934. Others followed. Although in the beginning these, too, started out as radically different kinds of stores which immediately appealed to a mass market, they found that they also had to start stocking clothing and other more prestigious goods in order to assure themselves of a stable customer base.

At the same time, this collapsing of differences in merchandise offerings between the dry goods stores and terminal depāto was accompanied by a marked shift in the type of customer patronizing old-style department stores. As we have seen, Mitsukoshi, Shirokiya and other stores in Tōkyō carefully cultivated certain kinds of high-class clientele, while the railway stores – precisely because they were mass-transit companies which built stores at the end of their lines – were much more down-market in their approach and aimed at the new middle classes. In fact, however, this latter tactic was already beginning to be taken on board by many of the old stores – mainly as a result of the great Kantō earthquake on 1 September 1923, and the accompanying fires that swept the centre of Tōkyō and brought department stores' business to a virtual halt.

In order to survive, Mitsukoshi and other concerns whose buildings had been gutted by fire began renting venues in which they set up temporary markets where they tried to sell as much as they could at low profit margins. This was not the first time department stores had done this. We have already noted that Mitsukoshi had held a bargain sale back in 1905, while Matsuya used to hold monthly bargain days from as early as 1908, when selected goods were discounted by up to twenty per cent. Still, these discount sales tended to be practised by stores that were somewhat 'down market' when compared with elite organizations like Mitsukoshi and Shirokiya. The latter's post-earthquake markets, however, attracted crowds of people since most smaller retailers had had to close down totally for renovation purposes, and the end result of this new retailing activity was that most stores soon became quite expert in mass marketing methods (Hatsuda 1993:175–8).

Once renovations after the fire and earthquake damage had been completed – Mitsukoshi reopened its Nihonbashi store for business on 7 April 1927 – Tōkyō's old department stores realized that they had little choice but to continue their newly-acquired mass marketing practices. The country was suffering from high inflation. Stores thus continued their practice of selling cheap goods to the masses and focused much more on products for daily use and everyday wear (something called a 'can can hat' was all the rage in June that year). This helped encourage mass (rather than prestige) consumption and so revitalize the manufacturing sector of the economy.

As part of this process, mass distribution – of both people and goods – became a crucial element in stores' success (and was, of course, what inspired the birth of the terminal depāto). In August 1920, in an attempt to cope with the increasing number of people who were coming to the city centre by train, Mitsukoshi inaugurated a fourteen seater, red bus service to ferry customers back and forth between Tōkyō Station and its Nihonbashi store. Five years later, it had to put on more buses to cope with the queues of people lining up to make use of this transportation service, and two years after that Shirokiya also instituted a similar service. By 1929, rather remarkably, some 30,000 passengers a day were being taken to and fro between Tōkyō Station and department stores located along the Ginza.[15]

This increase in railway traffic also encouraged stores to rethink their locations. For example, although it seemed at the time a somewhat risky decision, when faced with rebuilding after the Kantō earthquake, Isetan opted to leave its old Kanda location for the thriving new centre of Shinjuku. It was clear that, as a major commuting hub, with both national and private railway lines converging and several hundred thousand passengers passing through a single large station area, Isetan could hardly go wrong. Mitsukoshi soon followed by setting up a branch store in front of Shinjuku station in 1929, before moving to a newly completed building nearby in the following year.

A third aspect of this relationship between department stores and railway transport was the decision to build a subway line from Asakusa, in the old downtown area of Tōkyō, to the railway station of Shinbashi, at the bottom of the Ginza. The first section, between Asakusa and Ueno, was opened in December 1927, but the previous year Mitsukoshi had already approached the Tōkyō Subway Corporation to suggest that it build a line linking all the big department stores between Ueno and the Ginza. It also offered to finance the construction of its own station (called 'Mitsukoshi-*mae*', or 'in front of Mitsukoshi'),[16] provided that the corporation put in an underground passage connecting the station to the store. A contract was signed in 1931, with Mitsukoshi paying for virtually all the costs incurred in building the station, which was opened in April 1932, complete with the subway system's first escalator and a splendid art deco-style underground passageway with show windows and Italian marble facades. The obvious success of this strategy led to other stores coming to agreements with the corporation to finance the building of other stations: Matsuzakaya in Ueno; Shirokiya, Takashimaya in Nihonbashi; and Matsuya in the Ginza (Hatsuda 1993:205–6). Special tickets were issued allowing passengers to get off three times at three different stores en route between Asakusa and Kyōbashi, and the stores found that the number of customers visiting them increased considerably.

That stores were part of a wider cultural phenomenon than just travel and shopping can be seen, perhaps, in the fact that they soon became incorporated in early Shōwa guided tours of Tōkyō. Mitsukoshi, for example, ascertained that five per cent of its customers consisted of people who had come up from the country to Tōkyō and who wished to take in the capital's most prestigious store as part of their city sight-seeing.[17] A walking tour guidebook for lovers published in 1932 suggested that as one of its 'date courses', a young couple could visit 'The Five Great Department Stores by Subway'. After a rendezvous in the Ginza, the couple could start by shopping at Matsuya, before taking the subway to Nihonbashi for more shopping at Shirokiya and a memorial photograph at Takashimaya. They could then move on to Mitsukoshi where they could take advantage of the rest room and free tea service, before taking the subway once again to Ueno and having lunch together at Matsuzakaya. The great thing about this tour was that, even if it were raining, the young couple could do all this without even having to put up an umbrella (Hatsuda 1993:206) (*Figures 6.8* and *6.9*)!

Figure 6.8 Poster advertising the completion of Mitsukoshi's main Nihonbashi store, 1935 (courtesy of Mitsukoshi Department Store).

Strolling in the Ginza

Nihonbashi had been the heart of commercial Edo, the home of big stores like Mitsukoshi (then Mitsui) and Daimaru. With the building of the Tōkyō-Yokohama railway, however, the Ginza area to the south developed as a new centre where the old and the new, things Japanese and western, mingled to form a very special kind of chic modernity. In the meantime, the more conservative Nihonbashi area came to be seen

167

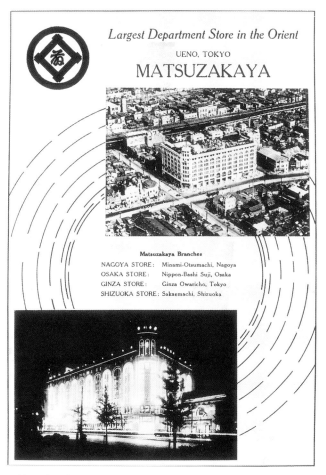

Largest Department Store in the Orient

UENO, TOKYO

MATSUZAKAYA

Matsuzakaya Branches

NAGOYA STORE: Minami-Otsumachi, Nagoya
OSAKA STORE: Nippon-Bashi Suji, Osaka
GINZA STORE: Ginza Owaricho, Tokyo
SHIZUOKA STORE: Sakaemachi, Shizuoka

Figure 6.9 Advertisement for Matsuzakaya Department Store.

as being at the forefront of the Meiji ideal of civilization and enlightenment and it is still the financial centre of the city and the country (Seidensticker 1983:186–97).

Ginza, on the other hand, was in a new style that contrasted strongly with the conservatism and moderation of Nihonbashi. Owing its name to the fact that at one stage it had been the 'seat' (*za*) of the Edo government's 'silver' (*gin*) mint, the street runs from Shinbashi station in the south to Kyōbashi in the north (which itself lies just south of

168

Nihonbashi). During the late Meiji and Taishō periods, the Ginza was seen by one and all as the city's 'centre' and it was here that people gathered in large numbers. This was partly because of the railway completed in 1872; partly because of its new 'Bricktown' opened two years later; partly because of the horse-drawn trolley service which linked it with Nihonbashi and Asakusa from 1882; partly because it was glitzy and madly innovative – the home of entrepreneurs like Hattori Kintarō, founder of the Seiko watch company, and the stamping ground of Meiji's *nouveau riche* (*narikin*) as well as the site for newspaper – and now other media – offices (Seidensticker 1983:199–204; see also Moeran 1996:1–2).

The department stores located along the stretch between Nihonbashi and the Ginza attracted people from both near and far, and their very presence contributed to the hub of activity and crowds of people. In the mid-20s, for example, it was noted that in the Ginza there were 35 per cent more pedestrians walking to and fro between the two department stores than there were in other parts of the street beyond the stores (Hatsuda 1993:203). Ginza soon became Japan's best known shopping street. Already early on (about 1912–1915), the term 'something something Ginza' had been used to refer to other shopping areas in various parts of Japan, from Iwate and Yamagata in the north, to Kagoshima in the very south of Kyushu. What really contributed to the area's popularity, however, was the decision by Matsuzakaya to set up a Ginza branch in December 1924, and by Matsuya in May 1925 to transfer its headquarters there from Kanda Imagawabashi. With Mitsukoshi's opening of a branch there in 1930, the atmosphere in the Ginza began to seem like that of the old days at the turn of the century when the kankōba emporiums had flourished. People thronged to see and be seen, as Matsuya in particular decided to push the Ginza name as part of its trend-setting marketing strategy, and the Ginza became *the* centre of fashion. As part of its strategy Matsuya bought up copies of two hit records ('Tōkyō Parade' and 'Ginza Serenade') which it then distributed to local tea houses and bars which were rewarded if the records were being played during store employees' random visits (Hatsuda 1993:207–9).

So, the Ginza became a fashionable place to be, the place in which to idle away one's time (ginbura) – in large part because of the presence of the department stores which offered fashionable, high quality, prestigious goods and entertainment. The Ginza was smart and the people who went there were smart, too, which made the Ginza even smarter – thanks to the efforts of the stores which did their utmost to foster this image by creating chic and fashionable trends. The fact that by the mid-30s, people frequenting the Ginza were coming from quite a long way away also showed that by this time fashions were by no means local in their distribution, but embraced the whole city of Tōkyō and even places further afield. Stores made sure to strengthen this nationalization of fashion by expanding into the provinces and setting up branches in provincial cities from the mid-1920s, and in this way served to bring these cities out of their time warp and make them culturally up to date.[18] But they also advanced dramatically in terms of their local economies, since the arrival of the big stores stimulated local demand and local manufacturers found themselves goaded into producing better, higher quality, more modern goods.

Conclusion

In this chapter, I have outlined the development of the Japanese department store, focusing in particular on the early history of Mitsukoshi and other traditional drapery stores, but also taking into account the emergence of the railway department store and the effect of transportation in general on the development of cities like Tōkyō in the pre-war period.

It has become clear from this discussion that the Japanese department store owed much to its counterparts in Europe and the United States. In the decision to display goods by means of display cases and shop windows, to initiate fashions, to put on art and other cultural exhibitions, to build ornate palaces of consumption, to adopt modern accounting methods, and so on and so forth, the Japanese department store depended heavily on the practices of well-established department stores in Paris, London and New York. Thus, although nowadays the Japanese department store can be said perhaps to occupy a rather special position in organizational and retailing practices, in its early days it was very much the conscious imitator of more advanced enterprises abroad.

There are other, less obvious, parallels to be found in the emergence of department stores in Japan and the west. For a start, these 'universal providers' share in common the fact that they were part of a 'big-city phenomenon', whose social and economic developments made them possible in the first place (Miller 1981:31). For example, just as the population of Paris doubled in the half century prior to the founding of the Bon Marché in 1867 (Miller 1981:35), so did the population of Tōkyō double during the

Meiji period to enable stores like Mitsukoshi and Shirokiya to expand so rapidly. This influx of people not only brought about a growing concentration of the market; it made necessary new systems of transport, in particular the overground and underground railway, that would enable food and other goods to be distributed from country to city, and people themselves to move to and from, and then about, these cities. In other words, the city was transformed in terms of its horizontal expansion outwards and the creation of specialized districts (for shopping, business, residence, and so on) as a result of the industrial revolution and railway transportation (Schivelbusch 1986:178). In Japan, the construction of the Minoo Arima Railway allowed the development of suburban Ōsaka and Kobe into such places as Tsukaguchi, Nishinomiya, Ashiya, and Rokkō, while a shift of the capital's terminus from Shinbashi to Tōkyō Station promoted the development of a new business district in Marunouchi, between the station and the Imperial Palace.

In general, railways increased 'the regularity, volume, and speed of the flow of goods and materials first into the factories and then out of the factories and into the markets' (Miller 1981:37). It was the flows of people through railways terminals like Ōsaka Umeda which gave rise to the world's first railway department store in Japan, and which then directly instigated the development of new 'centres' where people could go for shopping and other forms of entertainment. These centres – in particular Ueno, Nihonbashi and the Ginza in Tōkyō – were then made more central, more fashionable, by the construction of an underground railway line. As in other great cities of the world, Japan's railway system influenced the development of certain parts of cities and increased the volume of traffic to and from those parts – as we saw in the number of passengers being ferried daily to and fro between Tōkyō Station and Nihonbashi and Ginza department stores during the 1920s (cf. Schivelbusch 1986:180).

Thus, as Wolfgang Schivelbusch (1986:188–97) so clearly demon-strates for Europe, there was in Japan a close relationship between the development of railway transport and that of the department store. They both relied upon a high volume of people to buy their wares (tickets, in the one case; a whole range of goods and entertainment, in the other). But they also both encouraged in their customers what Schivelbusch calls a 'panoramic' perception of the world through which they passed. This panoramic view – of an outside world of valleys, hillsides, houses, fields, trees perceived from a railway compartment, on the one hand; and of a confused juxtaposition of objects and images experienced

171

inside a department store, on the other – was marked by a kind of evanescent, impressionistic appreciation of a world perceived as a heterogeneous totality, rather than in its individuality (Schivelbusch 1986:190–1). Here, indeed, was a new 'floating world' for Japanese of the late Meiji, Taishō and early Shōwa periods.

We have seen here how the Japanese department store, like the Bon Marché, 'became a permanent fair, an institution, a fantasy world, a spectacle of extraordinary proportions, so that going to the store became an event and an adventure' (Miller 1981:167). As in Europe and the United States, the Japanese department store stood at the centre of a new phenomenon – consumerism – and did its utmost to sell both itself and consumption by means of merchandise displays, fixed prices, returns, services, art exhibitions, music, theatre and other cultural events, in-house magazines, advertising campaigns, and architectural innovations. From the foods that it stocked in its basement to the views that it offered from its roof, anything and everything was for sale as stores sought to promote Japan's new consumer society (*Figure 6.10*).

As noted at the beginning of this chapter, Japan's consumerism has been marked by an apparently undisciplined penchant for things foreign and things Japanese. The Japanese department store has taken advantage of, and catered to, this hybrid taste. In so doing, Mitsukoshi and other department stores have disseminated the values and lifestyle of Tōkyō's upper classes to Japanese middle-class society as a whole and so have acted as 'bourgeois' instruments of social homogenization, in the same way that the Bon Marché did for France in the second half of the nineteenth century (Miller 1981:183). However, unlike European or American stores, the Japanese department store has not just shown people how to dress in what kinds of clothes for what event; how to furnish their homes with what kind of furniture in which rooms; how to eat what, where and when; which art to put where and why; and so on and so forth. It has been obliged to instruct Japanese how to behave in two somewhat distinct, almost schizophrenic, cultural contexts. The success with which they have achieved this task of Japanese and western eclecticism (*wayō setchū*) (Tobin 1992a:26) can be seen, perhaps, in the unconcerned way in which a geisha can blow bubbles from the gum that she is chewing in her mouth (*The Face*, April 1993), or in which a 'speed tribe' (*bōsōzoku*) Japanese youth will perm his hair, dress like a wise guy and gather with friends on his flashy motorcycle at the Meiji Shrine, in the hope of being recruited to a *yakuza* gang (Greenfield 1994:17) – without so much as the blink of an

Figure 6.10 'Oriental beauty' presenting Mitsukoshi Department Store to the world. Poster 1910 (courtesy of Mitsukoshi Department Store).

eyelid at some of the incongruities each might present to a Japanese born in the mid-19th century or to a European or American visiting Japan today. Thus, the new national middle-class culture that the Japanese department store has helped build floats between at least two worlds that are 'a pastiche of traditional Japanese and borrowed western elements' (Tobin 1992a:1).

As Tobin and his contributors point out in their various discussions of things 're-made in Japan', the Japanese have since the beginning of the Meiji period been intent on domesticating an imagined west. The end result of this domestication is a synthesis of things Japanese and things foreign which would seem to epitomize what Hannerz (1991:126) has called 'creolization'. The importance of such creolization is that it allows cultures to put old things in new ways (Hannerz 1992:265–7) and, in the case of Japan, to create a new hybrid cultural creole form which, like the department store itself (as we shall see in the chapter by Ueno Chizuko), now generates its own new structures which are in turn imitated by other Asian societies. In this respect, perhaps, the Japanese department store can be said to have made a major contribution not just to Japanese culture, but to many other Asian cultures, too.

Notes

1 Mitsukoshi Department Store, for example, employed 323 persons in 1905, 596 in 1907, and 892 in 1908. By 1915, the number of employees had risen to 2,245, and six years later this figure had doubled to 4,593. Thereafter, staff numbers continued to increase (in spite of the temporary setback caused by the great Kantō earthquake of 1923): 5,938 in 1927; 7,476 in 1930; and 8,710 in 1935 (Mitsukoshi 1990:304).

2 There is some confusion over exact dates here. Seidensticker (1983:111) correctly points out that Mitsukoshi was registered as the store's legal name on 15 October 1904. Kinoshita and Ashimura (1980:60–1), however, maintain that an advertisement was placed in the *Jiji Shinpō* Newspaper on 27 December 1904. Mitsukoshi's own records support Hatsuda (1993:60), as cited here in the text. They also note that a Mitsui-Mitsukoshi announcement about the impending department store was printed on Mitsui Gofukuten's New Year cards and sent to all business customers on 20 December 1904 (Mitsukoshi 1990:43).

Although Mitsukoshi used the English term 'department store' in its early years, a number of Japanese phrases were also used. For example, an internal report on American department stores gathered by a Mitsui Gofukuten employee in 1897–98 makes use of the phrase *zakka chinretsu hanbaisho* ('miscellaneous sales display place'), while *kouri daishō ten* ('large retail store', or *grand magasin*) was in fairly common usage by the end of the Meiji period (1868–1912). Each of these reflects different emphases on the most important characteristics of a department store.

By the beginning of the Shōwa period (1926–1989), a Japanization process was clearly under way, with two phrases *hyakka shōten* (hundred goods sales store) and hyakkaten (hundred goods store) being used interchangeably to define those stores which, like Mitsukoshi and Daimaru, had developed from former entities as kimono and dry goods stores; and terminal depāto (terminal department stores) to refer to stores which developed in tandem with their railway line businesses (Hatsuda 1993:61–2). Hyakkaten and depāto – the terms generally used for department stores in contemporary Japan – thus point to, and in industry circles maintain, a historical distinction between two types of department store.

3   In later years, people were allowed to enter the bazaars in their ordinary footwear. It is not known exactly when this change took place, but a May 1885 copperplate print depicts shoppers inside a store in their shoes (Hatsuda 1993:33). It was department stores' decision after the Kantō earthquake of 1923 to allow customers to come inside in their outdoor footwear that finally led to the mass circulation of consumers in city centres (Seidensticker 1983:113, 1991:30).

4   In those days, most stores would take their goods round to customers and attempt to persuade them to make orders which were then normally paid for twice a year: during the mid-summer *obon* ancestors' festival and before New Year. Echigoya's cash sales innovation made financial sense in terms of the time and effort otherwise spent in collecting payments due, as well as in terms of speeding up the circulation of goods and capital thanks to direct sales in large quantities and with low mark up (Kinoshita and Ashimura 1980:47–8; Mitsukoshi 1990:23).

5   For the sake of convenience, I shall henceforth refer to the store founded by Mitsui Takatoshi as Mitsukoshi.

6   Takahashi did not need to make an issue of fixed price tags because of the Echigoya policy of 'cash payment and no haggling over prices'.

7   The fact that these artists were used to working with painting materials and not woven and dyed cloth created certain difficulties, since they did not at first understand some of the technical problems posed by their designs. However, by obliging them to visit textile factories, learn to dye cloth for themselves, and generally acquaint themselves with the new medium in which they were being asked to work, Takahashi successfully achieved his aim of revitalizing the clothing industry.

8   Shirokiya, for example, went so far as to retitle its magazine *Ryūkō* (Fashion) in 1906 in an attempt to build on its regular customer base.

9   Mitsukoshi claims to have placed its – and Japan's – first newspaper advertisement for a bargain sale, in the *Jiji Shinpō* newspaper, on 15 May 1874 (Mitsukoshi 1990:31).

10 Who came to Japan in February 1906 to confer a Knighthood of the Garter on the Emperor Meiji on behalf of King Edward VII.

11 For example, the store obtained a license in 1915 to sell Johnny Walker whiskey, and in 1921 Burberry raincoats.

12 Takashimaya was an exception, keeping a traditional architectural style for its three-floor buildings in both Kyōto (where its headquarters were located) and Tōkyō, and thus marking itself as slightly different from its competitors – a difference that it maintained in merchandize by concentrating on Nishijin textiles manufactured in Kyōto (Hatsuda 1993:106).

13 Another great crowd-puller was air conditioning, which was first put in by Mitsukoshi in 1927 (the same year as it held Japan's first fashion show [Mitsukoshi 1990:97]), followed by Shirokiya in 1931, and Takashimaya and Isetan two years later (Hatsuda 1993:201).

14 Like Mitsukoshi's Takahashi Sadao, Kobayashi Ichizō had also previously been employed in the Mitsui Bank, but had failed to be accepted as part of

the management of Mitsukoshi, and had then moved to Ōsaka to run the Minoo Arima Railway Company.

15 Mitsukoshi was ferrying 13,023, Shirokiya 8,198, Matsuya 6,893, and Matsuzakaya 2,740 passengers daily between their stores and Tōkyō Station (Hatsuda 1993:181).

16 Mitsukoshi-mae is the only station in Tōkyō named after a particular corporation.

17 Unlike the Bon Marché, however, Mitsukoshi does not appear to have organized daily tours of its premises (cf. Miller 1981:169).

18 When Mitsukoshi set up a branch store in Sapporo, in the northernmost island of Hokkaidō, it was remarked that in one day the city had advanced ten years culturally (Hatsuda 1993:211).

7

SEIBU DEPARTMENT STORE AND IMAGE MARKETING

Japanese Consumerism in the Postwar Period[*]

Ueno Chizuko

Department stores are products of mass society. And mass society is a product of modernity which itself has structured the various ways in which department stores function and develop. One department store which has followed closely the developments taken by mass society in postwar Japan is Seibu. As part of the Saison enterprise group, Seibu has not merely reflected, but actively contributed to and planned, such developments by the injection of huge amounts of capital into the consumer market. This chapter seeks to discuss trends in postwar Japanese consumerism through the activities of Seibu Department Store and the Seibu Saison Group and focuses on two things in particular: the breakdown of Japan's mass market in the 1970s and 80s, and the use of mass media images to create and appeal to niche markets formed around the new urban consumers in the Tōkyō-Kantō megalopolis.

In order to meet with success in its attempt to create a new breed of consumer loyal to the Seibu name, the Seibu Saison Group has had to educate people in a new way of life and system of values. This it has done by means of commodities, events and information, all of which have been made readily available in such a way that Seibu Department Store has over the years been turned into a kind of space medium for public consumption (although there have been, of course, financial limitations on who could have access to such consumption). At the

* This chapter is translated and adapted by Brian Moeran from a much longer essay on Seibu Department Store and Japan's image market (see Ueno 1991), originally written to mark the 25th anniversary of the corporate history of the Saison Group. Ueno Chizuko wishes to acknowledge the cooperation of the Group and those individuals therein with whom she conducted interviews for her survey. For his part, Brian Moeran would like to thank Wong Heung Wah for his assistance in making a preliminary translation of most of the text of the essay in question.

same time, since consumer perceptions of a department store like Seibu tend inevitably to differ from the business realities in which it finds itself, the Seibu Saison Group as a whole has had to embark upon a comprehensive image strategy in order to bridge this perceptual gap. In Seibu's case, this strategy led to what is now known as the 'golden age' of Japanese television advertising starting a few years after the end of Japan's 'miracle' high-growth period and continuing into the early 80s. In this chapter, then, we will trace some of the changes that have taken place in the nature of mass society in Japan during these years and illustrate certain developments through a discussion of some of the Seibu Saison Group's advertising campaigns.

Seibu and Japan's Postwar Consumer Market

Seibu Department Store owes its origin to Tsutsumi Yasujirō's purchase of the Keihin Kyūkō Railway's Kikuya Department Store in Ikebukuro in 1940. Renamed Musashino Department Store, it went through various vicissitudes before, on 1 November 1949, being relocated in a new building as Seibu Department Store alongside Tsutsumi's newly renamed Seibu Ikebukuro private railway line terminus serving the north-western suburbs of Tōkyō (see Havens 1994:47–8). Unlike other more traditional Tōkyō department stores such as Mitsukoshi, Takashimaya and Matsuzakaya, Seibu was not located in the capital's prestigious Ginza shopping street, but was to be found in Ikebukuro, one of the less well-known centres that are to be found on the Yamanote inner-city loop line. In this respect, Seibu was like a number of other 'new wave' department stores that came into being during the first decades of the twentieth century – Tōkyū, Tōbu and Odakyū in Tōkyō, for instance, and Hanshin and Hankyū in Ōsaka. As noted by Brian Moeran in the previous chapter in this book, all of these started out as railway terminus department stores whose main clientele consisted of people who needed to purchase groceries and everyday items during their commute to and from work in Tōkyō. In this sense, and in spite of its clear emulation of industry leaders Mitsukoshi and Takashimaya, which also called themselves hyakkaten rather than depāto (Havens 1994:50), Seibu was very much a 'local' Ikebukuro store which was not widely known throughout the capital as a whole – just as Tōkyū was a local Shibuya, and Odakyū a local Shinjuku, store. Each was severely constrained by the characteristics of their locations, so that in the pre- and immediate post-war periods the metropolitan area of Tōkyō was essentially little more than a series of sub-centres such as Ikebukuro, Shinjuku and Shibuya, each with its own local department store(s).

Tsutsumi borrowed heavily from his railway company to help finance a new seven-floor building for Seibu Department Store, completed by 1954. This development was made possible, firstly, by the decision to build the Marunouchi subway line from Ikebukuro to Ochanomizu, Tōkyō Station, the west Ginza and, eventually, Shinjuku during the 1950s – a decision which helped transform the image of Ikebukuro, in Thomas Havens's words (1994:51), 'from pastoral outpost to bustling, in-town commercial district'. Secondly, during the same decade, a real-estate boom in the suburbs of Tōkyō enabled Tsutsumi's land business to thrive in the area served by his railway line, which itself became the fastest growing private railway in the region and so brought more and more customers into Seibu Department Store (Havens 1994:50).

Not all went well, however. Seibu faced a problem of negative 'low-class' image which it somehow had to overcome, even though its sales and profits continued to rise (to such an extent that they exceeded those of the Seibu railway line in 1956 [Havens 1994:52]). Then in 1963, the year in which Seibu founded its Seiyū supermarket chain, there was a major fire in the department store's Ikebukuro building. In the following year, which coincided with the Tōkyō Olympics, its founding president, Tsutsumi Yasujirō, died and was succeeded by his son, Seiji. This marked the beginning of a new era for Seibu, however, for as well as investing heavily in the long-term reconstruction of the Ikebukuro store, the new CEO decided to open a new store in Shibuya, half a dozen stations to the south along the Yamanote loop line. Located on the other side of Shinjuku, Shibuya was not only close to the newly-built Olympic stadium, Yoyogi sports complex and NHK national broadcasting centre, but was within easy striking distance of a number of upper-class residential areas and prominent higher educational establishments. By taking this decision to expand Seibu's activities into a new area, therefore, Tsutsumi made it clear that his department store was about to launch a marketing offensive that not only threatened the hitherto unrivalled business of Tōkyū Department Store (whose main railway terminus was located in Shibuya), but which attempted to eradicate its old 'Seibu of Ikebukuro' lower-middle class image by appealing to a wealthier and younger breed of consumer who – thanks to the development of areas along two railway lines terminating in Shibuya – was beginning to frequent this part of the capital.

At the same time, as part of the second phase of its development from a 'local' store, Tsutsumi decided to open new Seibu stores in other

179

parts of Tōkyō's outlying districts: Funabashi (1967), Ōmiya (1969), Hachiōji (1970), and even as far afield as the city of Shizuoka (1970). Prior to this, in 1963, the name of the store's supermarket was changed to Seiyū and – in order to combat the threat of the super-discount stores that were emerging during this period as a result of the first postwar revolution in distribution and retailing methods, and which were posing a major business threat to department stores in general – Tsutsumi set about building a chain of Seiyū stores across the country.

Another development was the founding of the first Parco store in 1969, right beside Seibu's Ikebukuro branch.[1] Parco was unique in its concept in that it housed a theatre, fashion boutiques, galleries, restaurants and bookshops, all in one building. It was followed by other Parco stores, first in the capital (in Shibuya in 1973), and then all over the country, in places as far apart as Sapporo (1975), Gifu, Chiba (1976), Ōita and Tsudanuma (1977), before returning to a suburb of Tōkyō, Kichijōji, in 1980. These developments were carried out as part – and in spite – of the painstaking and profound restructuring of the Japanese economy that followed the oil crisis in 1973 and which led Seibu to set up a number of speciality stores (like LoFt, which carried goods ranging from stationery to do-it-yourself products, by way of art materials, games, bicycle accessories and furnishings), to introduce what it called a 'cast' system of itemized goods displays,[2] and to embark upon a 'refreshment' of its already existing stores.

By first 'refreshing' its store in Shibuya, where it also set up further speciality stores during the 1970s and 80s, Seibu also contributed to the further popularity of this area of Tōkyō as a shopping centre.[3] Like Parco itself, many of these ventures did not bear the Seibu name, a fact which could create some difficulties for the Seibu Retailing Group (as the Seibu Saison Group was then called), but its management felt that it had little alternative but to proceed with these venture-type enterprises. It was kept afloat by an increasingly buoyant domestic market which from the end of the 70s and throughout the 80s permitted the retail sector of Japan's economy to explore all kinds of marketing activities and so to enjoy considerable growth. Thus, although Seibu bore considerable financial risk during these expansion years, it was able to take full advantage of a rapidly-growing mass consumer society and so to recuperate its previous investment before proceeding to embark upon each new venture.

Seibu's planned Shibuya store finally opened in 1968, and in the same year Phase Eight of the renovation of its main Ikebukuro store was completed. With the completion of Phase Nine seven years later,

Seibu for the first time became recognized as a major Tōkyō – as opposed to a mere local Ikebukuro – store. Not only was its total floor space now greater than that of either Isetan or Mitsukoshi, making Seibu the largest store in the capital; its clientele was now being drawn from all over the metropolitan area, as well as from the suburban areas of Chiba, Saitama and Ibaragi in the Kantō megalopolis. Many of these were undoubtedly attracted by Seibu's decision to include in Phase Nine its own Museum of Art, housed in a separate building beside the department store. In spite of the downturn in consumption as a result of the oil crisis in 1973, the Seibu Museum of Art was an innovative marketing idea which contributed enormously to the store's public image and reputation, since it showed once and for all how department stores could be a cut above the super-discount stores by attracting hundreds of thousands of visitors to its exhibitions. On the downside, however, the Museum's art exhibitions have not generally paid for themselves overall, as audiences for avant-garde exhibitions in particular have not gone on to spend their money elsewhere in the store.

Finally, in line with the overall diversification and disintegration of 'mass' consumption in Japan during the 1980s, Seibu opened its Yūrakuchō store just off the Ginza[4] in 1984 and so edged closer to being recognized as *the* premier department store of Tōkyō, and Japan. At the same time, however, the opening of the Yūrakuchō store marked a further stage in what was becoming a gradual metamorphosis of the very nature and character of Japanese department stores generally. The words 'department store' in Japanese literally mean 'one hundred item store' (hyakkaten), a function which such traditional businesses as Mitsukoshi and Takashimaya claimed to fulfil by offering something for everybody. Over the years, however, Seibu had embarked upon a gradual process of specialization – starting with its '70 item store' in Shibuya and ending up with its 'single miscellaneous goods' stores like LoFt.

At the same time, there was increasing demand for, and sales turnover in, services and events surrounding commodities, rather than for and in commodities *per se*. This led to the development of whole shopping streets, rather than just shops, to which each member of the Seibu Retailing Group contributed its individual expertise. As a result of the breakdown of Japan's mass market, therefore, the department store itself began to devolve its functions. In Seibu's case, this devolution concerned not just its business operations, but its own role within the Seibu Saison Group[5] which by 1988 comprised a total of several dozen companies, but to whose total annual turnover Seibu

Department Store's contribution had decreased to one third. It is this transition of internal function and external role which has to be dealt with in the decade leading up the year 2000, and which forms the focus of much of the discussion in this chapter.

Marketing and the Postwar Market in Japan

Once it had become Tōkyō's number one, largest department store, and so found itself catering to a clientele that came from all over the capital and not just from a local or regional market in and around Ikebukuro, Seibu had to deal with a number of difficult marketing problems. In a way, it was now selling to a truly 'mass' market where people for the most part shared similar lifestyles, consumption patterns and consumer behaviour – thanks to postwar technological innovations in production, sales and communications. At the same time, however, it was clear from the store's operations in Shibuya that there *were* differences in consumer demand and consumption cycles – differences which soon revealed that Shibuya was in many ways one of the capital's trendiest markets anticipating developments that later took place elsewhere in the Ginza, Shinjuku or Ikebukuro.

In this kind of consumer climate, marketing was a crucial weapon in Seibu's strategy. The store had always preferred to conduct its own market surveys rather than rely on external agencies when formulating its business policies, and to this end it early on recruited key personnel from Dentsu advertising agency. The latter established a number of basic steps in the collection and analysis of data, which they then classified as 'hard' (quantitative) and 'soft' (qualitative) marketing information and used to develop strategies that gave Seibu a distinct competitive edge during the 1970s and 80s.

The relatively homogeneous mass market that had existed in Japan in the 1960s reached saturation point by the end of the decade and was given a rude jolt by the oil shock of 1973 and the ensuing economic depression. By the mid-70s, however, it was becoming clear that there were all sorts of different markets to be targeted: suburban families who lived in areas well outside the Yamanote loop line; the so-called 'bulge' generation caused by the postwar baby boom who lived along the railway arteries emanating from Ikebukuro, Shinjuku and Shibuya; and single men and women – but mainly women – who had moved into the centre of Tōkyō during the rapid (sub)urbanization of the city in the 1960s. Awareness of these differing consumer groups prompted Seibu to develop a marketing strategy which, firstly, provided people with a range of brand commodities that corresponded to their changing lifestyles; secondly, delivered a wide range of goods suited to individual consumers' diverse needs; and thirdly, adapted itself to the changing values of Japan's ever-expanding postwar generations. The keywords used in this strategy were 'lifestyle', 'individualization' and 'diversification'.[6]

Such diversification was necessary because there was a marked shift in the expectations of consumers who were no longer prepared to tolerate manufacturer-led marketing in the way that they had done in the 60s. Rather, there was a strong feeling that trends should be dictated by consumers themselves and that manufacturers should then adapt production to suit consumer demand. In other words, there was a marked shift from 'upstream' to 'downstream' marketing. This gave retailers like Seibu a much greater say in the production of trend-setting goods, as well as in the merchandizing of coordinated goods.

Much of this change was due to a changing social environment during the postwar decades. During the 1950s and 60s, the 'miracle' decades of the Japanese economy, there was a massive migration of the rural population to the cities. This sparked off a period of enormous urban growth as the new arrivals gradually settled down and started their own families, and it was their children who came to form Japan's first truly urban generation – born and brought up in cities, with only tangential links to the countryside. Often referred to as the 'new families', this generation developed new and different values and behaviour patterns from those of their parents; it was also an affluent generation without experience of immediate postwar hunger and hardship; and a generation which was the first to grow up during the present era of electronic information. Unlike their parents, who tended to go for brand names when shopping, these baby boomers were much more concerned with quality and 'trendiness' and were often better informed about products than the sales staff there to serve them.

At the end of the 70s, as part of the development of its department store and other businesses in the Seibu Retailing Group, Tsutsumi turned his attention to an even younger age group, the 'new young' born in the latter half of the 50s, who – in Thomas Havens's words (1994:118) – 'took quality for granted and were much more interested in artistic and cultural fulfilment than previous generations of consumers'. Aware of the long-term benefits that would accrue from cultivating a 'bulge' generation that would itself in due course produce a second 'bulge' generation, Seibu started to educate its customers in the concept of 'lifestyle' – introduced to Japan from the United States during the first half of the 70s and soon sweeping through domestic marketing practices. By classifying consumers according to demographic, gender, age and employment criteria, marketers were able to promote the efficacy of what they liked to term 'cluster' marketing. For Seibu, this entailed a shift from single to coordinated product marketing that itself reflected and encouraged a total 'lifestyle'. This was then reinforced by the establishment of several speciality stores which allowed Seibu to adopt an overall 'zone' approach to merchandizing. Such zones included: home improvement (to make life enjoyable); hobbies and leisure (to make it entertaining, and not just filled with work as life had been for a previous generation disparagingly referred to in the western media as 'economic animals'); fashion (to make life beautiful); culture (to make it sophisticated and intellectual); tradition (to enrich consumers' lives); and convenience.

Seibu's rethinking of how best to target its customers was in part at least influenced by the overall situation prevailing in the retail industry at that time. The 1960s had seen a major retailing war between department stores, super-discount stores and supermarkets, and it had seemed at the time as if Japan's department stores would go into irrevocable decline. However, by branching out into the marketing of art and culture, on the one hand, and by paying close attention to consumer lifestyles and ensuring that people were educated in such lifestyle concepts as coordinated products, on the other, stores were not only able to defeat their rivals, but to gain an even stronger position than before in the retail market. This position they then secured and made virtually unassailable through the creation of a corporate identity.

Image Marketing

Seibu decided to give priority to its corporate image, rather than to sales as such, from the mid-70s. It thus embarked upon its so-called 'image strategy' which was energetically promoted by the store's CEO, Tsutsumi Seiji, who at the time put himself in charge of Seibu's Publicity Department. Since he was also closely involved in the management of the Merchandizing Department, which had hived off from the Marketing Department in 1963 as part of Seibu's initial restructuring, Tsutsumi was able to maintain direct control over two extremely important parts of the store's strategic planning – one concerned with the everyday operation and management of its sales floor activities, the other with the creation of the images that were designed to attract customers to those same sales floors.

Right from the start it was recognized that there was quite a gap between sales floor *practices* and consumer *images* of Seibu as a department store. Although initially attracted to the store as a result of its advertising campaigns, customers were immediately made aware of the difference between image and reality – partly because of the haphazard and unsatisfactory spatial arrangement of sales floors, partly because of the inadequate selection of goods displayed there, and partly because of the poor attitude of staff employed to look after customers. This conceptual gap produced a counter-image which Tsutsumi quickly realized had to be overcome since Seibu's advertising was actually broadening, rather than bridging, the gap between image and reality. Rather than adopt the customary policy of changing the image to fit reality, he decided to adapt reality to the advertising image, and so set about restructuring chaotic sales floor practices, localizing the merchandizing policy, and improving staff morale. In this respect, Seibu's image strategy revolutionized the store's practices, created a sense of independence and so had a thoroughly educational effect on both staff and clientele.

In general, the ratio of advertising expenditure to sales revenues in the retail industry as a whole in Japan is about three per cent, and that of department stores somewhere between two and three per cent.[7] In the second half of the 60s, however, Seibu's advertising-to-sales ratio rose from 3.1 to 3.9 per cent – a figure which not only contrasted strongly with its competitors, but with the store's own earlier policy (adopted during the regime of Tsutsumi Yasujirō) not to advertise more than an absolute minimum. As Seibu gradually built up both its image and its sales during the 70s and early part of the 80s, its advertising expenditure quintupled while its overall advertising-to-sales ratio dropped from a high of 3.9 per cent in 1969 to 2.5 per cent in 1983.[8] Compared with two other Japanese corporations also well-known for the quality of their advertising, the liquor and soft drinks manufacturer Suntory, and Shiseido cosmetics, which had advertising-to-sales ratios of 3.28 and 6.67 per cent respectively, Seibu can be seen to have enjoyed a relatively high effect on turnover for lower advertising costs.

When it first put its new policy of increased advertising into effect in the mid-60s, Seibu made primary use of newspapers and other print media, even though television was already establishing itself as a major new advertising medium – thanks to the live broadcasting of the present emperor (then crown prince) Akihito's wedding in 1958, followed by that of the Tōkyō Olympics in 1964. The main reasons that Seibu opted for newspapers as its main advertising medium[9] were: firstly, it had embarked upon a merchandizing policy which focused on local products for local stores, and so marketed none of those *nationally* known brand goods that were more suited to network television advertising; secondly, it focused mainly on particular goods and special sales which could best be advertised in leaflets and newspaper enclosures; and thirdly, it needed to make full use of print media, since it had to put across a lot of information which could not be effectively included in an image-based medium such as television (cf. Moeran 1996:242). In other words, like most other Japanese department stores until the oil crisis in 1973, Seibu regarded itself as a business which sold commodities and goods, and believed that their sale was most effectively increased by print advertising – newspapers, posters, and train carriage ads which, though strictly speaking a mass medium, were carried on specific railway lines serving particular local regions.

Gradually, however, Seibu came to change its choice of media. Although print advertising was the main medium used to promote the completion of Phase Nine of the Ikebukuro store reconstruction project in 1975, Seibu was already taking its first steps towards promoting a new corporate identity. It began to use a new Seibu logo, for example, on its wrapping paper and carrier bags; emphasized the store's interior design and staging of sales space; created an overall image strategy that was put out in all mass media; and made use of its new Museum of Art to act as a focal point for news and information. It also changed the colours hitherto used on all its promotional materials, as well as for staff uniforms, so that it was able to promote a total visual system as part of its corporate image packaging from about this time.

Nevertheless, the concept of corporate identity was still poorly understood and did not yet extend to the total packaging of the Seibu name, since 'image' was still seen to be more important than 'identity' as such. It is true that Seibu first advertised its enterprise group as a whole in 1973 – which in that year expanded to embrace 79 different companies – but the oil crisis put an end to this idea which was not resuscitated until the following decade when the diversification of the group's activities, as well as of Seibu's own department stores, was well advanced and needed some form of coordinating, unified image.

Still, these innovations required a reorganization among the store's creative staff and interior designers, as well as a realignment and gathering together of all those involved in its advertising and promotional campaigns. This led to the formation of a design committee whose members were for the most part outsiders and included, among others, Tanaka Ikkō and Yamaguchi Harumi. Together they oversaw all design work done on behalf of Seibu at that time.

The relationship between advertisers and creative staff is always a difficult one, since the former have to be able somehow to maintain objectivity and keep a certain distance from their copywriters and art directors, knowing when to use them, and when not to do so. A particular problem emerges in this relationship when – as in the case of designers Yamaguchi Harumi and Ishioka Eiko, who created through their distinctive style and techniques what is known as the 'women's era' of television commercials in the late 70s – creative staff for one reason or another themselves become famous and are then consumed as 'artists' together with their works. As a result, they need to be replaced from time to time, in the same way that a store's wrapping paper does. Thus, to stay ahead in the game of image marketing, a store like Seibu needed to be on a constant lookout for new talent and to employ only the best among art directors, photographers, designers, copywriters, and so on in order to ensure that its own advertising campaigns were ahead of the trends, rather than lagging behind them. This probably explains why neither Yamaguchi nor Ishioka was very deeply involved in Seibu's television commercials during the 80s. Their style, their art, had already been consumed by the public and was thus no longer as avant-garde as it had once been seen to be. In this respect, the commercialization of art that took place in Japan from the mid-70s – a commercialization to which Seibu later actively contributed by marketing and auctioning various kinds of art – has reduced that apparently uncommodifiable aesthetic activity into an ever-accelerating cycle of 'scrap and build'.

The construction of the Museum of Art as part of the Ikebukuro store's general refurbishment was a crucial element in Seibu's image strategy at this time. Although, as Millie Creighton points out in the next chapter, several other Japanese department stores had started to put on art exhibitions as a means of attracting customers to their premises (see Havens 1982; Moeran 1987; Creighton 1992), none had gone so far as to establish its own separate art museum. Seibu's innovation here attracted considerable attention on the part of media and the general public, and there was a mad rush of visitors to some of its early exhibitions, 160,000 people coming to see an exhibition of western art that included works by artists from da Vinci to Picasso, plus a further 70,000 attending a Kandinsky, and 60,000 more an Escher, exhibition. Other exhibitions of contemporary Japanese art and photography were also much talked about, so that the opening of the Museum of Art added considerably to Seibu's image campaign.

This was hardly surprising: as one of the highest forms of culture, art was (and is) a highly visible means of promoting a cultural image, accepted and admired by people who had never heard of 'Seibu of Ikebukuro' before, as well as among so-called opinion leaders who then influenced various different groups of consumers. Thus, whereas prior to the completion of Phase Nine, Seibu's Ikebukuro store drew about one quarter of all residents in the neighbouring Toshima and Nerima wards, half of whom had to travel no more than 20 minutes to reach the store, by 1976 it had transformed itself from a local to a metropolitan store which was attracting a wide range of customers from Shinjuku ward, as well as from stations along the Keihin Tōhoku line between Tōkyō and Yokohama. Moreover, these customers were no longer from a low-income bracket as before, but consisted of professional middle-class families in their 20s and 30s with comparatively high incomes. In other words, the metamessage communicated through its advertising campaigns that Seibu was a unique department store was having a telling effect, thanks mainly to the way in which the store ran an extremely prestigious (if for the most part unprofitable) Museum of Art, together with a culture centre, the Ikebukuro Community College attracting 35,000 members, cinema theatres, and various avant-garde artistic activities (see Havens 1994:235–41).

Advertising

By 1980, when Phase Ten of the Ikebukuro store refurbishment was completed, one third of Japan's 120 million plus population lived in the sprawling urban megalopolis of the Kantō plain – a demographic fact which led Seibu to embark upon what it referred to as a 'redevelopment of the city'. Following its victory in the distribution war with super-discount stores in the 60s, and with suburban shopping centres in the 70s, Seibu turned its attention back to the very place from which it had begun its expansion – the city centre – and started an ambitious building programme which saw the completion in 1979 of the Ikebukuro Sunshine 60 Building (to which it relocated its head-quarters), and the opening of Seibu Sports, Seibu Habitat and other big speciality stores in the Ikebukuro area during the 80s. During this process, Seibu revived the phrase 'department store' to refer not to departments within a single store, but to whole stores, each of which acted as a single department by focusing on one specialized range of merchandize – sports goods, interior furnishings, or whatever. In this way, it aimed to appeal to various different consumer targets and generations, but in particular to the new generation of 'singles' (especially single women) who had an increasingly large purchasing power and seemed intent on asserting themselves in a much more diversified manner than hitherto (cf. Skov and Moeran 1995). It was this new generation of young women which Seibu targeted in its 1979 advertising campaign, 'The Age of Women' (*Onna no Jidai*), whose visuals suggested 'women staging themselves', rather than the more customary 'women being watched' (in the manner first described by John Berger [1972]), and so imbued their messages with a sense of auto-erotic narcissism, rather than hetero-sexual coquetry. This sense of independence and individuality was reflected in the visual of a two and a half year old baby swimming on her own in a pool, accompanied by the slogan (by copywriter Itoi Shigesato): 'Myself – A New Discovery' (*Jibun, shinhakken*). This campaign, used for the completion of Phase Ten of the Ikebukuro store's refurbishment, was designed to make people realize how human beings – and thus, by analogy, Seibu itself – could make the impossible possible, and marked the beginning of Seibu's golden age of advertising (*Figure 7.1*).

During the 70s, the department store had certainly created its own particular advertising style – thanks in particular to the work of copywriter, Itoi Shigesato. From 1975 through to 1980, a number of slightly interrogative, inviting slogans were used to accompany the series 'My Own Expression' (*Watashi kara no hassō*)[10] – each of them somehow affirming an ultimate sense of self-centredness accompanied by a value-free 'me-ism' in which a dual relationship was established between advertiser and consumer, between Seibu and its clientele. Sometimes advertising slogans were instructive ('I want this year to be one in which I begin something' [*Nanika o hajimeru toshi ni shitai*]); other times they were more provocative ('What do you think?' [*Dō omoimasu ka?*]); but they were always forceful, and always kept Seibu one step ahead of targeted consumers.

What the latter found when they now went to the Ikebukuro store was not a 'new' or 'fresh' Seibu, but a 'new self' that they discovered for themselves – different for each different person visiting the store, and multiplying into numerous different selves within each customer. These messages emphasized non-conformity and self-confidence among contemporary Japanese, preparing them for a new age in which the previous conformity of postwar society was fragmenting in tandem with the 'disintegration of the masses'. People were being made to realize that human beings' potential was infinite and that it was all right to avoid competition with others and to be simply one's self.

Figure 7.1 'Myself - A New Discovery.' A baby at two years and four months old, swimming in the water, gives an amazing image of great human potential.

In 1981, the 'Mystery, I Love It!' campaign was launched (*Figure 7.2*). This came about as a result of the completion of Phase Ten of the Ikebukuro store's refurbishment, when one event planned was an exhibition of Egyptian art treasures, and it was decided to combine two previously independent campaigns to mark the completion of the latest phase of the store's refurbishment and the opening of the art exhibition. Tsutsumi Seiji is said to have been the one to suggest to the creative team that they 'go to Egypt' – hardly the most fashionable place in

不思議、大好き。

Figure 7.2 'Mystery, I Love It!' Two white women, dressed in safari wear, standing in front of an ancient Egyptian temple against a backdrop of local women, show the orientalist image of curiosity towards mysteries.

Japan in the early 1980s (even though the rising value of the yen made Cairo but a short trip away), but one which immediately conjured up an aura of mystery. The visuals used were not particularly mysterious – two tall Caucasian women in safari-style 'colonial fashion' clothing, standing in front of some ancient Egyptian ruins. Other than marking a variation on the old 70s theme of 'The Age of Women', this seemed like little more than western orientalism (of the kind later taken up in Ralph Lauren's *Safari* ads), while the juxtaposition of the two white

191

models with a group of black women could be interpreted as adding the slightest hint of racism.

In a way, then, the use of the background of ancient Egypt with modern western women was similar conceptually to the visuals used in Japan National Railways' 'Discover Japan' campaign of 1970 (Ivy 1988), where Japanese women dressed in fashionable brand clothes were posed in front of traditional Japanese places. The distance between then and now, tradition and modernity, was the same in both campaigns. The only difference was that, whereas the 'Discover Japan' campaign played on an exoticism of Japan, the 'Mystery, I Love It!' campaign for Seibu depicted an exoticism of the west.[11] After all, in this new age of 'internationalism' (the new buzzword of the 1980s), travelling abroad seemed as easy to most Japanese as going to visit a neighbouring town.

While messages used in the 'Myself – A New Discovery' campaign had been slightly didactic, those in 'Mystery, I Love It!' suggested that the city was a space beyond that in daily use, and that the department store was a space medium putting on offer all sorts of strange things. This echoed the way in which space had begun to take on unprecedented value in urban areas, particularly in the concentrated centralization of Tōkyō. Moreover, the increasing proliferation and density of communications served to enhance, rather than detract from, the meaning of space so that urban space moved into a kind of renaissance period in which its ceremonial and non-daily usages increased rapidly. The slogans 'Myself – A New Discovery' and 'Mystery, I Love It!' made use of imagery that acted as obvious invitations to the city.

But if this was, indeed, a new 'city age', the advertising campaigns put out by Seibu during this period were not so crude as to proclaim it directly to one and all. Rather, during the 80s, campaigns were clearly marked by an absence of message. Copywriter Itoi Shigesato, for example, in his single phrase 'Mystery, I Love It!' stripped visual images of both historical depth and geographical distance, but allowed them to evolve in a splendid media mix of music, television, print media and so on. The campaign initiated a whole series of similar, message-less slogans – from 'Tasty Life' (*Ōishii seikatsu*) to 'Happy, eh! Satchan!' *(Ureshii ne, Satchan)* (*Figure 7.3*), by way of a young woman muttering to herself 'So what?' in English. In each, there was nothing but a meaningless – if slightly exotic – murmur, in which the usual aim of an advertiser communicating a message to its targeted audience was totally ignored. That such non-communication worked

Figure 7.3 'Happy, eh! Satchan.' A small Japanese girl, Satchan, following Lisa Lion, a well-known female body builder, in the attempt to shape her body, thus indicating that a woman can grow strong - with the assumption that a strong spirit rests in a strong body.

can be gauged from the way in which 'Mystery, I Love It!' fuelled a whole series of television commercials around the theme of 'the seven new wonders of the world', as dreamed up by Seibu's Sales Promotion Department. What worked for the ancient ruins of Egypt, therefore, was also made to work for images as different as the mysteries of the universe, Edo mechanical dolls and surrealist paintings by René Magritte (not to mention the unlikely cultural combination of India, Nepal, China and Bali in one variation) (*Figure 7.4*). Each of these expressed an unrivalled astonishment at the wonders of the world, and at the same time suggested that visual advertising could indeed become a form of 'high culture'.[12] Thus Seibu came to be seen as a cultural patron that sponsored artistic television commercials that carried no message.

Figure 7.4 'Oh, The Origin.' Two young Indian girls dressed in traditional costume symbolize the origins of fashion, while at the same time reflecting the new consciousness of the time, i.e. back to Asia, back to earth.

Although, strictly speaking, the so-called 'golden age' of television advertising in Japan only lasted from 1980 to 1982, it was sufficient to propel a number of nameless advertising creative people into the limelight and transform them into publicly recognized artists – rather like the celebrities they were themselves using in their campaigns.[13] People like Itoi Shigesato, Nakahata Takeshi, Yamaguchi Harumi and Ishioka Eiko became household names in Japan, and the advertising industry suddenly seemed like an interesting place for young people to find employment, since there was a chance that their work might be appraised in terms of 'art' rather than as just a form of sales promotion. As mentioned earlier, such a transformation had its risks since both 'artist' and 'artwork' were now consumerable and thus subject to a process of differentiation whereby the talents of individual copywriters and designers became valuable consumer items in Japan's image market as a whole. They thus became subject to the ever-quickening cycle of build-and-scrap that gripped commodities in general and the technology used to make such commodities. The trouble here was that, while clients were institutions which could afford to speed up the endless renovation of their corporate images, creators were people with particular individual talents who could not really be subjected to the same processes. This led to the devouring and subsequent discarding of creative talent in the advertising world, so that when a client set about looking at which copywriter or designer might be best to take on a particular campaign, it also inevitably found itself making decisions about who it would *not* employ.

This meant that a rather subtle relationship emerged between clients and advertising creative staff. Among the so-called '3 S' of advertising at that time – Suntory, Shiseido and Seibu – the former two employed their own in-house creative staff. Seibu, on the other hand, relied totally on external art directors, like Tanaka Ikkō and Asaba Katsumi, to carry out its advertising according to a general strategy developed by its own Sales Promotion Department. These design rooms then employed copywriters and photographers to form a creative team for each campaign. Rather than deal with the person directly in charge of day-to-day details of the campaign schedule, or even with the head of the Sales Promotion Department (as is usually the case), these outside design rooms received their instructions directly from the top of Seibu's corporate hierarchy: that is, from Tsutsumi Seiji himself. It is the unusual role that the latter has had in his company's image strategy which has partly given rise to what may be called the 'Tsutsumi myth' in vogue in Japan during the 1980s.

The relationship between Seibu and its advertising creative teams was somewhat stand-offish. The store's Sales Promotions Department did its utmost to ensure that it contracted the most with-it and fashionable creative personnel whom it then tried to keep together as a team over a number of campaign seasons. In this respect, it brought them into close relations with those working in the department store, but also kept them at a certain distance since they were not, after all, themselves Seibu employees. Creative people for their part tried to protect their position by ensuring that they themselves did not get *too* involved in Seibu work, since that would merely brand them as a certain type of 'Seibu' copywriter, designer, photographer, or whatever.[14] This suggests that, as creative 'artists', they were very aware of the dangers of being themselves consumed by the frenetic pace of Japan's commercialism.

This shift from nameless creative personnel to famous artists marked a simultaneous independence of the image from advertisements themselves. This is most obvious, perhaps, in the Seibu Saison Group's advertising (to which many people who saw it responded by saying that they had no idea what was in fact being advertised), but there was more to this transformation than creators merely being given the freedom by a client to do as their moods inspired them. Rather, it was connected with Seibu's own self-assertion and sensitivity that emerged as a result of its image marketing. The way in which symbols began to float away from their meanings – and thus how the overdetermination of the signifier began to give way to an underdetermined signified – was happening not just with commodities, but with a whole range of consumer events and experiences. Television commercials were part of this independent 'market of images', and the 'meanings' which linked them to sponsors and their products rapidly became minimal during the early 1980s.

The End of the Department Store

In this chapter, we have traced the development of Japan's postwar consumer markets and focused in particular on the way in which Seibu's advertising campaigns in the 70s and 80s somehow latched onto the ethos of the period, hit a chord with the Japanese public and so helped create a special image for the department store and for the Seibu Saison Group as a whole. In this way, Seibu was able to move from selling merchandize to selling images, and both the department store and the enterprise group of which it was a part moved beyond the sale of mere goods and commodities to the provision of services, information and Culture (with a capital C).

This development was, of course, brought about in part by the changing nature of the Japanese economy – particularly following its restructuring after the oil crisis of 1973. By the latter half of the 70s more than half the working population was employed in the tertiary sector and there was a remarkable increase in 'invisible' expenditure on communications, education and entertainment. This meant not only a radical restructuring of the department store business itself, but a gradual decrease in the reliance of the Seibu Saison Group as a whole on the activities of Seibu Department Store. Thus, as a separate set of operations, Seibu began to open up new specialized stores such as Seibu Seed (1986)[15] and Seibu LoFt (1987) – an idea which then gained popularity as other similar stores were set up throughout Japan and then abroad. Similarly Mujirushi Ryōhin, the 'non-brand goods item' store founded by Seiyū, gradually developed its own outlets – Howdy Seibu (1981) in Shiraganedai and The Prime (1985) in Shibuya – which moved away from being 'department' stores as such. Parco, too, practised a similar diffusion, with forays into book publishing, magazines and mini-media (including its own TV channel [1983]). Just as the Seibu Saison Group began to detach itself from Seibu Department Store, therefore, so did these offshoots from Seibu begin to drop the Seibu (and Saison) name. Parco is one example; LoFt another; Family Mart, various hotels and leisure ventures are yet others. In this way, whether planned or not, the Seibu name has come to be hidden as consumers both within Japan and abroad (especially in Asia) unconcernedly patronize the Seibu Saison Group's various businesses.

As is well known, the department store business was begun in America by John Wanamaker in 1874. It was from this time that the ideas of cash sales for properly priced goods, returnable items, and 'one stop shopping' originated. The sales strategy of 'treating every customer on equal terms' practised by the first department stores clashed with the then-current business method of using personal connections and patronage to sell to different strata of a status-conscious society. In this respect, department stores were a product of, and developed in tandem with, mass society.

But if department stores are a product of a particular period of history – and so, inevitably, of a particular culture – then history itself must bring them to the end of their original mission at some point or other. It is at this point that Seibu now finds itself, in a number of different ways. First, there is clearly a historical limitation to the department store as a commercial institution since 'a store with several different departments' becomes comparatively less significant with the growth of other competitive businesses. Second, there has been a concomitant change in the corporate image of department stores in Japan, as consumers rapidly change their perceptions of 'Seibu' *vis-à-vis* those other stores together with which it forms a system of different possibilities for consumption activities. In this respect, the question arises as to whether or not Seibu's image strategy has really succeeded. Third, there is an internal problem of how best to maintain the structural organization of Seibu Department Store itself as it moves from growth to stability under the captaincy of successive generations of the Tsutsumi family. Related to this, fourthly, is the matter of how Seibu's corporate climate will be transmitted from one generation of staff to the next and of how employees will react to it. Fifth, there is the overall decline of Seibu Department Store's position within the Seibu Saison Group, and the fact that it can no longer act as the 'anchor' in the tug-of-war accompanying the Group's overall growth. This means, sixthly, that Seibu needs to consider how it is going to restructure itself and the extent to which it should collaborate with other members of the Seibu Saison Group. Is there, for example, going to be a shift in management style from Tsutsumi's individual leadership to a more corporate structure? Or will there be some kind of break-up of the Group? In which case, how will the Saison corporate image be affected? Finally, there is the general economic situation in Japan which has seen a series of transfigurations of the domestic market – including the final death knoll of the 'mass' market, on the one hand, and the bursting of the financial 'bubble', on the other – and which consequently obliges Seibu to consider how best to continue to maintain itself as an organization while creating the flexibility to deal with future changes in consumer demand.

Let us expand slightly on these points. As we have seen, as large-scale retailers and capital investors, Japanese department stores were able to take on and overcome the threat of the super-discount stores in the 1960s, primarily by creating for themselves an 'added value' over and above the goods that they offered for sale. At the same time, however, it seemed more than likely at one stage that these metropolitan 'boxes' would gradually lose their *raison d'être* and disintegrate entirely as their new-found entertainment value was taken over by those specializing in the operation of Disneyland, and various other kinds of 'events'. In other words, it seemed as if department stores' ability to introduce cultural events would be usurped by museums and art galleries; that its function as a meeting place for people would be taken over by hotels and restaurants; and that the consumption of goods itself would shift to mail order and cable TV shopping. In the face of such possibilities, Seibu encouraged the diversification and strengthening of its enterprise group, spurring on its own fragmentation. In one respect, then, the same drive that gave birth to the department store also accelerated its demise.[16]

Still, this organizational fragmentation was offset by a continued consumer perception that Seibu stood for 'innovation'. According to a special feature on Suntory, Shiseido and Seibu in the December 1989 edition of the marketing journal *Senden Kaigi*, Seibu Department Store's 'mind share' (that is, the number of people positively conscious of the store) had dropped by almost half, from 49 to 25 per cent, since 1985 – as had the number of people who wanted to work there (from 44 to 27 per cent). This drop in admiration for, and image of, Seibu was attributed to the rehabilitation of Mitsukoshi which once again emerged at the end of the 80s as the leader among Japan's department stores – possibly because of the 'neo-conservative' mood that prevailed in Japan during these years. In spite of the renewed respect for Mitsukoshi among consumers, however, Seibu still managed to maintain its 'bright', 'fresh' and 'outstanding' image so that most people believed that the store would keep its promise if it said that it was going to do something 'new'. Although there was no particular connotation to this 'something new', consumers felt vaguely expectant and convinced that Seibu would find the answer for them – all of which intimates that the store had indeed been able to impress this image on the Japanese public during the two decades or so since its Ikebukuro branch fire.

Now it could be argued (as it has been by the copywriter, Itoi Shigesato) that the reason this was at all possible was that Seibu had 'neither history nor tradition', thereby giving it a clean slate so far as the building of corporate image was concerned. However, this could have a negative, as well as positive, effect since consumers might shift to wanting something more than either the history or tradition that they might otherwise acknowledge Seibu now possesses. Still, either way, Seibu can rely on its corporate image since the idea of 'something new', repeated time and time again, does in fact give rise to a 'tradition'. In this respect, there is great strength in the Seibu Saison Group's option of dropping the Seibu name entirely, as it builds up and develops external businesses and structures which are preparing Seibu for life as a 'post'-department store. It would seem, therefore, that the Group does not suffer from the kind of weakness characteristically revealed by late-developing businesses when trying to cope with even later developing competitors. The Seibu Saison Group has taken on an enterprise structure appropriate to its consistent growth, in spite – or because – of Seibu Department Store's continued capital investments in new business ventures. It has also managed to retain stable management, thanks to Tsutsumi Seiji's refusal to put his company on the stock market and thereby subject it to pressures from investors.

But this is about the only limitation imposed. The Seibu Saison Group has really and truly embarked on a capitalist path that aims at regenerating its productive growth *ad infinitum*. Given this opportunity, it has not once looked back and is, as a result, at present suffering from a chronic shortage of human resources since business developments at first took priority over personnel management. Recently, however, things have changed, so that Saison has no rivals in Japan when it comes to trial-and-error innovations in personnel management, although, so far as staff quality is concerned, Seibu has lost out to older, well-established stores like Mitsukoshi and Takashimaya. The Seibu Saison Group remains committed to such innovations, however, and is unflinchingly determined not to lose its self-confidence regardless of their success or failure – a fact which intimates that differences in personalities between those charged with the development of separate business spheres and those who at present occupy positions of senior management in the Group have been overcome for the betterment of a corporate environment.

But even if the Saison sense of 'corporation' is sustained by each of the individuals employed therein, the question remains: how is this corporate culture to be passed on by those who are currently charged with its care? Hitherto, the sense of innovation prevalent during Saison's high growth period has been successfully created by employees in their 40s and above. Also remarkable is the pride with which Seibu and Seiyū store managers, as well as those in charge of various project developments, competed among one another (with an appropriate sense of competitiveness) to be the most original in the work that they did for the Group. This was partly because Seibu did not adopt a franchise system, but encouraged each store to develop a 'local' character as part of a dual-structured regional and national business, and so made all those concerned aware of, and receptive to, differences within the Group. Such a policy served to set the Seibu Saison Group off from most other major retailers who tended to market a single 'package' of goods that ignored regional tastes. It also discouraged the kind of complaisance affecting most regional concerns, since those in charge of Seibu and Seiyū outlets found themselves drawn into a conflict of claims from national and regional distributors and so were obliged to clear the difficult hurdles in which such a double-bind often placed them.

Still, one cannot help but sense a certain anachronism here. After all, every company creates its own ethos and tends to move from a period of high growth to one of stability, so that there is always a question of how things are going to be passed down from one generation to the next. These problems tend to emerge, firstly, when a gap opens up between the company concerned and a new generation of ('neo-conservative' or 'new breed') consumers; secondly, when those in charge of recruitment and personnel shift from innovative to established patterns of staff deployment with the rise in status of their company; thirdly, when the company itself moves into a stable state and ceases to be so innovative; and finally, when the market changes and ceases to welcome innovations as previously. In Japan, one or two of these problems have already emerged, thereby threatening the Seibu Saison Group's corporate continuity and thus what it means to be a part of 'Saison' in general.

And what *does* it mean? We have seen that there has been a gradual decline in the share of goods sold by the Seibu Saison Group as a whole, in the same way that there has been a shift in the department store business from the sale of 'goods' to that of 'non-goods'. Thus, while it has planned to hive off its functions, first to '70 item' and then 'individual miscellaneous goods' speciality stores, Seibu has also succeeded in overcoming its image as a mere 'department store' and become instead a kind of 'super' department store. One particular characteristic of Seibu, then, not found among other Japanese department stores, is its ability to deny its department store function while still being a department store. This has been helped by the fact that the Group as a whole has fortified its image as a 'developer' – particularly through its 'zoning' of complexes of shops and stores, and its simultaneous shift of competition from city to regional centres.

Still, as the Group has expanded, its overall future has become less and less clear. It is probably for this reason that Tsutsumi Seiji – the only person with a real grasp of all Group activities – suddenly announced his retirement as chief executive officer in January 1991. Needless to say, this caused considerable public comment and criticism at the time, but it transpired that Tsutsumi's so-called 'retirement' was little more than a charade which allowed him to relieve himself of his title of CEO, while allowing little else to change. His idea appears to have been to administer some kind of shock therapy to the Seibu Saison Group and prepare those concerned for a shift from individual to corporate management leadership.

Even though Saison is an enormous enterprise group which, in 1989, comprised some 89 companies and had a total paid-up capital of ¥65,800 million, taken individually these companies are little more than small to medium-sized businesses. However, because they have all been gathered together under the crowning name of 'Saison', they have enjoyed the continued confidence and trust of consumers and have been able to employ talented personnel whom they would never have been able to attract as individual corporations.[17] At the same time, however, the more the Group as a whole has expanded and the more diverse the activities of its individual members have become, the more ambivalent its corporate image has come to be seen. In general, a corporate image can exercise a kind of stranglehold on the innovations that capitalism continually demands of companies, so that once the Seibu Saison Group had created for itself a stable identity promoting value and style, it found itself being left behind by unpredictable changes in the market. And since there are never rules when it comes to market changes, the one rule that companies need to adopt as part of their corporate existence is themselves to have no pre-planned rules with which to deal with such shifts in the market. The moment a company creates some kind of 'ism' about its activities, it is bound to be shaken up by the market. In a way, then, the Seibu Saison Group is a model of how an enterprise group ought to work in the way that it adapts itself to market situations, since its corporate image advertising slogans of 'novelty' and 'leadership' act as metaphors for change and instil public confidence in the Group's ability to adapt successfully to changing circumstances.

In practical, concrete terms the Group developed its business from 'goods' to 'non-goods' in reaction to amoeba-like changes in the Japanese market. Thus, as we have seen during the course of this chapter, its internal structure adapted in such a way that it no longer relied on the activities of Seibu Department Store alone, while also developing its various businesses so that they did not depend totally upon such potentially trendy, and thus unstable, concepts as 'value' and 'lifestyle' alone. On the one hand, it led the way in promoting activities connected with the culture industry; on the other, it could out-pace such economy-oriented organizations as the *Nihon Keizai* Newspaper by launching its own financial magazine, *Money Japan*.[18] Similarly, it could simultaneously promote such contrasting goods as 'no brand'

Mujirushi Ryōhin and the kind of specialized gadgetry sold in LoFt, as well as manage high-class western-style hotels in whose rooms it freely televised soft-porn videos. Such contrasts are too numerous to mention here, but should not be taken to imply that Saison had no 'identity'. After all, the corporate character of such an enterprise group consists of an overarching identity beyond the sum total of the individual companies operating therein. Saison thus makes use of and discards such 'convictions' and 'styles' as it sees fit in order to deal with the market's knotty changes.

The problem with its corporate character, though, is not these separate parts, but the future of the system as a whole and how that system is to be preserved. The Seibu Saison Group nowadays has to tackle all those 'different kinds of values' that first emerged within Seibu Department Store, so that if it goes into gourmet cuisine, it must also enter the fast-food business, and if it targets professionals, it must also cater for those merely interested in gadgetry. In other words, Saison as a group is trying to establish itself as an all-round 'hundred item' business and so secure an independent Saison realm. To talk about Seibu in these terms is thus to talk about the workings of Japanese capitalism itself.

Notes

1 Parco is an Italianate name designed to mesh in with the fashion goods (mostly with French and English names) that it sells by means of a boutique system of space rental. In this respect, it is not so much a department store as such, but a rent-a-building, or real estate, business which leases out space to tenants. The single commodity in which it deals, therefore, is space, and the market that it targets consists primarily of young working women with their own incomes – in the 1980s, employed in the growing service sector.

2 The 'cast' system (based on the idea of 'casting' actors for parts in plays or films) was introduced by Seibu's Personnel Division which employed specialists on contract terms, with relatively higher incomes for specified periods of time. This enabled the department store to avoid the financial burden otherwise imposed by the more traditional hiring practice of 'lifetime employment'.

3 It also set a precedent which others were keen to emulate, and thereby initiated what came to be known as the 'refresh boom' among Tōkyō department stores at the end of the 70s.

4 Although Yūrakuchō is part of the greater Ginza area, and although Seibu is located very close to the Ginza shopping street itself, local Ginza merchants campaigned successfully to stop Seibu from using the title of 'Ginza branch' for its new store, but to identify itself by its postal address (Yūrakuchō) (see Havens 1994:173).

5 The Seibu Retailing Group was renamed the Seibu Saison Group in 1985, and Saison Corporation in 1987, when Tsutsumi Seiji intended that the new corporation act as an 'ideological gemeinschaft', an 'agglomeration of ideas' rather than of capital, to 'coordinate group policy, develop large-scale projects, and serve as a steering committee for the core firms' (Havens 1994:143) which were themselves reconstituted in seven enterprise clusters.

6 A number of different 'generations' have been singled out for attention by Japanese observers:

(1) Baby boomers, or the 'bulge' generation, who were born right after the war between 1947 and 1959, mainly in rural areas. This was the first generation that went through mass higher education and spent their student days in urban areas. Since they could not afford to live in city centres, they later settled down in the outskirts of metropolitan areas.

(2) The 'in-between' generation (*tanima no sedai*), relatively small in number and born in the 50s, for the most part in rural areas, before the period of rapid urbanization in Japan in the latter part of the decade.

(3) The 'new breed' (or *shinjinrui* electronics generation), born during the 60s into an environment characterized by media and information technology. The first truly urban generation, born and raised in urban areas, who experienced television right from the start of their lives.

(4) The second baby boomers (known as the post-shinjinrui generation), born in the 70s after the first baby boomer marriage rate peaked in 1973. Usually only children or with just one sibling close in age.

7 In 1983, Tōkyū Department Store spent 2.14 per cent of its sales on advertising (the lowest ratio), and Takashimaya (the highest) 2.91 per cent.

8 At the same time, advertising marked a steady decline as a percentage of overall sales expenses, from a high of 19.6 per cent in 1968 to a low of 10.9 per cent in 1983.

9 In the mid-60s, Seibu had a contract for one hundred columns per month in the *Asahi* Newspaper alone.

10 For example, 'Did you have a hearty laugh today?' (*Kyō, ōki na koe de waraimashita ka?*); 'Is there a lyric you've come to like today?' (*Kyō, suki ni natta uta ga arimasuka?*) (both 1976); 'How sensitive are you? Bzzzz!' (*Kandō ikaga? Pippi*); 'For the one who wants to fly' (*Tobitai hito no*) (both 1977); 'More imagination' (*Motto imagination*) (1978); and 'Body and soul – shape up' (*Karada to kokoro, shape up*) (1979).

11 Or a Japanese interpretation thereof. For discussions of Japanese advertising in this respect, see Moeran and Skov (1996a and 1996b).

12 A similar approach was adopted by Parco in its advertising campaigns, where a 15-second television commercial, for example, might show no more than Faye Dunaway eating a boiled egg, adding at its end the single phrase in English: 'This is a film for Parco'.

13 Witness Woody Allen taking part in 'Tasty Life' for Seibu in 1982, and Faye Dunaway endorsing Parco in 1979.

14 Tanaka Ikkō, for example, made sure that Seibu contracts never amounted to more than half his design room's total advertising work.

15 Seibu Seed itself set up a second speciality store, Capsule, at the end of the decade.

16 Seibu is the exception here. In 1988–89, during the heady years of the 'bubble' economy, I conducted a general survey of Japanese department stores and found, time and time again, that my informants proudly (and, to my mind, quite groundlessly) believed that their stores had no rivals in the retail industry and that they would thus continue 'forever'. This presumption was based on burgeoning consumption stimulated by the bubble economy (which was to come to an abrupt end in 1991–92), when each department store's turnover increased in proportion with the growth of the consumer market as a whole, regardless of the effort and confidence, or lack thereof, of those employed therein. The only person to express any reservations about the future at that time was the representative from Seibu.

17 From 1986, all new employees for companies in the Seibu Saison Group were recruited by the Group as a whole.

18 In July 1985, five months before the launching of the *Nihon Keizai* Newspaper's *Money* in December of the same year.

8

SOMETHING MORE

Japanese Department Stores' Marketing of 'A Meaningful Human Life'

Millie Creighton

Their employees and customers agree that department stores in Japan do not just exist to sell goods or display merchandise; they offer 'something more'. This 'something more' encompasses, as Mitsukoshi puts it, the role of department stores in promoting 'the revival of learning and culture' (Mitsukoshi 1986:18). It includes an entertainment and an educational function; it involves the sponsorship of the performing arts, and an attempt to revitalize community crafts; it offers an attempt to fulfill the cultural and intellectual needs of the populace, not just their desire for consumer goods. In some cases the emphasis on 'something more' has led department stores to an attempt to deal with philosophical issues, to address questions of human purpose and meaning.

Understanding certain underpinnings of the Japanese retailing context such as the development of a merchant ethic of social accountability, the high-ranking status niche of department stores among retailing institutions, and these stores' desired prestige image-positionings can help illuminate why Japanese department stores constantly strive to offer something more, given that they exist primarily as profit-oriented institutions for the sale and distribution of consumer goods.

Department stores in Japan boast long histories and traditions. Many, such as Mitsukoshi, Takashimaya and Matsuzakaya, developed from dry goods stores existing 300 or 400 years ago during the Edo period (1600–1867). Such department stores trace their beginnings to the commercial houses developing then, and their stated corporate philosophies echo the ethics of the Edo merchant guilds that spawned them. Newer department stores, developing from the railway tradition, such as Seibu, gained admittance to the esteemed ranks of department stores and in doing so claimed membership in this merchant tradition.

At the beginning of the Edo period the pursuit of profit, the core of the merchantile trade, was deemed inconsistent with righteousness and held in low-esteem. However, along with major changes in the organization of life and society, a 're-definition of the sacred' (Bellah 1957:8) occurred, allowing for the greater pursuit of commercial activities, reflected in the developing merchant ethic. This ethic justified the pursuit of monetary gain, but at the same time called for a sense of social responsibility on the part of merchants. The open pursuit of economic gain was justified to the extent that merchants also struggled to enhance their communities and their societies. The realization of wealth brought further responsibility to, in a sense, return something to their public through involvement in activities geared toward fostering general social welfare.

This was also seen as consistent with recognizing economic advantages. As Tsuda points out, 'there must be customers before a merchant can make money' (Tsuda 1970:168). Thus the role of department stores in contributing to social values, educating the populace and providing enlightening services had historic precedence in the precursors to department stores, and has continued to be well-developed since their emergence in the following Meiji period.

In theory the merchant ethic of accountability is not limited to department stores, but remains the ideal for all Japanese retailing. However, this ethic is embraced more strongly by department stores because of their high-ranking, or prestige, niche in Japanese retailing. Institutions and individuals in Japan are not equally responsible for upholding asserted social values. In general, people and institutions holding higher stations are accountable to a greater extent than those in lower positions. A parallel can be drawn with department store service offerings and extension of polite behavior toward customers. Standards of service and politeness are not defined differently for different institutions. However, in order to retain their status as Japan's higher prestige retailers, department stores are expected to uphold these standards to a much greater degree than are other types of stores. Expectations of polite behavior or service offerings are much lower at a supā (a combination supermarket and variety store), and discount stores can practically ignore these concerns.

My purpose here is neither to assess whether stores or their personnel truly believe in a merchant ethic of accountability, nor to suggest that cultural explanations override rational economic concerns. I did, in the course of my research, meet many department store employees who, in espousing these ideals, seemed to be doing more than granting them lip service. They seemed to believe that the offerings and programmes made available by their stores served the public and therefore made a 'return gift' for the gift of patronage. This belief helped such employees define their work as meaningful and creative. However, even if only offered in the guise of social service, the 'something more' department stores give their customers is both in keeping with cultural expectations of their higher status, and economically rational. In order to maintain their reputation as Japan's sophisticated, higher prestige retailers, department stores must offer their clientele something more. By doing so, they show that they at least publically endorse the merchant ethic and hence are willing to take on the obligations of their high-class retailing niche. Although many of the offerings are costly to the stores, they are economically rational in the long term by helping to maintain department stores' desired image positioning, and thus contribute to long-term sales and profits. Moreover, in the short term, cultural activities – particularly art exhibitions (Havens 1982:140–2; Moeran 1987; Creighton 1989) – encourage a 'spillover' effect as customers purchase unrelated goods in other parts of a store.

It is hardly surprising, then, to find that Japanese department stores are not unique among the world's department stores in staging exhibitions or offering their customers shows and amusements (see Williams 1982; Bowlby 1985; Benson 1986) or other forms of 'edutainment', events and services that are both entertaining and redeemingly educational (see Creighton 1992:49–51, 1994). American department stores experienced their golden days of retailing in the 1920s. In its centennial publication of 1926, the American retailer Lord & Taylor also proclaimed that department stores held an important role in serving society, while enhancing human life:

> The original department store was merely a clearing house for merchandise. . . The modern department store is also a clearing house, but it is a creative and educative influence as well. . . This evolution in store keeping is due to two things. First, to the creative impulse of industry to redeem the monopoly of mass education by adopting ideas from twenty centuries of art, and second, to the wider diffusion of prosperity and knowledge and a corresponding development and diffusion of taste.
>
> (Lord & Taylor 1926)

Such passages reveal that showmanship has gone hand in hand with salesmanship for other department stores in other parts of the world during their own golden days (see also the chapters in this volume by Yen and Chan).

However, department stores are also embedded within a particular cultural milieu, reflecting long espoused social values, patterns of economic organization, and the specific concerns or issues of that society at that point in its history. In terms of their high public profile and emphatically high service orientation, the 1980s can be thought of as Japan's golden days of department store retailing. Japan's so-called 'economic miracle' had within a few decades transformed a poverty-stricken nation into an affluent one, and catapulted Japan into a new international prominence. However, it was also an age of 'things other than things' ('*mono igai no mono*') (Creighton 1992:53), an age in which Japanese consumers found their desires for material goods sated and were a bit disillusioned upon the realization of the society's long-sought economic advances. Many Japanese began questioning whether economic growth could continue to be equated with success, and began to feel that affluence had been bought at great social cost (Hidaka 1984; Hein 1993). By the mid-1980s Japan's per capita personal consumption had reached that of the U.S. (Hernadi 1990:186), but now that Japan had fully arrived as a consumer society, consumers were more than ever yearning for something more than consumer durables.

In order to illuminate the intersections of Japanese department stores and contemporary Japanese identity during this time, this chapter will explore how these stores extend 'something more' to their customers in the following three ways. First, it will provide a general discussion of department store offerings in museum exhibitions and other cultural events. Second, it will focus on Seibu Department Store's attempts to move beyond being a distributor of goods to being a distributor of philosophy for modern life. Third, it will explore three different branches of Seibu created as 'theme stores' to help communicate Seibu's espoused philosophic marketing ideal of a 'Life Worthy of Human Beings', in which each store becomes a pavilion addressing pertinent concerns of Japanese society in the mid-1980s.

Department Stores as Culture Brokers: Exhibitions and Museums

Department stores in Japan present cultural and artistic exhibitions of every kind imaginable. There are frequent special exhibitions in various sales areas. On a visit to a department store in one of Japan's urban centers one might find an exhibition of folk instruments from around the world in the music department, textiles from India in the fabric department, famous utensils for the tea ceremony or exquisitely crafted miniature villages made of decorative sugar cubes on the food floor. There may be craftspeople engaged in demonstrations or musicians giving performances anywhere in the store.

Department stores have a primary role in the circulation of art in Japan. Most stores have art galleries and art forums, where craft and art works are exhibited and sometimes sold. Moeran (1987:32) and Havens (1982) discuss how 'making it' for Japanese artists and craftspeople requires having one's work exhibited at department stores. Some department stores have legally designated museums of art. Whether the art works are Japanese or from abroad, more of them circulate through department stores than through museums (Creighton 1989).

Many department store employees emphasize that the cultural and artistic offerings are part of the department store tradition in Japan. The director of cultural events at Isetan says that,

> This is not something that has come about in recent years but has a long history in Japan. It goes back to the beginning of department stores in Japan. Isetan, Takashimaya, Mitsukoshi, they all held exhibitions [and] other special events.

Every floor frequently has 'mini-exhibitions' or shows directly associated with merchandise sales, the purpose of which is to directly enhance sales by making shopping entertaining. There are also art or craft shows where works are exhibited with the primary goal of selling them; the department store receives a percentage of the sales. However, there are also exhibits which industry people insist are staged simply to satisfy a need. A buyer for Matsuzakaya says that 'these are true exhibits, the store isn't trying to sell the goods but give the customers a chance to see cultural treasures'.

Providing cultural or artistic treasures is related back to the belief that merchants have the responsibility to respond to social needs. Tsutsumi Seiji, chairman of the Seibu Saison Group, says that,

> when social needs develop faster than government can respond, the department store must take the lead in meeting these needs. It is part of our social responsibility and we aim to make these services pay for themselves in the long term.
>
> (quoted in O'Donnell 1982:54)

This statement refers to social accountability, but another sentiment also emerges. For the stores there is no contradiction between wanting to make money and supplying the populace with culture and intellectualism. It is fully expected that providing for social needs should indirectly increase profits. Seibu releases commonly mention that,

> The Seibu Saison Group aims not only to generate profit, but to balance material and mental well-being through a lively engagement in art and cultural activities.
>
> (Seibu Saison Group 1985:30)

Department stores do not expect to make money on the exhibitions, but they are not shy about the fact that they hope to attract people to the stores (cf. Moeran 1987), thereby increasing general sales.

Museums and galleries are typically placed on the upper floors as an acknowledged strategic plan to encourage people to shop throughout the store rather than only on the lower levels. Putting a museum on the top floor is, according to one department store museum staff member, like putting in a fountain:

> By getting more people to come to the exhibitions, more people come to the store. The museum is at the top of the store, so people might go to the museum first but they must come down – through each floor – and maybe they'll buy something on the way down. We say it works like a shower. Think of a fountain. First the water goes up but it must come down and as it does some of it splatters out at various places. It's just like that.

Thus their profit-motivated economic aims are presented as consistent with attempts to further the quality of life, and vice versa.

The emphasis on providing cultural, artistic and intellectual offerings has affected personnel training programs. Employees involved in managerial training sessions at some department stores are expected to study the performing and visual arts. During their training period they will attend museums and concerts together, view presentations of traditional Japanese art forms, engage in philosophical and religious discussions. According to the personnel director of one store this is because department store managers are expected to have a 'knowledge of culture'. Seibu sent one of its museum staff employees to the U.S. to work at the Philadelphia Museum of Art for two years. She indicated that she was interning at the museum to learn more about American art, to learn more about curatorship, and to gain the personal contacts that would be helpful in arranging fine art exchanges in the future.

Japanese department stores project different images and since exhibitions are part of stores' marketing strategies, their exhibitions differ in style. With an image seeped in idioms of traditionalistic Japanese identity, Mitsukoshi tends to provide a lot of exhibitions of what are considered traditional Japanese arts and crafts. Once Mitsukoshi hosted a special exhibition of *sumō* wrestling articles for fans of the traditional sport, and a food fair in which all companies represented had to have a history of at least one hundred years. When it comes to foreign exhibitions, Mitsukoshi often chooses impressionists, artists well-liked by their conservative clientele.

Other stores do not feel compelled to present such highly intellectual topics or renowned great artists. Seibu, for example, likes to take the occasional risk as part of its innovative image and so deals with artists who are, in the eyes of its staff, 'controversial' and 'contemporary'. Tōbu Department Store, on the other hand, has an image which does not aim to be particularly intellectual, and the store specializes in popular culture exhibitions which a member of Tōbu's special events staff calls 'amusement-oriented'. In July of 1986 an eerie poster with a black cat and broken china doll advertised their latest – a mystery exhibition. The young staff member proudly announced that he had 'heard it's the first mystery exhibition done in Japan; Tōbu is the first to do it!' It followed on the smash success of the previous year's horror exhibition, and contributed to a marketing image that set Tobu apart from rival stores like Seibu or Odakyū.

Exhibitions of famous art usually run from six to eight weeks. They can take years to plan and millions of dollars (O'Donnell 1982:54) to produce. Although entrance tickets are usually sold for the exhibitions, staff indicate that the revenue generated by these does not cover costs. The time commitment involved in staging exhibitions is much greater than for displaying merchandise. An exhibition of Japanese art usually requires at least a year of planning and a foreign exhibition requires two to three, sometimes up to five years. The staff first choose a subject and a title, then decide what selections they want to gather. If it is a foreign exhibition they must contact museums around the world. Arrangements must be made to insure and transport the pieces. All of these things need to be finished at least one year prior to the exhibition. Then a catalogue is made, explanations of the exhibits and biographical sketches of the artists written, the works gathered and photographed, all for an exhibition that will probably last just six weeks.

Wrapping up after an exhibition is over can usually be done fairly quickly, but this, too, requires more work than handling merchandise. Again, there are particular difficulties with a foreign exhibition. It takes longer to make the arrangements to return the items and staff members are sometimes expected to accompany the art works back.

Exhibitions of foreign art are common at department store galleries and museums. A member of Isetan's art museum explains that,

> The Japanese have known Japanese art for ages, but looking at foreign art – this is still a relatively new phenomenon. . . Even now, the Japanese have an intense interest in viewing foreign culture.

By offering foreign art, store museums claim they serve an educational function, consistent with the role they have historically held in educating Japanese about foreign goods, holidays, and customs (see Creighton 1991). As expressed by the museum employee above, department stores present foreign art so that Japanese people can learn more about it and develop a greater appreciation for it. It is also a way of introducing children to art, something this museum director cites as lacking in Japanese public schools:

> Europeans and Americans were taken to museums from the time they were children. Even now, children in Japan have less of a chance to see art. Now schools are starting to do this a little but there is still not much emphasis on taking children to museums. Here we help people develop a sense of art appreciation.

In this sense, exhibitions of foreign art are again seen as a way department stores provide 'something more' as a response to social needs.

The main Seibu and Isetan stores both have what is designated as a 'museum of art' (*bijutsukan*). In order to be granted the 'museum' designation certain legal requirements must be met. An employee for Seibu says that,

> It's funny, in Japan it's very difficult to get the name 'museum'. We can use 'gallery' or 'show' but if you can use the word museum, bijutsukan, it has a lot of meaning.

In both cases the stores claim that their museums compensate for the dearth of public facilities. The two busiest areas of Tōkyō are the central Shinjuku area, where Isetan's main store is located, and the Ikebukuro area, home to Seibu's flagship store. According to department store lore, Seibu became the first to host an in-store museum in Japan after Tsutsumi Seiji proclaimed at a board meeting that although the Ikebukuro district had plenty of places for socializing and entertainment, what the area really needed was a museum (O'Donnell 1982:53). The director of cultural events at Isetan echoes similar sentiments, saying that,

> The art museum is considered a service to the customers. It also fulfills a sense of service to the society. Whether it's Shinjuku or Ikebukuro, there is no public museum. At Ikebukuro, Seibu has a museum and at Shinjuku, Isetan does. There are still few public museums in Japan compared to the U.S. or Europe, so it is the department stores that take this role. . . If lots of good public museums are made perhaps the need for department store museums will diminish, but this hasn't happened yet.

Japanese values assert that to be the recipient of some resource or the beneficiary of someone's generosity brings with it obligations. Likewise store philosophy asserts that the store itself, by accepting profits from customers, also has an obligation to society. Department stores in Japan assert that they are a place of culture, not just a showplace of consumerism. Holding exhibitions, maintaining galleries, providing in-store art museums help them achieve this image in the public's eye. A museum director for Isetan claims that having a museum raises Isetan's image. A member of Seibu's art museum staff agrees claiming that,

> The museum is very different from the general department store activity. The museum is not conscious of making money. The important thing is to present and make a good impression of Seibu by introducing good artists' works to the public.

For these designated exhibitions, the emphasis is not on sales. The stores claim that they help fulfill the social obligations they have incurred by accepting profits, but the hope that good exhibits will encourage greater customer allegiance and ultimately raise sales is also openly admitted. A member of Seibu's art museum staff sums up the purpose of her store's exhibitions this way:

> I think to have a good show, to get people to think, 'Wow! So Seibu is this kind of a place', I think that is the whole point. Even if it doesn't make enough money immediately, for the future it builds a good corporate identity.

Ultimately Japanese department stores offer something more in the way of exhibitions and museums to enhance their reputation, to cause people to stand up and take notice, and thus to reinforce their desired image positioning as Japan's high status retailers.

Seibu as Philosopher: Going Beyond Material Goods

In addition to staging shows and events, department stores also enter the philosophical arena, making efforts to define meaning in human life. The chairman of Seibu has asserted that retailing is an activity requiring philosophers as well as economists (Seibu Saison Group 1985:3). Providing philosophical statements is an arena more often associated with religious institutions, or, with growing secularization of values, educational or cultural institutions. However, since department stores in Japan have long been mainstream providers of educational and cultural offerings, it is not inconsistent that they have become involved in philosophical issues of concern to the Japanese public. Following its image positioning as Japan's innovative retailer, Seibu in particular has positioned itself as a transmitter of philosophy, thereby offering its customers something more in terms of a pathway to meaning through consumerism. This section will focus on the presentation of philosophical statements by Seibu in its efforts to define and distribute a meaningful human life.

Japan has undergone huge economic and lifestyle transitions in the last fifty years, shifting from the poverty and material deprivation of the early post-war period to an age of affluence in which many people now feel their desires for consumer goods to be sated. According to many marketing analysts, this transition has been accompanied by a rising disillusionment with material possessions as a source of self-fulfillment, and an increasing demand for services, educational offerings, and leisure pursuits. Hernadi (1990:189) notes the increasing demand for 'sporting, educational and hobby activities', concluding that, 'having reached material affluence, a kind of qualitative affluence became the target of Japanese consumers'. Modern Japanese, tired of the consumer utopia, seek to go beyond material goods in search of values, self-fulfillment and a meaningful human life. Such a trend might not seem likely to be a great boost for the nation's large retailers who developed primarily to sell consumer goods. However, in a seeming paradox, department stores have asserted themselves as the vehicles through which consumers may pursue their quest away from material goods towards 'spiritual intangibles'.

Tsutsumi Seiji discusses this paradox, noting both consumer desires to transcend material values and the emergence of department stores as a means to transcendence:

At a time when material prosperity has grown, Japanese consumers are asking for more. They are looking beyond things to psychological self-fulfillment, aesthetic satisfaction and meaningful human relations. People want to discover something new. The term 'breaking away from things' appears frequently in analyses of consumer trends in Japan. I interpret this to mean a transcendence of material values, and I believe the retail industry must provide the means to achieve this transcendence.

(quoted in O'Donnell 1982:54)

For Seibu there is no contradiction involved in the distributors of material goods aiding people to transcend materialism. Like other department store concerns, Seibu actively asserts that it has an important social role beyond selling goods. Tsutsumi claims that department stores have a potential social utility that is 'obvious as long as they are used in accordance with the needs of the time' (Seibu Saison Group 1985:4). As critical issues to Japanese society of the 1980s and 1990s, Seibu Saison Group (1985:6) identified an aging population with concerns for health and security, an educated population interested in continuing education, an increasing number of women 'entering the world outside the home', increasing leisure time but limited recreation facilities, concerns with problems of industrialization and attempts at internationalization. Seibu Saison Group (1985:10) contends that the ruptures of meaning arising from these has left everyone 'trying to search for his or her own values'. Seibu Saison Group (1985:7, 12, 14, 16) asserts its own role as being to aid Japanese lead a better life, a 'Life Worthy of Human Beings'.

One way that Seibu claims it is contributing to a 'Life Worthy of Human Beings' is by enhancing the use of leisure time. Once more renowned for their tireless dedication to hard work, Japanese are experiencing a rise in leisure time. There has been an increase in legal holidays, and a shift to a five-day work week. Seibu contends that this increasing leisure time should no longer be viewed as time 'to relax in anticipation of work'. Like work time, its philosophy asserts, leisure time should be productive; put to use 'creatively and culturally, in more diverse ways, outdoors and indoors' (Seibu Saison Group 1985:12):

Some devote their leisure time to life-long learning, to history or archeology. Some spend their leisure time engaged in volunteer activities. Some are participants in the arts, others are viewers. For all, the Seibu Saison Group provides the means by which they can make the most of their interests.

(Seibu Saison Group 1985:13)

Making the most of one's leisure time suggests education in the sense of personal development. The Japanese have long asserted a preeminent value on education. 'It's educational' (*benkyō ni naru*) is frequently cited as the justifying rational behind diverse activities. Japan's Ad Hoc Council on Education in 1986 stressed 'the importance of providing various opportunities for lifelong education' to 'free [people] from the idea that school education is self-sufficient' (Kawabata 1986). Seibu had already embarked on a similar campaign to nurture independent learning when it annexed to its main store what it called a 'community college'[1] offering over 400 courses. According to Seibu Saison Group (1985:12), the goal of the center was to provide a 'very extensive range of courses to satisfy people's needs for culture', self-education and the creatively productive use of time.

A second way that Seibu seeks to build a 'Life Worthy of Human Beings' is by fostering security (Seibu Saison Group 1985:14). According to Seibu philosophy, feelings of insecurity threaten to intrude on the Japanese sense of well-being because growing affluence has not been able to foster a true sense of security. Instead, Seibu observes, 'it seems that the wealthier we grow, the more we seek reliability and security'. An aging populace and increasing social complexity have contributed to a world in which people are 'undeniably . . . uneasy about the future', a world in which 'the need for security is taking on a new importance'. Seibu purports to bolster reliability and security by offering 'systems and goods which by their nature are information' (Seibu Saison Group 1985:14).

A third way Seibu claims to help create a 'Life Worthy of Human Beings' is by promoting health. Seibu identifies health issues as a growing concern because of the lengthening average Japanese life span, defining 'healthiness' as not just 'living a long life, but living a long life happily and healthfully' (Seibu Saison Group 1985:16). One attempt to promote healthy living was the creation of an herbal medicine shop at the flagship store. Another was the construction of a special pavilion dedicated to enhancing health. Emphasizing the concept of 'renewal', the huge complex housing 'facilities for refreshment of mental and physical health' (Seibu Saison Group 1985:17), christened the 'Re-Born Pavilion', offers the faithful options for exercising. Noting that Japanese people are increasingly exercising Seibu philosophy suggests that 're-birth' not 'weight loss' is the valid goal of such discipline, asserting that the Japanese 'aim in exercising is not to lose weight, however, but to refresh themselves, to gain mental and physical health' (Seibu Saison Group 1985:16). Japan's new-found affluence has brought new concerns. In a society which once considered obesity a foreign problem, there are growing concerns with the increasing numbers of individuals who are overweight, particularly among the young. Despite Seibu's disclaimers, it is likely that the popularity of such health centers does involve concerns with physical attractiveness, with being overweight and desiring to lose weight; a desire Seibu re-frames in the more socially legitimate goal of refreshing mental and physical health.

In addition to the 'Re-Born Pavilion' and Herbal Medicine Shop, Seibu Saison Group (1985:17) proclaims its commitment to promoting health in a diversity of other ways. Included among these is the manufacture of 'fertilizer, an important component to healthy living'. Seibu's identification of 'healthiness', as a focus of consumer industries, and its extension of this idea to a concern with fertilizer, comes at a time when some Japanese are asserting that issues such as pollution, urban congestion, and inadequate social infrastructure must be taken into account when assessing whether Japanese consumers have adequately benefitted from rapid economic growth (Horioka 1993:63).

Many of Seibu's philosophical statements suggest that commu-nication is the key to recovering the humanity that was an inherent component of the traditional order, a humanity that industrialization and urbanization have threatened to erode. A Seibu brochure warns that 'communication is essential if we are to recover the humanity in our lives' (Seibu Saison Group 1985:10). The traditional order did not require that one's attentions be lavished, and hence dissipated, on those outside of specified relationships. Ties were to be nurtured among relatives, intimate associates, members of the community. Contemporary Seibu doctrine likewise encourages humanistic communication to support established relationships, claiming to provide 'venues for improving communication amongst generations, friends, neighbors' (Seibu Saison Group 1985:11). Venues offered by Seibu include community fairs, area craft promotions, entertain-ment, vacation villages that help facilitate intergenerational fun, and a 'gathering of friends' (*tomo no kai*) or shopping and personal interest clubs that are used as networking foci for groups of member friends.

These forays into philosophical statements of a meaningful human life are all part of Seibu's image marketing. They project a public image of Seibu as social philosopher, a role Seibu defines as consistent with its role as an economic institution. With growing affluence, and a sense of saturation of material items, many Japanese consumers began experiencing a disillusionment with the pervasiveness of consumption as a definer of modern existence. By providing philosophy oriented toward framing meaning in human life, Seibu co-opts this disenchantment, redirecting the search for fulfillment back into diverse consumer venues, while further imbuing its own image with an aura of lofty intellectualism.

Three Seibu Theme Stores

By the mid-1980s, Japanese consumerism had shifted from an emphasis on the masses (*taishō*), to the 'segmented masses' (*bunshū*). Instead of campaigns directed at everyone, retailers began targeting groups of people, with what Ivy (1993:253) calls 'varying value orientations'. 'Lifestyles' became the buzzword of Japanese advertising and consumerism. Concurrent with its emphasis on philosophy in the 1980s, Seibu began to place more emphasis on educating consumers about diversified lifestyle possibilities (see the preceding chapter by Ueno).

As part of its lifestyle marketing, certain Seibu stores were designed with a new orientation. Rather than attempting to carry the entire range of merchandise customary to department stores, these stores imaged particular lifestyles while serving as statement stores grappling with specific philosophical concerns of the age. Seiter (1992:233) contends that the physical space of store layouts constitutes cultural objects. This recognition is at the foundation of a forthcoming volume that explores these physical spaces, analyzing how they define the meanings of 'servicescapes' for different types of retailing institutions in different parts of the world (Sherry et al., forthcoming). Store layouts and definitions of store space establish a physical reality heavily imbued with symbolic meaning; they 'create a setting for behavior' (Mukerji 1983:15). Allison (1994:36–41) discusses the importance of spatial arrangements and definitions of space in another venue of Japanese consumerism, nighttime hostessing clubs. The three Seibu store settings which will be discussed here are Yūrakuchō Seibu in the Ginza area of Tōkyō, the Seibu store located in Tsukuba, and Seibu SEED, all established in the mid-1980s, and all reflecting social concerns of Japan at that point in its history. Each of these stores struggles with a social issue, expresses a world view, or affirms existential meaning. Each one is a store with a theme, a store with a statement.

Aiding the information society: Yūrakuchō Seibu

Japan in the late 1970s and early 1980s had as its a goal becoming an 'information society' (*jōhōka shakai*). If communication was the means to revitalizing a lost humanity, information was the key to establishing meaningful communication. When information became a significant social issue, department stores entered the debate expressing concern for open access to information. The chairman of Seibu was convinced that department stores were a potential avenue of information dissemination:

> I cannot help feeling that there are still important, but untouched ways we could use the department store as a base for information exchange.
>
> (Seibu Saison Group 1985:4)

Joining the efforts to create an 'information society', Seibu designed and constructed a new store with a special thematic approach. The Yūrakuchō Seibu, built in the upscale shopping area known as the Ginza, was visualized as 'embodying a new information traffic center role for the department store' (Seibu Saison Group 1985:20). In Havens' words (1994:173), the store was designed as 'a theater of the mind' offering 'the future now: information and new media'. The New Year period is considered a particularly auspicious time for new beginnings in Japan and thus the three-day grand opening of the store was planned for the first days of 1985. In these three days an estimated two million people visited the Ginza area, a notable increase over the same period of previous years. A Seibu publication for 1985 explains the conception and reception of the new store as an information networking center:

> This store is an important information gathering and relaying point in the Seibu Saison network. . . The opening of the Yūrakuchō Seibu is more than the opening of a new Seibu Department Store outlet. . . Information from around the world concentrates at the Yūrakuchō Seibu which is linked with [other] shops by an information network. In the end, then, it means that the store is a forum for information exchange.
>
> (Seibu Saison Group 1985:1, 4)

Thus the Yūrakuchō Seibu was christened, not a department store, but an information forum, a store with the stated purpose of disseminating information rather than carrying a full line of consumer merchandise.

The Yūrakuchō Seibu started out with less floor space than a typical department store. Instead of reducing the size of some departments as an adjustment to space limitations, Seibu cut departments entirely, such as toys and children's wear. Eliminating whole departments freed space for information centers. An example is the entire eighth floor which is not a sales floor, but an information center, with information on consumer durables, results of research on items for sale in Japan, comparisons of different brand items in quality and price. There is information on non-material consumer goods such as insurance or vacation possibilities available to the Japanese. For many of the items Seibu is directly involved in their sale or distribution, but information is also available on goods, services, and activities not handled or sold by Seibu concerns.

Another designated information center is located on the fifth floor and is oriented toward non-Japanese clientele. This is the Foreign Customer Liaison Office, the first of its kind in Japan. Office staff assist foreign customers in making purchases. They will deal with questions about merchandise or other problems related to shopping, but also provide information services that have nothing to do with sales. For example, the staff will assist foreigners research school possibilities for their children or obtain alien registration cards, they will provide clarification of the Japanese legal system and information on health care facilities, or explain how to go about having a phone installed or buying a train ticket for a weekend outing to a hot spring. A foreign resident or traveler may bring almost any concern or question to this office and receive assistance, whether Seibu is capable of realizing any direct profit from the interaction or not.

While asserting the central importance of information in meaningful human life, the Yūrakuchō store functions as a statement warning against limiting information access. As expressed by Seibu's chairman,

> As long as we offer the information people want, they will come to the store. Let me add that it is important that new media not be monopolized, but rather be used by many. In that way, the social value of new media will be enhanced.
>
> (Seibu Saison Group 1985:4)

Thus the Yūrakuchō Seibu expresses a philosophical concern that Japan's 'information society' embrace consumer issues and address the needs of all its members.

With the inauguration of its Yūrakuchō store, the first of Seibu's theme stores, Seibu announced the incorporation of information into its

221

espoused world view. According to this world view, information is an essential tool that will enable people to lead meaningful lives, or, as a brochure asserts, 'by assimilating such information into their lives, people will enrich their lives'. Rising affluence, according to Seibu philosophy, has ushered the Japanese populace towards lifestyles of choice, in which, guided by the use of information, people 'must clearly define how they want to lead their lives' if they are to pursue a meaningful existence (Seibu Saison Group 1985:7–8).

Coming to terms with technology: Tsukuba Seibu

The next Seibu theme store was also opened in 1985. Its opening was planned to coincide with the International Science Exposition, Expo '85, held in Tsukuba. Prior to 1985 Tsukuba, a rural area north of Tōkyō, had been selected as the base for a nationally planned academic and research community. The World's Fair marked the realization of Japan's planned research community, as well as Japan's status as a technological giant, a leader in patented scientific research. With the science exposition, Tsukuba took on the new role of Japan's 'Science City'. In hosting Expo '85, Japan as a society affirmed its continuing commitment to technological development.

Seibu expressed its support for this societal affirmation of technology by dedicating its new Tsukuba store to service-oriented technology. Store pamphlets, advertising and in-store posters all deal with the conflicts created by technological advance. The store takes a philosophical stance on whether technological advance is a threat to job security and meaningful human relationships or a blessing to all people. The Tsukuba Seibu's stated world view asserts that technological change is nothing to fear, but should be seen as the route through which human beings will be freed from mundane or dangerous work to dedicate themselves to creative pursuits.

While building its Tsukuba store, Seibu asserted that a task for Japan is building a comfortable society for everyone where scientific developments go hand in hand with helping human beings. Tsukuba Seibu was dedicated as an expression of Japanese retailing's contribution to realizing that goal. Store pamphlets echo themes of Expo '85. Rather than a store, the building is referred to as a pavilion, echoing the language of the world's fair, such as in the advertising slogan, 'The Whole Building is Now a Life Information Pavilion'. Promotions for the Tsukuba store loudly proclaim it to be 'different':

> Different from department stores you're accustomed to, Seibu implements advanced scientific technology. You can draw on the wisdom. . . Seibu is setting its roots deeply in Tsukuba and assists your daily life with mechatronics and service.
>
> (Seibu Department Store 1985a)

Tsukuba Seibu highlighted various advanced technologies in its operations in an effort to prove that emerging technologies could be directly applied to consumer service and that a department store could operate with the dual nature of 'humanlike heart and mechatronic stage' (Seibu Department Store 1985a). As part of the mechatronic stage, the Tsukuba Seibu store is located in the Creo shopping mall, which boasts of a technological first in the world's only spiral-shaped escalator.[2] Another new technological application introduced by the Tsukuba store was 'Roporter'. Roporter (or robot porter) is a computerized robot shopping cart. The signal intercepting Roporter follows a customer around the sales floor and will transport purchases to the check-out counter or exit without being pushed or even touched by the customer. From the store exit the customer is assisted by 'Solarporter', a car operated entirely by a solar energy battery. According to the store's explanations, 'Solarporter is an active helper. A Solarporter car delivers. . . purchases from the exit to the parking area' (Seibu Department Store 1985a).

Other technological applications assist customers in particular store areas. The food department is the home of a meat slicing robot. As the robot cuts, it keeps a running tally of price totals and customers can stop the order at any time. The kimono department employs a unique system called the 'amiputer' (a 'knitting' [amu] computer). The 'amiputer' enables people to see what they would look like in different kimono without actually trying them on. This system is particularly popular since most expensive kimono are custom-made. For custom-made kimono, customers make selections from displays of bolts of kimono cloth (kijaku) and so are not able to try the actual kimono on before deciding on a purchase. The record department contains a computerized information system listing information on over 50,000 records whether or not the store sells them.

Some of the most interesting technology adopted by the Tsukuba store is not directly intended to assist customers but to aid store operations. A high speed automatic cashiering system, billed as a 'futuristic system', sends cash and sales receipts orbiting across the ceiling from the customer to a central cashier and back again. Store floors are swept and mopped at special times by the store's own robot cleaning team. The robots epitomize Japanese consumerism's infatuation with cuteness (see Kinsella 1995). The cute robot cleaners are a special attraction for store customers. Vehicles that deliver goods to homes are equipped with computerized delivery aids. The computerized system indicates the location of the customer's home and gives driving instructions.

There is one computerized system that customers would have little opportunity to observe, but it is one mentioned in store guides and promotional films emphasizing the scientific nature of Tsukuba Seibu. The store has installed a robotic system capable of unloading incoming merchandise, delivering it to appropriate sales floors, and arranging the merchandise on the sales floors, all done mechanically at night without the presence of human beings. When this automatic conveyance system is set into motion, it first unloads in-coming merchandise into carts. Each cart has a sensitized plate indicating the sales floor where the goods are to be sent. A detector at one end of the warehouse reads the marked plate and a crane goes into automatic operation. The goods are sent to the specified floors and the type and quantity of merchandise delivered is registered on computers. The goods are automatically retrieved by robots at night and transferred to the appropriate areas of the floor. Seibu proudly advertises this system as contributing to the betterment of human life by eliminating tiresome work. A Seibu film highlighting the Tsukuba store claims that with the introduction of this 'high technology' the transfer of merchandise which used to involve 'hard work' has been completely automated, exemplifying how 'advanced technology is contributing to labor saving'.

I watched the entire process described here on a Tsukuba Seibu promotional film (Seibu Department Store 1985b) during a research visit to the store. One of the employees assisting me mentioned that although the system had been in use during the fair and for sometime thereafter, it was at that time no longer used because the store found it more economical to have the process carried out by human labor rather than running the complicated technology. This suggests that Seibu's dedication to the use of technology for saving human labor was to some extent a promotional ploy; at least it did not outweigh other economic concerns for cost-effective maintenance. However, the fact that Seibu developed these technological systems as a promotional means of enhancing its image suggests that issues of technology and its possible use in human life were major issues in Japanese society at the time, and therefore the Tsukuba Seibu store can be seen as a mirror of this concern within Japanese society.

Expo '85 addressed issues of technology in contemporary Japanese life. When the Expo was over, Tsukuba's planned research community remained as a testament to Japan's commitment to technological development. Travel and recreation brochures still proclaim Tsukuba as the 'science resort city' of Japan. The pavilions constructed for the exposition have been dismantled, but in the heart of Tsukuba a department store remains that professes to be a 'Life Information Pavilion' equipped with the latest in technological innovations. Tsukuba Seibu customers are no longer exposition enthusiasts interested in artificial intelligence, nor are they primarily researchers or academicians. The bulk of Tsukuba Seibu's clientele are rural farm families representing a conservative clientele. Instead of the glitz and glamour of its Tōkyō stores, Tsukuba Seibu projects a more 'down home' Japanese family-oriented lifestyle. The staff jokingly suggest that the image marketing of Tsukuba Seibu is the '*onigiri*' (hand-rolled rice balls) lifestyle. The store's message is that technology need not threaten the values of the 'onigiri life' but that instead a seamless joining of technology with traditionalistic forms of Japanese humanity is possible. Tsukuba Seibu as a servicescape located in the heart of 'Science City' embodies the possibility of combining a 'humanlike heart and mechatronic stage'. The Tsukuba store sends Seibu's statement that this can also be a goal for Japanese society if it pursues the use of scientific developments to help human beings realize a more meaningful human life.

Nurturing the creative life-shopper: Seibu Seed

The Yūrakuchō and Tsukuba Seibu stores both had themes that dealt with specific social concerns. In 1986 Seibu opened a store that addressed the question of ultimate meaning in human life. The store, named SEED, sends the message that as humans we struggle to develop into creative beings. Creativity is both the affirmation of existence and a reason for being. SEED soon became closely tied to the world of Tōkyō's visual and performing arts. The eighth floor of the building is devoted to exhibition space, while the tenth floor houses a theater for the performing arts known as SEED Hall. However, the whole SEED building is posited as a vehicle for creative expression, including the sales floors. Consumerism is proffered as a means of creative expression. SEED consumers do not just shop, they create through selective purchasing choices.

The name of the store was chosen to reflect this emphasis on creative development. A seed is a promise, something that when nurtured develops into a new being. As a director at SEED explains that,

> The name was selected to fit the image. We're trying to suggest the idea of a seed. A seed is something that grows, develops and finally emerges into the new reality of tomorrow.

Before entering the store, SEED shoppers encounter a huge brown pod jiggling up and down in space. The pod has cracked slightly and inside interspersed kernels are visible; others have already emerged from the pod and lie waiting on the ground.

The SEED experience is suggested to be one of growth and development. One arrives a seedling to enter through SEED Gate, as the entry level is called. The seedling shopper is met by SEED employees dressed in flowing ethnic garments, refractions of other flowers from distant fields, who distribute brochures that serve the double purpose of merchandise location guides and guides to spiritual development. Every floor in the SEED building has a name – The Wave, The Microbeam, The Relation, The Next, and so on. These floors are conceptualized as fitting into three different levels, each representing one stage of development (Seibu Saison Group 1986).[3]

From SEED Gate one is channeled toward the escalator to begin one's ascent to the upper realms, floor by floor. Near the escalator is an immense mural, an artistic presentation of SEED's message of human development. The mural depicts seeds growing, developing, emerging into the new reality of tomorrow. These are human seeds. To the left is a seed barely cracked from which a human head has emerged and burrowed its way up through the top soil. From another seed a human head with torso has burst forth, while from a third a nearly complete human being has emerged with head, arms, torso, the beginnings of legs, but no feet. This one will soon be able to cast aside its empty seed husk and walk away a free, creative being. Freedom in this case does not imply total independence. In consumerism, as in other arenas of Japanese life, an insistent refrain is 'the fundamental connectedness of human beings to each other' (Kondo 1990:9). The artist's depiction recognizes the interdependency of the three beings in their various stages of development, as it recognizes the need for nurturance for development to proceed. The head is being carefully watered by the near-complete human body.

The building's floors, like the human seeds, are grouped into three stages of development. The journey upward through each floor is metaphorically linked to a journey of human development; the vehicle of one's journey is the store escalator. Tobin (1992b:26) claims that in Japan 'the process of growing up and becoming a person was thought to take place metaphorically if not literally on the road'. To become a mature human being a person needed to 'embark on a journey'. As the vehicle of the shopper's journey SEED's escalator is analogous to a train, which both Ivy (1988) and Robertson (1988) have discussed as a symbol of travel and journey in Japan. In addition to the suggestion that customers travel the escalator as they would a train, other metaphoric associations with trains are made. For example, one Seibu publication (Seibu Saison Group 1986:15) says that SEED is the spot from which new designer goods will start their journey, using the expression 'SEED*hatsu*' (start off from SEED), a take on train lingo for starting off from a particular station.

The consumer aspiring to become a creative life-shopper leaves SEED Gate by stepping on the escalator, leaving the seedling identity behind and becoming a 'Spearhead'. The seedling shopper remains in the 'Spearhead' level of development until transcending to a floor called 'The Parts'. The middle level of development is designated as 'Sensitive', while in the upper echelons the consumer reaches the 'Creative' stage.

The use of English subtitles for floors and stages of growth are part of SEED's attempts to create an aura of lofty intellectualism. Merchandise lay-out and visual stimuli also help create an unusual style for a retail outfit. One of the lower floors, designated as 'The Wave', is devoted to records, videos and equipment sales. Videos (*Rocky III*, *Rocky IV*) run throughout the floor, colored spotlights flash back and forth at several locations, and employees wear black sweatshirts and tight jeans instead of the customary Seibu uniform. The videos shown on upper floors tend to be more uplifting. *The Uemura Story*, a movie about the life and presumed death of one of Japan's honored adventurers, was a common item on the 'Sensitive' level. Mannequins in the store are far from ordinary. Some are made from plaster, others from granite. They may or may not have heads and other body parts. Sometimes there are no mannequins where they are usually expected; stepping off the escalator onto a floor called 'The Office', the SEED shopper meets three suits, unencumbered by the usual mannequin wearers, relaxing under the shade of ferns. A video behind them shows excerpts from *Picnic at Hanging Rock*.

The emphasis on creativity at SEED extends to dressing rooms and rest rooms. On one floor the dressing rooms are arranged to look like stables. On another floor what at first appears to be a mirror comprising an entire wall turns out to be several entrances to fitting rooms. Upon entering the mirror one is greeted by oneself in another mirror opposite the opening. Closing the door provides one with the privacy to change or the opportunity to play in a labyrinth of reflected images. Restrooms at SEED are not marked by written signs; instead the indicators for toilets are all holograms, each containing a floating, multi-colored humanoid form. Following the seed metaphor, these are somewhat suggestive of adult-looking yet fetal figures.

A question that arises when considering Seed is whether it is possible to forego the heavy intellectualism, the philosophical inquiry into human existence, the spiritual quest to develop oneself into a creative being. The answer is yes. It is possible to go to SEED, ride the escalator down to 'The Wave', pick up the latest hit record, pay for it and leave without paying particular attention to the store's philosophical statements. In fact Seibu has provided various entertainment-oriented options for those who prefer to keep their shopping on the light side.

However, even these fun activities are related to themes such as information access or the utility of modern technological developments to consumer activity. Toward one end of the first floor of SEED Gate there is an area billed as an information corner where eight video screens act as 'message boxes' from which customers may retrieve store information by use of a touch screen system. Screens not being used as a store guide show popular videos. Customers can also write or leave messages on the screens, and the SEED guide points out the utility of the 'message box' in enhancing communication, and of keeping communication private. The 'message box' is described as:

A very useful visual message board for those who wish to meet others. You can make secret messages with your own secret numbers.

(Seibu Department Store 1986)

The videos may also be used as a creative forum. Customers can retrieve filed images or create their own artwork. On the day of my first visit to SEED, someone had drawn a cartoon entitled 'English *Sensei*' (English teacher) that bore the scrawled caption: 'This is a pen', echoing the sarcasm about English lessons spoofed on prime time commercials. The video screens are connected to a copier so that customers can have their messages or artwork printed out. Near the 'message box' is an area designated in *katakana* as 'graffiti spot', created and operated in conjunction with the broadcasting station Television Tōkyō. 'Graffiti spot' contains three video screens connected to a computer that allow customers to select their own video programming.

SEED decor and merchandise arrangement, floor titles and designated levels of developmental growth serve to convey the idea that a visit to SEED is not just a shopping outing. SEED's statement is that consumerism, regarding either what is purchased or where it is purchased, can be a form of creative expression, an intellectual encounter, a quest for spiritual development. SEED is a store, but a store where the emphasis is not on goods *per se*, part of Seibu's effort to show how the retailing industry will provide the means enabling Japanese consumers to transcend materialism.

Conclusions

As Japanese shoppers seek greater meaning in consumerism, depart-ment stores attempt to redefine the meaning of consumerism. Helping consumers transcend materialism seems a contradictory role for department stores which originated primarily to sell and distribute material goods. Those in the Japanese retailing industry suggest a way to mediate the contradiction. The time has come, they assert, to redefine the nature of buying and selling. The Chairman of Seibu claims that, 'We have to go back to square one and rethink the absolute basics, such as the meaning of "consumption"' (Seibu Saison Group 1985:3). According to those in the Japanese department store industry, consumption involves much more than satisfying physical, or even social, needs. Consumption is a form of self-expression, a form of communication; it communicates an attitude, a philosophical orienta-tion, a sense of identity. The purchasing choices people make reflect their values and world views. Where people choose to buy may also be a statement of world view. Consumption, at least as espoused by stores like SEED, is a potentially creative endeavor. With the development of consumer societies, the necessity to participate in the production of items used in daily life, even the preparation of foods consumed in daily life, declines, and the retailing world in Japan responds to the resulting sense of lost meaning in human life, in part, by asserting that selective consumption is itself a form of creativity. It also responds by offering customers more than goods; it offers them cultural engage-ments, self-development through 'edutainment', and philosophical statements regarding social issues and definitions of a meaningful human life. Even though there seems to be growing dissatisfaction and disillusionment with consumerism as a route to human fulfillment in Japan, department stores' ability to co-opt this dissatisfaction, and to redirect the search for a more meaningful human life back into consumer avenues and industries reveals how deeply consumerism is enmeshed in contemporary Japan.

The time has come when Japanese department stores emphasize their offerings in 'things other than things' ('mono igai no mono'). Department stores, once showplaces for merchandise, are now national suppliers of cultural activities, ritual participation and secular values. Few in the industry would go so far as to assert that salvation will ever be found at a department store cash register. But many assert that the department store is a vehicle through which people will be able to define and affirm a meaningful existence in the information society, the technological age, the consumer utopia that constitute the reality of contemporary Japan.

Notes

1　This educational center is called Seibu's Community College, with the English words community college written in *katakana*. It is not an accredited two-year university as the words might suggest. The courses involve instruction for a paid fee, and cover a broad range of topics. In some cases the instruction can lead to a type of licensing or accrediting, such as for the courses in ham radio operation.

2　This escalator, which received much attention in Japan, is located outside the premises of Tsukuba Seibu in the shared mall area connecting Seibu with the other stores in the mall. Strictly speaking, the escalator belongs to the Creo complex and not to Seibu. Pamphlets and advertising brochures for Tsukuba Seibu frequently mention the escalator, and although they do not claim that the escalator belongs to Seibu, they are written in such a way that readers might gain this impression.

3　For a more detailed discussion of SEED as a servicescape and of each floor, see Creighton (forthcoming).

Part III

A Japanese Entrepreneur in Hong Kong and China

9

THE YAOHAN GROUP

Model or Maverick among Japanese Retailers in China?

Lonny E. Carlile

The Yaohan Group traces its roots to a small vegetable stand in Japan's Izu Peninsula during the early 1950s. Currently it operates approximately 350 stores and numerous shopping centers worldwide, with most of them located in areas with large Chinese populations. In 1990, Yaohan moved its headquarters from Japan to Hong Kong and began expanding into mainland China itself, with a target of 1,000 stores by 2005 and ¥1 trillion in sales by 2000. It has already opened what is claimed to be Asia's largest shopping center in Shanghai. Yaohan is widely recognized as being at the forefront of Japanese retailing in Greater China, and its chairman, Wada Kazuo, a 'guru' of entry into the China market.

This chapter analyzes the strategy, structure, process and impact of Yaohan's expansion into the Greater China market within the context of the development of Japanese retailing over the last fifty years and China's current policies on the modernization of its distribution system as a medium for understanding the forces that are shaping retailing and consumption in China and elsewhere in East Asia. Specifically, it asks the following questions: What were the circumstances that gave rise to Yaohan's entry into the China market? What was the nature of Yaohan's business strategy as it expanded? In answering these questions it is useful to go backwards in time and trace the roots of the internationalization of Japanese retailing. Subsequent sections will then focus specifically on Yaohan's internationalization and the goals and modalities of China's liberalization of its retail sector while placing these developments in a comparative historical perspective.

The Internationalization of Japanese Retailing

Prior to 1971, overseas investment on the part of Japanese retailers was a rare and exceptional occurrence. Strict controls on the export of capital certainly had much to do with this situation, but there were other fundamental factors at work as well. The late 1950s and the entire decade of the 1960s were the years of Japan's postwar 'consumption revolution' and Japanese retailers had their hands full servicing a rapidly expanding domestic market. A core activity associated with this was the wholesale importation and domestication of mass marketing and distribution techniques developed in the 'early developer' in the mass consumption arena, the United States (*Chain Store Age* 1988; Uemura 1993; Havens 1994). The few exceptional instances of overseas operations by Japanese firms were, if anything, the kinds of exceptions to the rule that help to highlight the importance of these fundamentals.

The first major Japanese retailer to set up a branch overseas was Takashimaya, which opened a store on New York's Fifth Avenue in 1958 (Uemura 1993; Okamoto 1995). The store was devoted almost exclusively to the sale of arts and crafts and various 'traditional' Japanese goods like kimonos. The opening of this store was said to have been encouraged by the Japanese government as a device for combating the image of cheap Japanese workmanship overseas. The store, however, was not profitable and in 1966 it was moved to a different location when its original lease expired. The amount of floor space was reduced to about half that of the original store and its merchandise line was changed to concentrate on Japanese food items, dinnerware and cooking utensils. Tōkyū also opened a store under the Shirokiya name in Honolulu in 1958, with the target market in this case being members of the sizable Japanese–American community in that city. The emphasis in its merchandise line was comparable to that of Takashimaya's New York City stores.

In 1962, Seibu opened a large, 10,000 m^2 store in Los Angeles that sold Japanese and 'regular' American merchandise in roughly equal proportions. The store was established with the ambition of serving as a demonstration of how Japanese retailers could compete in the mainstream American mass market. The venture, however, proved to be an immediate money-loser due to the poor sales of American merchandise. Seibu pulled out after just two years, cementing the view that Japanese retailers were simply not competitive in the mature mass markets of the advanced industrialized countries (Uemura 1993; Havens 1994:73–4).

A rather different tack was adopted by Daimaru, which opened medium-sized department stores in Hong Kong and Bangkok. Initially, sales at the Hong Kong store were poor, but picked up in the latter half of the 1960s as the store developed a customer base among the rapidly growing number of Japanese tourists visiting the British colony. If anything, the emphasis in Daimaru's Hong Kong operations was on the procurement of mainland Chinese goods to be imported for sale in stores back home, utilizing connections with Chinese merchants that the company had developed prior to the Second World War when it ran stores in Tianjin, Singapore and Penang. The Bangkok store was opened at the invitation of the King of Thailand and found a comfortable market niche serving the wealthy elite of that country. Between 1964 and 1971 there were, in fact, no other major overseas investments by Japanese retailers.

Capital liberalization on the part of the Japanese government in the early 1970s opened the way for increased retail investment overseas (Uemura 1993:91–2). Despite this, the levels of such investment remained modest and directed at specific target markets. Mitsukoshi, Daimaru, Takashimaya, Isetan and other established Japanese department stores set up shops in Hong Kong, Paris, London, New York, and other major North American and Western European cities. In most instances these stores were small (sales areas of under 500 m^2) and were leased from an existing local department store or shopping center. Though profitable, the level of sales at such stores was generally quite modest and, as in the case of Daimaru's earlier store in Hong Kong, such sales were used to help defray the costs of maintaining overseas bases for the collection of market information, the purchasing of products for import into Japan, and the entertainment of business partners.

The one major exception to this general trend can be found in the store that Isetan opened in Singapore in 1970. With Isetan owning a minority interest (40 per cent) in Isetan Emporium, the venture was rather localized to begin with. Localization was taken a step further when it was quickly discovered that the Japanese goods sold at the store were considered too expensive by the local population, and the merchandise mix was shifted from one in which half the goods stocked were Japanese in origin, to one where Japanese products, local products, and goods imported from elsewhere were stocked in roughly equal proportions. After this, the Singapore joint venture did well and a second store was opened in 1979. The venture was listed on the Singapore stock exchange in 1981, opening the way to further expansion.

The experience of Japanese retailers overseas prior to 1980, then, gives rise to a number of generalizations. There is little doubt that controls on capital export by Japan served as a major damper on the overseas expansion of Japanese retailers. However, the modest levels of investment even after liberalization suggest that other factors were also involved. As the Seibu experience in Los Angeles illustrates most clearly, Japanese retailers were simply not competitive in the mainstream mass market of the advanced industrialized countries of the west. They were, however, in a position to take advantage of a specialized market niche – namely, the overseas Japanese consumer market consisting of local populations of Japanese descent and the expanding number of Japanese tourists abroad. The experience of Daimaru in Bangkok and Isetan in Singapore suggested one further market niche where Japanese retailers, with the appropriate strategy, might be potentially competitive. This was among Asian consumers with high income levels. As a number of other writers have emphasized, the competitive advantage of Japanese retailers here seems to have been not in the area of price or efficiency of operations, but rather in image, prestige, shopping experience, and other more amorphous and intangible 'cultural' dimensions. A large part of the Japanese competitive advantage rested on the contrast between its 'advanced' forms of packaging, presentation and store ambiance that contrasted sharply with the minimally processed, unmarketed and unstaged bazaar-style retailing that predominated among existing local retailers (*Chain Store Age* 1988; *Asian Finance* 1989; Creighton 1992; Ching 1996). Indeed, it is often remarked that Japanese retailers were instrumental in making shopping a recreational experience in these countries (Okamoto 1995:42). The following characterization of the contrast between the retailing practices of one Japanese supermarket chain in Hong Kong and its local competitors could be applied to Japanese department stores and supermarkets throughout the Asian newly industrialized countries (NICs):

> Its supermarkets offered a clean, spacious shopping environment filled with a huge variety of fresh, well-packaged vegetables, meats and sashimi – a contrast to the colony's cramped supermarkets and dingy wet markets.
>
> (Cheng 1996)

Japan's early 'Asianization' of western modes of marketing and distribution thus provided Japanese retailers with a competitive advantage in the upper income market segments of Asian NICs. Prior to the 1980s, however, this market niche was both extremely limited due to the small size of the population with sufficient disposable income to purchase from Japanese retailers, and difficult to access due to restrictions on foreign investment in the retail sectors of Asian countries. As Isetan's Singapore experience illustrates, once access was attained it was possible to expand a store's customer base somewhat to the upper-middle and even middle income segments if a process of localization took place.

The decade of the 1980s saw a substantial increase in the amount of Japanese retailer investment overseas (Uemura 1993; Okamoto 1995). From the beginning of the 1980s, this investment concentrated in newly industrializing East and Southeast Asian countries as they liberalized foreign access to their retail sectors. Japanese supermarkets began to join department stores during this period. Among the 'pull' factors making Southeast Asia attractive were a substantial appreciation of the yen that lowered the relative cost of real estate and labor in the target countries, and the expansion of the local consumer markets as a result of rapid economic growth in NICs. 'Push' factors included the relative stagnation of consumer demand in Japan that accompanied the economic slowdown in the wake of the second oil crisis and a tightening up of the Large Scale Retail Stores Law, a measure that protected small-scale retailers by making it extremely difficult for supermarkets, department stores and other large-scale retailers to open new stores.

During the latter half of the 1980s, these push and pull factors increased in strength and created a veritable 'boom' in the entry of Japanese retailers into Southeast Asian markets. The rapid economic growth of the Asian NICs expanded the size of the potential customer base of overseas Japanese retailers (Robison and Goodman 1996). Making these exercises attractive to Japanese retailers was the huge differential between a four per cent domestic growth rate and the often double digit growth rates in the NICs. The relaxation of entry rules proceeded in countries where investment was already allowed and liberalization occurred for the first time in a number of other countries, thereby increasing Japanese retailer access to these growing consumer bases. Adding fuel to this trend was a further dramatic appreciation of the yen in the wake of the Plaza Accord of 1985. In addition to making investments in these countries that much cheaper, the yen's apprecia-tion spurred a major boom in overseas Japanese tourism, thereby expanding the size of an already important customer segment for these stores (Carlile 1996).

An illustration of the consequences can be seen in the experience of Taiwan. In 1986, Taiwan opened up its domestic market to foreign retailers. By the following year, a joint venture of Sogō Department

Store had opened the first Japanese-style department store in Taipei, which proved extremely popular and profitable. Sogō's venture was quickly followed by the entry of Isetan and Mitsukoshi. The story was similar around Southeast Asia, with the liberalization of domestic markets being followed by the opening of competing stores by retailers from Japan. Japanese retailers tended to stick to formulas already proven at home – so much so that it was often remarked that Japanese department stores overseas were virtual clones of the home institutions (Uemura 1993:99). And although investments overseas became a growth sector for major Japanese retailers during the 1980s, this internationalization never proceeded to the point where overseas operations became the core concern.

Pre-China Yaohan

As discussed above, overseas operations on the part of major Japanese retailers were of marginal concern for them up until around 1980 and were never elevated to core strategic concerns for these firms, even after interest in investment overseas increased from the 1980s onward. For Wada Kazuo, president of the Yaohan Group (and Yaohan itself), by contrast, overseas operations came to have a critical place in overall strategy, and it was Yaohan's very marginality in the Japanese domestic market that drove it to grant centrality to its overseas strategy (Osawa 1990; Wada 1995:60–62; Gargan 1996).

During the early 1960s, a period in which Japan was experiencing a 'consumer revolution' spurred by rapid economic growth, Yaohan was able to capture a share of Japan's growing mass market by establishing a chain of mass merchandise, supermarket-style stores in the Izu region. However, Yaohan soon found its regional market niche under siege from deep-pocketed national supermarket chains like Daiei and Itō-Yōkadō. Wada's 1969 decision to venture overseas was less an aggressive effort to expand than a defensive measure to counteract the chain's sinking fortunes in its home market:

> One could not help but see that throughout the country retailers and small and medium-sized supermarkets were being swallowed up, one after the other, by the big firms. It was out of a sense of crisis derived from the knowledge that these trends would surely reach the Izu Peninsula that Yaohan turned its gaze overseas and decided to start by going to Brazil.
>
> (Wada 1995:71, 74)

With only five stores and an annual sales figure that was three per cent of that of the industry leader, Wada had little confidence in Yaohan's ability to survive the shake-out that was underway among Japan's supermarkets.

Yaohan's initial overseas entry, into the Brazilian market, involved the pursuit of a tested strategy in an untested market. Like Tōkyō's Shirokiya store in Honolulu, Yaohan's target market was an overseas Japanese community – in this case, the 100,000-strong Japanese-Brazilian community centered in Sao Paolo. Precedent notwithstanding, Wada was unable to obtain financial backing for the venture from Japanese banks, although he was able eventually and after great difficulty to get a loan from the Overseas Economic Cooperation Fund, a Japanese aid agency. By providing Japanese goods and higher standards of service than were the norm in Brazil at the time (including Sunday operations, for instance) the Brazilian venture did well initially, and Yaohan was able to expand its original store and open three others. However, in the latter half of the 1970s, Brazil experienced a bout of severe inflation that defused the Brazilian 'economic miracle'. Faced with a collapsing currency in the face of dollar-denominated loans, the sudden imposition of import controls that prevented Yaohan's Brazilian stores from obtaining critical merchandise (a third of Yaohan's merchandise was imported from Japan), and even a ban on Sunday shopping (an important element in Yaohan's competitive strategy), Yaohan fell into a severe financial bind that eventually led to the liquidation of its Brazilian ventures. The losses accrued have been estimated at nearly ¥300 million (Miyashita 1994:152). Despite the ultimate failure of the Brazilian experiment, Wada did gain from the experience an appreciation for a strategic variable that would come to characterize his later ventures – that is, the importance of being the first major entrant in a new market. Early entry helps to ensure capture of something which Wada stresses repeatedly in his writing: 'pioneer's profit' (sōgyōsha rieki). Also, mentioned by Wada is the importance of the character of the political leadership and economic policies of the host country government (Wada 1995:12–23, 82).

Yaohan's entry into the Greater China market dates back to its decision to locate in Singapore during a period when its Brazilian venture was beginning to take off. Like the emphasis on pioneer's profits, another key element in the strategy that Yaohan has been following in mainland China was already in evidence in its Singapore venture – that is, the attunement of corporate strategy to the development strategy of host governments. Yaohan Singapore was established as a joint venture with Yaohan holding 45 per cent of the company's equity and the Singapore government holding the other 55 per cent. At that time, the state-guided Singaporean 'miracle' was just getting underway, and the venture involved Yaohan in the establishment of a 'model' shopping center that the government was constructing with the aim of modernizing the country's distribution system. The distinctiveness of Yaohan's position on such matters relative to other major Japanese retailers can be seen in the fact that Nomura Securities, which mediated the relationship between Yaohan and the Singaporean government, turned to Yaohan only after being turned down by other larger Japanese department stores. As a result, Yaohan opened in 1974 in what was at the time Southeast Asia's largest shopping center on Orchard Road, and this in turn paved the way for Yaohan to move beyond just supermarket operations to real estate development, specialty stores, restaurants, and a wide array of other tangential enterprises. Yaohan did extremely well in Singapore and opened four more supermarkets in the country over the next nine years (Wada 1995:81–83).

A second major Singaporean national development project that Yaohan participated in was the construction of its International Merchandise Mart. This was also established as a joint venture with the Singaporean government (the state held a ten per cent stake in the venture) in 1988. Opened in 1992, the Singaporean IMM began full operations shortly thereafter. Described as a 'comprehensive distribu-tion center', the IMM is the second largest building in Singapore and houses a huge number of overseas and domestic manufacturing representatives, wholesalers, freight forwarders, transport companies, and so on in a five story complex with 172,000 m^2 of floor space (Miyashita 1994:158). Like Yaohan's initial venture, the Singapore IMM represents a coincidence of needs, in this case between Yaohan, which wanted to rationalize its procurement operations in order to make them more competitive, and the Singaporean government's desire to modernize what it felt to be an as yet backward distribution system. According to Wada, it was at the insistence of the Singaporean government that Wada tripled the size of his planned complex (Wada 1995:132–4).

Yaohan's next step in its expansion in the Greater China market occurred when it entered Hong Kong in 1984. Thanks to the British colony's open economy, the Hong Kong retail sector represented a field already crowded with Japanese-owned retailers, many of whom were by this time also pursuing local consumers in an economy that was beginning to show signs of a NIC-style 'take-off'. Indeed, according to one estimate, Japanese firms accounted for 20 per cent of total sales by department stores and supermarkets as early as 1982. By 1988 this figure had jumped to 35 per cent and then to 44 per cent in 1990 (Okamoto 1995:34). Yaohan distinguished itself from the other Japanese retailers and reaped its 'pioneer's profit' by avoiding the central city and high income areas that were the target sites of most Japanese retailers, and by concentrating its energies on opening stores in suburban areas and new housing developments (Gargan). There, reflecting Yaohan's earlier experiences, its stores were able to capture a competitive niche based on a more 'advanced' and westernized (albeit with a Japanese flavor) system of marketing relative to existing local competitors.

During the late 1980s, when Yaohan was focusing on its Hong Kong operations, Wada made it a point to establish connections with the Hong Kong economic elite, including the multi-billionaire tycoon Li Kashing, 'sugar king' Robert Kwok, and Macau's 'casino king' Stanley Ho. It was at this time, in particular, that Wada apparently deepened his understanding of Chinese business practices, and it was on the basis of this newfound knowledge that he and Yaohan gradually developed both a new philosophy of management and ambitions to enter the mainland China market. In Wada's own words:

> I was able to get to know the bigwigs among the overseas Chinese and was blessed with the opportunity to study their ways of thinking for a period of five years. If I had not had this experience and had continued to think like a typical Japanese, I would not have considered engaging in various kinds of negotiations with the Chinese government or engaging in various kinds of business transactions in China.
>
> (Wada 1995:103)

Among the lessons that Wada claims to have learned while in Hong Kong were the importance of personal connections with key decision makers, a top-down style of management that allows for a quick response to emerging opportunities, a stress on profit margins rather than on market share, entrepreneurial boldness and a willingness to take and absorb risks, and a strong faith in the future economic prospects of the Chinese market. Aside, perhaps, from the last, all of these, it might be noted, represented characteristics that were foreign to the consensus-based, market share oriented ideal that typified the Japanese firm. Applying the knowledge that Wada was gaining in Hong

241

Kong, Yaohan expanded during the late 1980s into several other Asian countries with sizable ethnic Chinese populations (e.g. Malaysia, Brunei, Taiwan and Thailand).

The tentative culmination of the Sinicization of Yaohan, however, occurred in May of 1990 when, in the midst of a post-Tiananmen slump, the headquarters of the Yaohan group was moved to Hong Kong. In the process, Wada also made it much easier to adopt a 'top-down,' quick-to-seize-an-investment-opportunity style of management – with a three-pillared emphasis on retail stores, restaurants, and real estate development – by organizing a diversified corporate group, Yaohan International Holdings, with an initial capitalization of HK$50 million. It ultimately shifted US$450 million in working capital (Ozawa 1990; Wada 1994). The holding company, a form that is legally prohibited under Japan's Antimonopoly Law, was incorporated in part with a financial cache earned by selling assets in what was at the time a booming Japanese stock market. Although the move was to Hong Kong, the target was mainland China, of which Hong Kong would become a part in 1997. Wada himself described his motivation in doing so as follows:

> The Twenty-First Century will be the century of Asia. Asia will surely follow the path that Japan took when it experienced its high economic growth and became an economic power. The eye of this big typhoon will be China. I chose Hong Kong as the best site for an Asian strategy that will include China in the Twenty-First Century.
>
> (quoted in Miyashita 1994:154)

Ties with mainland Chinese interests deepened, as is evidenced by the China International Trust and Investment Corporation's (CITIC)'s 1993 acquisition of ten per cent of the stock in the Yaohan holding company (*Asahi Shinbun* 1996:13). The flip side of this Sinicization was a de-Japanization of Yaohan. The company's relations with Japanese bankers deteriorated to the point that no bank was willing to claim to be the group's main bank, thereby further marginalizing its status within the Japanese business community (Nishimura 1996:53).

The Liberalization of China's Retail Sector and Yaohan's Global Strategy

Japanese retailers, like their non-Japanese and non-retailer counterparts, have not been immune to the 'China dream' of doing well in a market that encompasses one quarter of the world's population (Carroll 1996). China's stellar economic growth performance and the consonant development of mass popular consumption in recent years have only whetted these dreams further. One fundamental problem for Japanese retailers, and retailers from any other country for that matter, has been that foreigners were formally prohibited from entering the retail and distribution sector in China, although it was not impossible to get around the regulations by setting up small-scale ventures with Chinese partners. In 1992, however, it became possible on an 'experimental basis' for foreign firms to open stores in six cities (Shanghai, Beijing, Guangzhou, Tianjin, Qingdao, and Dalian) as well as in China's special economic zones (Shenzen, Zhuhai, Shantou, Xiamen, and Hainan). A number of conditions were attached to entry: stores were required to take the form of a joint venture with a Chinese partner; although these ventures could apply for import-export licenses, they could not engage in trade agency activities or in wholesaling; nor could the amount of merchandise imported exceed 30 per cent of turnover. As of 1996, fourteen stores had been authorized, with the size of the ventures involved ranging from $4.5 million to $100 million and 21,000 to 100,000 m^2 in sales area. Six of these involved Hong Kong partners, four of them Japanese, two Thai, and one each from Singapore and Malaysia. In June 1996, a further rule change made it possible to have foreign participation in joint ventures involved in wholesaling, albeit under relatively tight supervision (*JETRO* 1994; *Keizai no 'me'* 1996).

Behind this change in policy is a conscious national development policy. Prior to the period of economic reform after 1979, the production and consumption of consumer goods were deliberately de-emphasized, with the result that a large and sophisticated consumer goods distribution system was not required. As in producer goods, the state sector dominated the production and distribution of manufactured consumer goods and therefore suffered from characteristic bureaucratic rigidity that created tremendous inefficiencies and inflexibility for the procurement of merchandise. Supplementing the formal system was a bargaining-based informal system of private distribution in fresh produce and less sophisticated consumer items, but this informal system was rudimentary and extremely limited in scope. With the reduction in the role of the state sector and the rapid rise in the level of mass consumption after the economic reforms were initiated, the need for efficient and flexible distribution channels increased dramatically. The state had attempted to address some of the problems, but in the past there was a tendency to emphasize the 'hardware' aspect of the problem – that is, roads, railroads, harbors, airports – while ignoring the 'software' of distribution services (Negishi 1994). The result has been that distribution remains a serious bottleneck in the development of large-scale commercial ventures. Indeed, one chronic problem that retailers have faced is that of maintaining stocks of well-selling items, since, once an item runs out, it can take weeks or months to obtain a replacement supply (Matsudaira 1994).

The importance to the development of a market economy of a well-developed and efficiently functioning private distribution system, especially in its 'software' aspect, was belatedly recognized in recent years and it was precisely this kind of recognition that led to the opening up of Chinese retailing to foreign ventures. In the words of one Chinese government spokesman:

> Until now China has held the 'four modernizations' [of industry, agriculture, defense and science] as our goal. . . Recently we have come to understand that we cannot realize a market economy unless we have development in the distribution sector and without modernization of distribution we have little hope of attaining the modernization of industry and agriculture.
>
> (Zhang 1994)

A policy of modernizing the distribution system was incorporated into a document entitled 'The Decision of the CCP Central Committee on Some Issues Concerning the Establishment of a Socialist Market Economic Structure (14 Nov. 1993)' that was passed at the Third Plenary Session of the Fourteenth Central Committee of the Chinese Communist Party. This was followed by the establishment of a Ministry of Internal Trade (which fused the earlier division of functions based on the distinction between production and consumer goods) to oversee the development of an effective and efficient internal market system.

The way in which the desired direction of reform has been expressed has been that of moving from a distribution system that is closed, small in number, and multi-leveled to one that is open, great in number, and minimally layered (Xin 1994). That is, previously a given distribution channel tended to handle only a limited number of products from a limited number of sources heading toward a limited number of destinations. It could not be used for the distribution of other goods (i.e., it was 'closed'); there was one or a limited number of channels to choose from for a given product (channels were few in number), and the number of transactions involved in moving from the point of origin to the final consumer was great in number (multi-leveled). The purpose of the reform of the distribution system has been to increase the flexibility and efficiency of the system, by encouraging channels that are open (i.e., products are not restricted to one particular channel), great in number (alternative channels can be chosen depending on the need), and characterized by a small number of steps. Domestically, this transformation is being encouraged in the following ways: the formation of privately owned and private-state joint ventures to fill various distribution niches, the privatization of state distribution functions (to the point that 90 per cent of consumer goods are handled through market rather than state-controlled transactions), a reduction in the number of regulations and controls on the flow of goods, and the establishment of specialized wholesale markets (Zhang 1994; *Keizai no 'me'* 1996).

The opening up of the retail sector to foreign interests fits into this larger scheme for the modernization of China's distribution system. Foreign participation in China's retail sector – particularly through the joint venture format – would provide not only capital but also an opportunity to attain technological transfer in that elusive 'software' aspect. In addition, since foreign-linked department stores and other large-scale retail outlets would presumably have a substantial proportion of their merchandise imported from overseas, such ventures are considered useful in tightening the previously institutionally estranged linkage between China's international trade sector and domestic distribution, thereby facilitating more effective integration of China into the world economy. Foreign retailer investment in the area of chain stores is particularly encouraged as these are seen as institutions that effectively combine wholesaling and retailing in a unitary fashion.

Yaohan's move into the mainland Chinese market has been remarkably attuned to this development strategy. It has been reported that representatives of Yaohan first met with Chinese government officials to discuss the possibility of a Yaohan investment in mainland China in October 1990, just five months after Yaohan set up its Hong Kong headquarters. The result of this initial meeting was a joint venture restaurant project. Yaohan then opened a 1,450 m^2 department store in Shenzhen in September 1991 – also a joint venture in which Chinese investors held a majority (51 per cent) interest, the only feasible means of investing given that the retail sector had not been opened to foreign capital (Miyashita 1994:157). Both of these, it might be noted, predated the change in regulations opening up the retail sector to foreigner investors, but they were considered justifiable in light of Shenzhen's role as a laboratory for testing reform policies.

Initially, Yaohan's investments in China focused on commercial developments in the Beijing area, where Li Kashing was also active. The centerpiece here was a joint venture between Yaohan and China Venturetech Investment Corporation, a state-controlled company backed by the Ministry of Finance and the State Science and Technology Commission. The Beijing department store, which opened in 1992, experienced a number of problems, and Yaohan eventually cut back on its activities in the capital (to the point of liquidating its interests in key ventures) (Sender 1995). Yaohan then shifted its attention to Shanghai. The move may very well have involved a shifting of personal allegiances based on a politically astute reading of the Chinese political context. Jiang Zemin moved from Shanghai to his current post following the Tiananmen incident. It was only after this move that economic liberalization and marketization began to take off in Shanghai, previously a rather conservative city commercially. Among the core projects associated with Shanghai's rise to a status as the center of commercial development emphasis was the Pudong development district, where Yaohan would participate actively and eventually move its headquarters. Beijing's star, by contrast, declined along with that of key backers of Beijing projects like Chen Xitong.[1]

In any event, when the formal rule changes did occur, Yaohan took advantage of them immediately and then integrated these into an ambitious global strategy aimed at making it the largest retailer in Asia shortly after the arrival of the Twenty-First Century. Its expansion into mainland China so far has been built on three interlinked pillars. The first such pillar is the establishment of a Yaohan commercial presence in China centering on its massive NEXTAGE complex in Pudong where construction began in September 1992 and the store opened in December 1995. As a demonstration of the seriousness of its claim that it will become China's largest retail chain by that time, Yaohan moved its headquarters from Hong Kong to the NEXTAGE complex in July 1996. The second pillar is the opening up of a large wholesale and distribution center (IMM) that, as will be discussed in greater detail in a moment, is the hub of a global Yaohan distribution and retail empire. An agreement with Beijing officials to construct the IMM in that city was reached in June 1993, but Yaohan subsequently changed its plans and chose to build the site in Shanghai. The $54 million IMM opened in the Min Xing district in June 1995. The third pillar is an ambitious plan announced during the summer of 1992 to open a chain of 1,000 Yaohan supermarkets in China by the year 2010, beginning with four stores that were opened in Shanghai in 1994. The date of the plan's completion was subsequently moved forward to 2005 (Miyashita 1994; Wada 1995:6–35).

Given the preceding discussion, one can easily spot parallels between Yaohan's Singapore strategy and the approach that it has taken in China. Like Yaohan's initial Singaporean entry, it is a strategy that has been geared toward realizing commercial advantage and early entry by attuning the company's investments to the development priorities of the host country. We have already discussed how, as in the Singaporean state, a key rationale for liberalizing foreign investment in the retail sector on the Chinese side is to benefit from technology transfer and obtain capital that can be used to modernize the retail and distribution sectors of the host country. It is thus no coincidence that Yaohan's massive shopping complex is located in Pudong, a huge state-run urban development project that aims to create, virtually from scratch, a brand new and highly modern financial district. The Shanghai IMM, the construction of which made Yaohan the first foreign company to establish a wholesaling operation, involved it in contributing to state modernization efforts in distribution, by building and operating a new wholesale market outlet that will, if current plans are implemented, play an important role in advancing the integration of China into the global economy. This it will do by creating distribution channels not only for Yaohan but for other Chinese marketers as well. On Yaohan's part, as a number of observers have pointed out, Wada's connections with key Chinese officials have served him well in accomplishing feats such as the opportune obtaining of the multiple licenses required from several different agencies. It has also given him a chance to reap the 'pioneer's profit' that has been an essential feature of Yaohan's business strategy in the past.

At the same time, however, Yaohan's China strategy goes beyond that which it pursued in Singapore, for China in the Yaohan vision is not just another market, but rather a linchpin in a grand Asian strategy that is aimed at making Yaohan the largest retailer in Asia (Miyashita 1994; Wada 1994, 1995:132–44). As Wada outlines in a recent book, the Shanghai IMM is conceived as an export hub for distributing low-cost Chinese products to be sold in Yaohan stores around the world:

> It is our intention to make the Shanghai IMM the base for product development for Yaohan as a whole which aims to create 'the world's most inexpensive products'.
>
> (Wada 1995:134)

Given the tremendous price differentials between Japan and China, and the fact that Japan remains Yaohan's home market, it is not surprising to find that Japan figures prominently as a target market. It is precisely for this reason that Yaohan, with the proposed participation of CITIC, is currently promoting the construction of the so-called Asia-Pacific Import Mart (AIM) or, alternatively, the Kitakyūshū IMM, in the south-western Japanese city of Kitakyūshū. Like the Kitakyūshū facility, the Singapore IMM would then serve as a trans-shipment point for Chinese products servicing stores in the ASEAN region. Yaohan plans to build a fourth IMM in Seoul, with the participation of the Samsung group, as a distribution hub for products in the mid-level price range. Both the Seoul and the Kitakyūshū IMMs are scheduled to be completed in 1998. Should these bold plans become a reality, China, as both Yaohan's largest and primary customer base and as its primary procurement base, would truly become the functional center of the corporate group's global empire.

Yaohan's China Strategy in Comparative Context

Yaohan, then, has elevated the expansion and diversification of its operations in China to the status of linchpin in its overall global strategy. A number of insights that are useful in assessing the viability of this strategy, and in determining the variables that are likely to shape its unfolding, can be derived from a brief comparison of China's current situation with the political economy of Japan's 'retail revolution'.

Much like China's retail sector prior to the economic reforms, extensive government controls, a heavy-handed de-emphasis on consumption, the forceful mobilization of manpower into other sectors (in Japan's case into the military and war-related industries), and the resulting lack of consumer goods characterized Japan's commercial sector during the war years between 1937 and 1945 and brought retailing as a viable profession to a virtual standstill (Ishihara 1993; Katayama 1993). The revival of retailing in postwar Japan took the form of the black markets that sprouted all over Japan's metropolitan areas in the interstices between the breakdown of the state-administered rationing system and the population's need to meet at least minimum biological requirements in food and clothing. Under conditions where unemployment was rampant, near hyper-inflation existed and where jobs provided only minimal purchasing power, there was a massive influx of population into black market occupations. 'Legitimate' retailing was revived after 1947 as wartime economic controls were rapidly dismantled. Since the revival of manufacturing failed to generate sufficient employment to absorb the unemployed and under-employed population, entry into the retail sector continued to surge. For the decade between 1947 and 1957 the service sector, and within that retailing, was the single largest source of new employment in the Japanese economy.

The significance of this overpopulated retail sector was recognized quite early on as a critical voting bloc and as a social shock absorber. During the early 1950s, a number of measures were adopted to protect and assist this mass of small-scale retailing operations, including the Department Store Law of 1956 that placed restrictions on the location and operations of departments stores.[2] Since the department store was the primary modality for large-scale retailing in Japan at the time, one outcome of this law was to constrain, for the time, the expansion of large-scale retailers. Another was to facilitate a cartel-like order among department stores that helped to alleviate competition and maintain profitability. Both the small-scale retailers and the department stores benefited from legal restrictions on foreign investment that effectively prevented the entry into Japan of foreign mass marketers.

During the late 1950s and early 1960s, two trends that fundamentally shaped the structure and character of Japan's distribution system predominated in the retailing sector (Ishihara 1993; Katayama 1993). One was the increasing control of manufacturers over 'downstream' wholesalers and retailers through their provision of a wide range of commercial assistance services (credit, capital, managerial consultation, and so on) in exchange for agreement on the part of affiliated wholesalers and retailers to honor the guidelines imposed by manufacturers in the areas of pricing, servicing policies, goods and models stocked, and so forth. This kind of manufacturer control over pricing and other aspects of marketing, it might be noted, also typically applied to goods sold in department stores. The second trend, and one which created great instability in the retail sector, was the spread of the supermarket format that was imported from the United States. The turbulence in the industry produced a number of nationwide chains that came to dominate the supermarket segment and threatened the fortunes of existing small retailers and department stores. Among the more prominent supermarket chains to emerge at this time were the current industry leader Daiei, Tōyoko Store, Seiyū, and Itō-Yōkadō. In addition to clashing with the small retailers themselves, the discounting practices of the national supermarket chains provoked the ire of manufacturers of consumer goods in the electronics, cosmetics, and a variety of other product markets with chains of exclusive or affiliated retail outlets. Legislation, entitled the Large-Scale Retail Stores Law, was passed in 1974 to close up various loopholes that supermarkets and other would-be large-scale retailers had utilized to get around the restrictions of the Department Store Law (Upham 1993). This law went quite far in dampening competition and facilitating the survival of Japan's small-scale retail outlets. Some sense of the consequences of the law and various other restrictions on large-scale retailing can be had from the oft-remarked fact that Japan has approximately the same number of retail outlets as the US, a country with roughly twice Japan's population.

As in Japan, the 'retail revolution' that is currently accompanying the restructuring of the retail sector in China involves a transition from a state-controlled, consumption-unfriendly system of distribution to one that is market oriented and dominated by private sector actors. Between 1958 and 1978, 90.7 per cent of goods are said to have been sold through state enterprises. By 1996, this figure was reduced to 55 per cent, but state-owned enterprises still controlled two-thirds of all wholesale transactions *(Keizai no 'me'* 1996). Although the direction is similar to that of Japan in the late 1940s and early 1950s, the degree to which the privatization of the retail sector has occurred is considerably less. Large, state-owned enterprises continue to play a large role in the system (Miyashita 1994). And despite the rather dramatic increase in both the absolute number of individuals involved in the commercial sector, the relative significance of employment in the sector as a percentage of the total population – currently estimated at 2.4 per cent – is a far cry from the situation in Japan in 1950 and 1960, where those with occupations in the retail and wholesale sector accounted for approximately 5 per cent and 7.5 per cent of the population in the respective years.[3] The lesser political significance of this group is further highlighted when we consider the dramatic difference between the postwar Japanese situation and the current regimes run by the Chinese Communist Party, in the degree to which they are sensitive to electoral and other mass political pressures. Finally, the Chinese regime since the reform period has, unlike the Japanese regime, chosen actively to encourage foreign investment as a key instrument for economic modernization.

What all of this adds up to, it seems, is a situation in China that is far less resistant to large-scale mass retailing than was the case in Japan. The slower pace of decontrol and privatization in China, combined with the eventual embrace of state-led development of the retail and commercial sector, has meant that there are rather substantial agglomerations of local capital in the retail sector, particularly at points where state capital and private interests meet. The smaller relative size of the commercial population in China, together with the undemocratic character of the regime, means that resistance to mass retailing will not have the same degree of political impact that it has had in Japan. Indeed, it is arguable that the state can promote retail sector modernization via foreign investment precisely for this reason. And the state's decision to invite foreign retail investment, along with the continuing role of state-owned enterprises, means that there will be a large accumulation of investment capital and readily available models for stimulating innovations in retailing and distribution.

As our earlier discussion makes clear, Yaohan has tried very hard to position itself to take advantage of China's current modus of retail sector modernization. Nevertheless, its position is not exclusively rosy. With the arrival of the 1990s, the profitability of Japanese larger-scale retailers in Southeast Asia has begun to slacken. There are a number of reasons for this. First, in many markets the rush by Japanese firms in the late 1980s led to a saturation of the market and keen competition among Japanese and local retailers (many of whom had adopted techniques from Japanese retailers) aiming for similar market segments. In Hong Kong, for instance, eleven large Japanese retailers were operating some 21 stores (Uemura 1993:97). Similar situations could be found in other Southeast Asian markets, albeit in less acute form. Even booming Shanghai shows signs of commercial saturation. With liberalization leading to a greater availability of western brand name items at more reasonable prices in Japan, the high-quality famous-maker brand luxury goods sold at these stores are no longer as attractive to Japanese tourists. And the very economic development that on the one hand had proven a source of attraction, is also taking its toll in the form of drastically increased rents for store space and a rapid growth in personnel costs throughout the major cities of Asia. In line with this, in the early 1990s a number of Japanese retailers pulled out of key markets.

Yaohan has not been not immune to these pressures and is currently facing strong demands from its financial backers in Japan to cut back on what are perceived to be overly ambitious and risky overseas expansion plans and to put its financial affairs – which in fact appear to be stretched to their limit – in order (Nishimura 1996; Kato 1996; Shirouzu and Warner 1997). Yaohan's operations in Japan, in particular, have faced severe losses in recent years and are the object of financier concern. In a bid to ease its financial woes, in May 1997, Yaohan announced that it would sell 16 supermarkets, one quarter of its retail stores in Japan, to supermarket chain Daiei for ¥33 billion (US$265 million) (*Far Eastern Economic Review* 1997). Not surprisingly, in light of our earlier discussion of Yaohan's global strategy, the group remains extremely reluctant to give up on its globalization plans.

Despite a dramatically increased level of interest in expanding into China, other Japanese retailers have not displayed the kind of aggressiveness that Yaohan has demonstrated in integrating its operations into China's development strategy. This is certainly true of Japan's often conservative department stores, although two Japanese supermarket chains (Daiei, the market leader, and Nichiei) have expressed plans to establish chains of markets in China (*Shūkan Tōyō Keizai* 1994:37). And though the current 'experiment' of the Chinese state probably guarantees a presence for the foreseeable future for those foreign retailers already in the market, just how far the Chinese government is willing to cast its net in receiving any further Japanese (or, for that matter, any other foreign) retailing presence remains an open question whose answer will determine the fate of future would-be entrants. In this situation, Yaohan remains well ahead of the crowd among Japanese retailers and if it can keep its financial coherence it does indeed appear to be in a strong position to reap the 'pioneer's profits' that Wada so frequently touts. However, it also remains in a precariously balanced position as an only partially de-Japanized, partially Sinicized enterprise. 55 per cent of its sales still come from Japan, as do critical banks loans. Should its lenders in Japan pull the rug from under it, Yaohan's global ambitions may never be realized. In the long run, it may very well be that the ultimate winners in this situation will be the large-scale Chinese retailers, as the situation in Chinese retailing today would seem to be ideally suited to a combination of fairly rapid modernization and 'Sinification' of both Japanese and western mass marketing modalities.

Notes

1 I would like to thank Kate Zhou for alerting me to these points. In addition to those in the Shanghai city government, Wada presumably also had connections with Deng Xiaoping and his family (see Rapaport 1995).

2 Another 'threat' to small-scale retailers that was controlled through legislation was consumer cooperatives.

3 The Chinese figure is from *Keizai no 'me'* (1994:44); the Japanese figure is derived from Andō (1984:5–6).

10

FROM JAPANESE SUPERMARKET TO HONG KONG DEPARTMENT STORE[*]

Wong Heung Wah

This chapter is a historical account of a Japanese regional super-market chain, Yaohan, and of its venture into Hong Kong's retail market[1]. Following Sahlins (1990), I see this venture as a dialectic between human practice and social structure, on the one hand, and between Yaohan and Hong Kong society, on the other. Each of these mutually affects the others in such a way that three methodological implications follow. Firstly, Yaohan's Hong Kong venture should be regarded as a multi-faceted historical process which takes into account not only the socio-cultural endowments of both Yaohan and Hong Kong, but the consequences for both of such endowments. Secondly, we cannot treat Yaohan as just another anonymous agent in the global expansion of Japanese companies. Its peculiarities need to be spelt out because their interaction with the local socio-cultural context very much orchestrated Yaohan's venture into Hong Kong. Finally, as this suggests, a comprehensive study of such a venture needs to begin in Japan.

The first part of this chapter, then, takes place in Japan and explores the context in which Yaohan's position within Japan's retailing world should be understood. Here I will examine the company's internal power structure as well as its corporate ideology (based on a Japanese 'new' religion), which together will help us discover and understand the corporate strategy, cultural categories and ideological baggage that Yaohan was to take with it into an unfamiliar Hong Kong market.

* This chapter is based on research conducted for the doctoral degree at the University of Oxford and funded by the Swire/Cathay Pacific Scholarship (89/90 – 91/92), the Overseas Research Student Award, U. K. (89/90 – 91/92), and the Sasagawa Scholarship (1991). The support given by Swire & Sons Ltd, the ORS Award Scheme, and the Sasagawa Foundation is gratefully acknowledged.

The second part will show in concrete terms how, on the one hand, Yaohan's position as a regional supermarket in Japan affected its locational strategy, merchandising policy, and clientele in such a way that it reproduced itself as a Japanese *supermarket* in Hong Kong; and how, on the other, Hong Kong Chinese perceived Yaohan according to their own pre-existing local categories, and embraced the newcomer as a Japanese *department store*. I will show, firstly, how Wada Kazuo, Yaohan's chairman, was instrumental in transforming the company from regional supermarket, first to international retailer, when he made the (to an outsider, somewhat idiosyncratic) decision to start Yaohan operations in Brazil in 1971, and later elsewhere outside Japan; and then to international conglomerate, when he moved the company's headquarters to Hong Kong in 1990, a year after the Tiananmen 'incident' in Beijing, and diversified the company's business there. Secondly, I will show how larger relations and forces – such as the attitudes of Hong Kong Chinese toward Japanese military actions in China and Hong Kong during the Second World War, as well as the politically uncertain future of Hong Kong – created a strong and positive reaction to the arrival of Yaohan in 1984, as well as to its subsequent move of headquarters to Hong Kong, contributing considerably towards the company's success there. Finally, I will show at the micro-level how Kazuo's manipulations of political sentiment in Hong Kong following the 'incident' in Beijing brought about an unintended consequence at the macro-level: Yaohan's advance into China in 1991.

Department Stores and Supermarkets in Japan

My point of departure is the way in which an apparently objective entity like a retailing venture is in fact constituted according to cultural norms. The following discussion is needed here because it helps establish the marginality of Yaohan. The Japanese use two words for department store: one, hyakkaten, is used to describe the old traditional 'dry goods' stores (as discussed by Moeran in this volume); the other, depāto, is a truncated version of 'department store (Larke 1994:166) and is used generically to refer to all such stores in Japan today.[2] Like depāto, *sūpā* is also a truncated loanword and is used to refer to supermarkets which devote themselves not only to food sales but also to the sales of a wide range of merchandise, including textiles, household goods, furniture and electrical appliances. Therefore, the term supermarket refers to a sort of combined self-service food store and mini-department store, similar to department stores in form, and known as general merchandise stores (Takaoka and Koyama 1991:11).

Department stores and supermarkets are different in three major ways: the organization of their operations, the number of their outlets, and their social prestige. Supermarkets are self-service operations with chain-style organization, in other words they separate merchandising and store operations. Department stores, unlike supermarkets, do not differentiate between these functions (Sato 1978:232–3). The second characteristic of supermarkets is their large number of outlets. Supermarket chain stores dot residential areas all over Japan. In contrast, major department stores operate far fewer stores. Departments stores and supermarkets are also different in social prestige, a status rooted in their histories and in the physical location of their stores (Larke 1994:169). Department stores, especially those like Mitsukoshi or Daimaru from the so-called 'kimono tradition', can boast longer histories than supermarkets[3] and, in Japanese business generally, a long corporate history tends to be related positively in consumers' minds to quality and prestige. The 'goodwill created and sustained by stores over a long period of time as a result, for example, of cultural marketing as discussed by Creighton in this volume, leads to a good corporate image (*Table 10.1*).

According to a 1979 *Nihon Keizai Shinbun* survey on the corporate image of retail companies, of the top twenty companies regarded as the most prestigious retailers, sixteen were department stores. Thus, as Larke notes, supermarket chains 'can offer everything that a department store can, except the name and the prestige (Larke 1994:184).

Name	Rank	Type of retailer	Original business	Original business founded	Modern business founded	No. of outlets
Itō-Yōkadō	n.a.	Supermarket	Drug store	1920	1958	149
Daiei	n.a.	Supermarket	Variety store	1957	1958	348
Mitsukoshi	1	Department store	Dry goods store	1673	1904	14
Daimaru	7	Department store	Dry goods store	1717	1920	7
Takashimaya	2	Department store	Dry goods store	1831	1919	10

Table 10.1 Data for Selected Supermarkets and Department Stores in Japan

255

Looking at differences in their business strategies suggests some meaningful connections between the categorical distinctions of prestige and such elements as merchandising policies, prices, locational strategies, and clienteles. Japanese retail experts classify merchandise into two categories according to consumers purchasing behaviour: the first is luxury merchandise *(kaimawari hin)* which, according to a dictionary of commercial Japanese, refers to such items as high fashion, jewellery, musical instruments, and so on. The purchasing frequency of luxury merchandise is low and customers tend to be choosy (Shiono 1989a:73–4). The second category consists of daily necessities *(moyori hin)* such as food, daily items, and household utensils. Unlike luxury merchandise, the purchasing frequency of daily necessities is high and customers tend to shop in stores convenient to them such as those close to their place of residence (Shiono 1989b:314; Okada 1994:14–5).

In order to match their high status, most department stores adopt a merchandising policy which centres on luxury merchandise, and is supplemented by daily necessities. In contrast, supermarkets focus mainly on daily necessities. We can therefore say that the merchandising policies of supermarkets generally stress daily necessities, while those of department stores emphasize high quality luxury goods. High quality goods and comprehensive customer services result in high prices (Creighton 1992:44), which themselves contribute to prestige. As Creighton points out, '[d]epartment stores are not patronized because they are inexpensive (Creighton 1988:91). Supermarkets, due to their emphasis on daily necessities, are less expensive than department stores. In fact, low prices were the *raison d'être* of supermarkets when they started to flourish in the 1960s (Havens 1994:75).

Moreover, consistently with their high status, most department stores, especially those from the 'kimono tradition', have located their stores in the earliest established central business districts, such as Nihonbashi and Ginza of Tōkyō (Creighton 1988:85). Locations at the heart of the most established business areas give department stores an atmosphere of tradition and exclusivity which attracts rich customers. Supermarkets, on the other hand, have located their stores outside the downtown areas and close to residential areas in order to be more easily accessible (Creighton 1988:92; Larke 1994:221). The key point considered here is not an aura of tradition and exclusivity, but convenience, so wealthy customers never constituted their core clientele.

Position of Yaohan Within Japan's Retail World

Despite its international business, Yaohan is still classified in Japan as a regional rather than a national supermarket. A national supermarket must, by definition, operate outlets across more than four prefectures and must have a network of outlets in two or more of the following cities: Tōkyō, Ōsaka, and Nagoya (Nikkei Ryūtsū Shinbun 1993:2). The Daiei, Seiyū, Itō-Yōkadō, Jusco (Aeon), and Uny groups are several well-known examples of national supermarkets.. These companies enjoy a significant share of the market and are invariably on the list of the 'Big Four in Japan's retail industry. Regional supermarkets, on the other hand, are smaller and less well-known.

Yaohan only operates in Shizuoka, Kanagawa, Aichi, and Yamanashi Prefectures and does not run stores in Tōkyō, Ōsaka or Nagoya. Therefore, it is classified as a regional supermarket. As such, it cannot compete with national supermarkets. The difference in corporate strength and reputation between the company and national supermarkets has been significant throughout its history. In the 1960s, for example, Daiei recorded sales of ¥100 billion, while Yaohan's sales were just ¥3 billion (Wada 1995:73). Given its tiny market share, Yaohan, not surprisingly, has never been listed among the 'Top Ten' of Japanese retailing. Even today, although Yaohan has become famous for its success in Southeast Asia, most Japanese living in Tōkyō or Ōsaka are unaware of its existence.

We can see that Yaohan is marginal because it is small in size, has a tiny market share, and operates regionally. More importantly, just as supermarkets generally are less prestigious than department stores, as a regional supermarket Yaohan has the lowest status within the supermarket category. But Yaohan's position in this cultural scheme of Japanese retailers, while important to any further analysis of the company, is in itself inadequate as a cultural explanation to help us understand either the internal dynamics or the corporate strategies of the store in overseas markets such as Hong Kong. Here, we need to look also at the domination of the Wada family over the company and at Seichō-no-Ie, a Japanese 'new' religion which informs company ideology.

Domination of the Wada Family over Yaohan

In December 1930, Wada Ryōhei, funded by his father-in-law Tajima Hanjirō who was the founder of Yaohan, opened a branch store in

Atami, a hot spring resort town fifty miles west of Tōkyō. At that time, Ryōhei's branch was just a village grocery store that delivered groceries to customers in bamboo baskets slung over the ends of a shoulder pole (Wada 1988:35–6). However, it was this branch that grew into an international conglomerate over the next 60 years. This sixty-year span was characterised by one persistent feature: the combined ownership and management by the Wada family.

During the first 30 years, overall management was divided into three spheres: general, operational, and merchandising management. These spheres of management were headed by immediate Wada family members. In 1932, for example, Ryōhei's wife was in charge of general management, Ryōhei himself was responsible for operational management, while his father-in-law sourced merchandise for them from Tōkyō (Wada 1988:54–9). At that time, the fusion of ownership and management had more to do with the size of what was essentially a 'family' enterprise than with the intentional closure of family business to outsiders.

The company expanded to include product lines other than groceries as more of the Wadas joined the company. Ryōhei's eldest son Kazuo joined the company in 1951 and took over his grandfather's job as the company's buyer (Tsuchiya 1991:102). In 1957, having worked in a bakery shop for one year, Ryōhei's second son Terumasa followed Kazuo and helped to establish the company's bakery business (Wada 1988:220–3). In 1962, his third son Naomi became a member of the company and helped to set up the fish, textile, and houseware sections, thereby turning the company into a general merchandise store (Wada 1994:94). At almost the same time, the company started to formalize its managerial system. In 1959, a Board of Directors was established, with all places occupied by the Wadas (Tsuchiya 1991:98).

In 1961, as senior managing director, Kazuo went to the United States to survey retail businesses there. Returning from thc trip, hc advised his father to convert the company into a modern store. Convinced by his son's arguments, the latter appointed his eldest son company president, and himself became chairman (Tsuchiya 1991:138–40). Kazuo then started to build a supermarket chain within Shizuoka Prefecture. In order to fund this expansion, the Wada family decided to sell 30 per cent of the company's shares to employees who had worked in the company for more than three years.

With the employees' investment, Kazuo managed to open ten stores from 1962 to 1970. In 1965, Hanjirō's store merged with Kazuo's branch to become Yaohan's Odawara branch and Hanjirō and his eldest son joined the company's Board of Directors (Wada 1988:233). At the same time, in 1969, the Board expanded and recruited two more members – Mitsumasa, Ryōhei's fourth son, who was responsible for the company's chain store expansion, and the first director who was not a Wada relative.

In 1971, Kazuo started Yaohan's first overseas outlet in Brazil, with the support of the local branch of the new religion Seichō-no-Ie in which the Wadas were devoted believers. This marked the beginning of the third phase of Yaohan's development. Although the company was forced to close its Brazil business in the second half of the 1970s, it continued to open stores in other countries, so that by 1995, the company was operating 57 stores in twelve countries and regions (*Table 10.2*).

The rapid overseas expansion forced the Wadas to start delegating authority to outsiders. The company recruited more and more non-family connected Board members, and by 1977 these exceeded the Wada family members in number. However, the Wadas did not lose their control over Yaohan, since throughout this phase, they occupied the most important positions on the Board, including those of chairman, president, and vice-president. Moreover, in a manner typical of pre-war Japanese *keibatsu*, the Wada family continued to place relatives in important positions.

Funding Yaohan's overseas development also required a great deal of capital. The company was first listed on the Nagoya Stock Exchange

Country	No. of outlets	Year of first operation
Singapore	4	1974
Costa Rica	2	1979
Hong Kong	9	1984
U. S. A.	9	1985
Brunei	2	1987
Malaysia	5	1987
China	19	1991
Thailand	3	1991
Macau	1	1992
Canada	1	1993
U. K.	1	1993
Taiwan	1	1994
Total:	57	

Table 10.2 Yaohan's Overseas Outlets, 1995

in 1983 and on the Tōkyō Stock Exchange in 1986 (Yaohan International Group 1993:47). Although Yaohan thus went public, the Wadas still remained the company's largest shareholders. According to the company's Annual Report, in 1989 five of Yaohan's ten largest shareholders were Wadas, who collectively owned 15.5 per cent of its shares, while institutional shareholders together held another 15.4 per cent of the company's shares (Yaohan Department Store Ltd 1989).

These institutional shareholders were the company's stable share-holders and, as is often the case with Japanese corporate shareholdings, chose not to interfere in the management's handling of company affairs. Instead, they formed a coalition with management and approved virtually anything it proposed. As a result, the Wadas were able to consolidate support from the ten largest shareholders who collectively held 31 per cent of the company's shares.

In 1990, Kazuo moved Yaohan's headquarters to Hong Kong as part of his plan to develop the company from being simply a retailer into an international conglomerate by diversifying its business there. He changed Yaohan's organizational structure according to the *zaibatsu* multi- subsidiary system which, as Morikawa (1992:xxiii) has argued, is the most conducive to the strategy of diversification. Kazuo established in Hong Kong a holding company through which he controlled three newly created groups: the Hong Kong, China, and Macau group; the Japan group; and all other countries group. This third group has its headquarters in Singapore.

Despite the changes, the Wada family still maintained a majority sharcholding of 71 per cent of the holding company which, in turn, owned the company's other subsidiaries (see *Table 10.3*). For example,

Name of shareholder	Percentage of shares held
The holding company	8.3
Sumitomo Trust & Banking	4.1
Long-Term Credit Bank of Japan	3.8
Tokai Bank	3.8
Nippon Fire & Marine Insurance	3.8
Sanwa Bank	2
Wada Terumasa	3
Three other financial institutions	5
Total:	32.8

Table 10.3 Ten Largest Shareholders in Yaohan's Japan Subsidiary, 1990
Source: Yaohan Department Store Ltd., 1990 Annual Report.

the ownership structure of the company's Japan subsidiary in 1990 reveals that the Wada-controlled holding company, together with Terumasa, held 11.3 per cent, while the other stable institutional shareholders collectively owned 21.5 per cent of shares. In other words, the percentage of shares that the Wadas commanded increased from 31 per cent to 32.8 per cent, actually strengthening the family's control of Yaohan's Japan subsidiary.

The Wadas have not only occupied the top management positions but also held effective power. Kazuo was chairman of the whole group and of each of the group's domestic and overseas subsidiaries. He himself also oversaw the Hong Kong, China, and Macau group, while his two brothers, Terumasa and Mitsumasa, were in charge of the Japan and all other countries groups, respectively (Wada 1992:198–9). Other Wadas were also heads or senior members of boards of directors of the group's subsidiaries. Moreover, Kazuo founded a new control mechanism called a supreme council (*saikō kaigi*) which made all major decisions. The supreme council consisted of five members: Kazuo, Terumasa, Mitsumasa, Hanjirō's grandson Tajima Shōichi, and Yamada Zensuke (Wada 1992:196–7; Yaohan International Group 1993:14). With a four-fifths majority in the council, the Wadas were able to dominate the management of the whole group.

The Wada family has thus dominated the management and ownership of Yaohan throughout the company's history. Such domination gives Kazuo, the eldest son of the family, the power to enforce his own mission. But it is important to stress that the Wadas' domination is two-fold. It has been as much a matter of the politics of perception and experience as it has been an exercise in formal management and ownership. The Wadas have been explicitly trying to impose on the company's employees a particular way of seeing and being, to colonize their consciousness with the signs and practices, the axioms and aesthetics of the Seichō-no-Ie religion. That is to say, the Wadas want not only the employees' labour, but also their souls.

Yaohan as A Religious Group

Seichō-no-Ie is one of Japan's so-called new religions (*shinkō shūkyō*). It started in 1930 under the leadership of Taniguchi Masaharu, a former active member of Ōmotokyō, another new religion from which Seichō-no-Ie can be said to have 'branched' (Thomsen 1963:153). Not unlike the founders of other new religious movements, Taniguchi was a charismatic leader who assumed absolute authority over his followers.

Moreover, Taniguchi's whole family – including his wife Teruko, his only daughter Emiko, and his adopted son-in-law (*muko yōshi*) Seicho – managed the entire Seichō-no-Ie organization (McFarland 1967:158).

The core doctrine of Taniguchi's teaching, as laid down in his 40 volume 'Truth of Life' (*Seimei no Jissō*), is that 'human beings are children of God; they have boundless power' (Taniguchi 1962:xii). From this basic doctrine derive several patterns of action. First, since humans share with God the same boundless power, they should have strong self-confidence even in the midst of misfortune. Second, since all human beings are children of God, they should be kind and grateful to one another (Taniguchi 1962:48–9). Third, humankind should develop and internalize an attitude of gratitude, both to and for all persons and things. Fourth, this gratitude is elicited by the repayment of favours. The teaching of Seichō-no-Ie: ' Please give, for if you do, your giving will be reciprocated' (*Ataeyo, saraba ataeraren*) epitomises the spirit of this utilitarianism. Finally, this gratitude is further sanctioned by being linked to the health of the human body. Originally, as children of God, human beings should be '[f]rom the beginning, free of sin and free of disease' (Taniguchi 1962:xii). However, since they did not realize their divine nature and also were not able to be grateful for everything, they became vulnerable to sickness. In other words, to cure their disease, they should feel gratitude and realize that they are the children of God.

Kazuo's wife Katsu was the first Wada to be converted to Seichō-no-Ie. Her husband soon joined her, working very hard to spread the message of the religion. Under his influence, his four younger brothers were also converted to Seichō-no-Ie. Wives of the Wada brothers were either members of Seichō-no-Ie or became believers after marrying them (Wada 1988:110–1).

In 1964, Kazuo formally announced that the teachings of Seichō-no-Ie had become the company's management philosophy and that he had established a complete set of employee training programmes introducing the religion's teachings (Tsuchiya 1991:140–5). This set of programmes has helped establish a hierarchy among Yaohan's employees since it presents a world view drawn from the teachings of Seichō-no-Ie and conducive to high productivity, high morale, and labour discipline. Thus, as they are taught that they are spiritually superior and have the ability to overcome any difficulty, employees of Yaohan can be motivated to accept economic and physical hardship. Such motivation has been particularly useful to Yaohan, as throughout its first two phases, material factors were seldom in its favour.

Moreover, the teaching that since humans share with God the same boundless power, they should have strong self-confidence even in the midst of misfortune has helped Yaohan's risky overseas expansions. This set of programmes remains unchanged in the 1990s, and continues to be used by Yaohan both in its domestic and overseas subsidiaries.

From 1964 onward, every employee of Yaohan has been required to be a believer in Seichō-no-Ie (Tsuchiya 1991:140). As a result, the standards of behaviour and thought usually applied solely to believers in the religion have been extended to the whole company staff with ritual phrases from Seichō-no-Ie such as 'Put hands flat together, thank you very much' (*Gasshō, Arigatō gozaimasu*) becoming not only the orthodox ideology of the company but part of the dominant daily discourse of the employees. Every article published in the company magazine must start with this phrase, which, according to one of my Japanese informants, has even been printed on Yaohan's letterhead. The broad and sustained application of these religious standards to all Yaohan staff has been a distinctive feature of the company, which has become not just an international conglomerate but also a religious group.

The three features of Yaohan reviewed above – its position as a regional supermarket in Japan's retailing world, the Wada family's dominance in the company's organizational structure, and the adoption of Seichō-no-Ie beliefs as the company's ideology – then articulated with another set of elements, such as the socio-political context of Hong Kong and the local categorization of department stores and supermarkets which together have affected the history of Yaohan's venture into Hong Kong. At this point, we make a radical jump in setting from Japan to Hong Kong, where Yaohan established its first outlet in 1984.

Yaohan's Arrival in Hong Kong

At the beginning of the 1980s, Sino-British negotiations over the future of Hong Kong brought a sharp downturn in economic growth. The prices of shares, land, and real-estate plummeted between 50 and 70 per cent from their peak in 1981 (Jao 1987:58). The Hang Seng Index (the Hong Kong equivalent to the Financial Times or Dow Jones Index) plunged 63 per cent, from 1810.2 in 1981 to 676.3 in December 1983. Land values dropped by an average of 60 per cent in 1982. Capital investment in plants, machinery, and equipment reached a negative 4.2 per cent in 1983 (Sida 1994:150).

It was during this period of crisis that Yaohan tried to establish outlets in Hong Kong. It is said that a famous local property development company, Sun Hung Kai, was about to complete a shopping centre in Shatin but could not find a large-scale retailer to operate an anchor store there because of the political uncertainties. The developer then turned to Japan. However, many giant retailers there were worried about the future of Hong Kong and unwilling to investment there. Finally, the project was brought to Kazuo who expressed an interest, and both sides started to negotiate terms in 1981.

Negotiations did not proceed smoothly, however, and both sides failed to reach an agreement on the rent, but two years later, when the crisis of confidence in Hong Kong was at its peak, Sun Hung Kai agreed to reduce the rate to half the initial offering price. Yaohan got a 10-year lease from Sun Hung Kai at a very favourable price.

Wada Kazuo: the main historical agent

Kazuo was the driving force behind the Hong Kong project. Many directors of Yaohan, including some of his brothers, opposed the project because they thought that it was too risky to invest in a politically uncertain Hong Kong. However, so far as Kazuo was concerned, risks also meant opportunities. Firstly, opportunities which arose from the political uncertainty that enhanced Kazuo's bargaining power in negotiating an attractive, long-term lease with Sun Hung Kai; secondly, when the developer expressed a willingness to lease to Yaohan most of the shopping centre's space, large enough to enable the company to operate a general merchandise store with which no rival in the Shatin area could compete; thirdly, the company could make use of its experience from Singapore, where it was already operating several outlets, and so ensure its success in Hong Kong which is similar to Singapore in terms of economic growth. Indeed, three members of its Hong Kong project team had previously worked in Singapore.

Given the low rent and the promising market, Kazuo was confident that he could recover his entire investment within nine years, that is, five years before the handover of Hong Kong to China in 1997. Therefore, even in the worst situation, he seemed unlikely to lose money. More importantly, he had the power to enforce his personal decisions, in the first place, by virtue of the structures of the Japanese company in which as chairman he was the most senior person. Secondly, the Wada family not only dominated the management and ownership of the company, but also through the teachings of Seichō-no-Ie influenced the hearts and minds of the company's employees. Kazuo's action was supported by the twin systems of a society and a religion in which the male head of an extended family is accorded respect and power. As a result, Kazuo was empowered as the Wada family's main historical agent, whose own life represented that of the company as a whole and who thus had a disproportionate historical effect on the destiny of Yaohan. 'If I change, the world will change too', he has said (Wada 1992:23).

From regional supermarket to international retailer

Let me cite an example of this. At the beginning of the 1970s, Kazuo adopted a strategy that was somewhat different from that of other regional supermarkets. During the previous decade, while Kazuo was building his chain stores within Shizuoka Prefecture, supermarkets such as Daiei and Seiyū started to go national, establishing stores throughout Japan. This expansion threatened the survival of many regional supermarkets. For example, at the beginning of the 1960s Hoteiya and Nishigawaya were the first and second most prominent regional supermarkets, respectively, in Aichi Prefecture. However, by 1966, Daiei had entered the Prefecture and become the highest ranking supermarket, leaving Hoteiya in fifth and Nishigawaya in seventeenth place in terms of market share. In order to protect their market share from being further eroded by Daiei, Nishigawaya merged with Hoteiya and in 1971 formed a giant supermarket named Uny. This new company regained first place ranking in Aichi Prefecture.

In Shizuoka, Yaohan faced the same threat from national super-markets. However, instead of merging with other regional super-markets, or being taken over, the company chose to go overseas. Yaohan, Kazuo repeatedly stressed, should keep its own identity (Ono 1992:34–6). Most of the employees, including Board members, opposed the plan at the time, arguing that the company should concentrate on its domestic market instead of spreading its already limited capital base by moving into an unknown overseas market (Itagaki 1990:105–6). Kazuo tried to convince his subordinates with Sony's 'gap theory'. He recalled that,

At that time, the big names in the Japanese distribution circles had developed powerful retail chains yielding a turnover of over ¥100 billion per year. While thinking there would be no other way for Yaohan to survive unless we managed to advance to Tōkyō, but faced with the knowledge that we lacked both the capital and staff to do so. . . It was at this point that I learnt of the Sony Corporation's "gap theory". . . When Messrs Masaru Ibuka and Akio Morita of Sony were repatriated to Japan after the Second World War and attempted to set up an electrical home appliances company, the leading manufacturers in this field already possessed vast sales networks existing from pre-war times. Sony, perceiving the existence of an "opening gap" in that none of these makers had ever thought of advancing overseas, promptly began to do so, *with the result that the reputation the company acquired in foreign parts was fed back to Japan and enabled them to close the "gap" between them and the existing networks.* . . Following this example set by the Sony "gap theory", I then sought to find a way to ensure Yaohan's survival by adopting an overseas advancement strategy.

(Wada 1992:10–1 [emphasis is added])

In the end, as both company president and head of the Wada family, Kazuo successfully suppressed the overwhelming opposition from employees and Board members and made his first overseas investment in the early 1970s (Itagaki 1990:113–5).

The interesting point here is that although Yaohan's marginality in Japan's retailing world drove it to go overseas, Kazuo's ultimate goal, rather like Sony's, was to return to Japan with a reputation gained in foreign countries that would enable Yaohan to compete with national supermarkets and even department stores. That is to say, Japan was still Kazuo's reference point, at least at the beginning of his overseas mission, so that, at the time, 'de-Japanization' was ultimately a means for Yaohan to become a 're-Japanized' number one.

This point becomes particularly important when we look at why Kazuo attributed general meanings to the consequences of Yaohan's Brazil venture and pronounced the company an international retailer. As we have seen, Yaohan's marginality is both economic and social. In order to become central to Japan's retailing world, Yaohan must succeed not only in its business but also enhance its reputation. From the late 1970s, Japan underwent a period during which so-called 'internationalization' (*kokusaika*) began to replace modernization (*kindaika*) as a powerful political and business rhetoric (Goodman 1993:221). Yaohan itself was granted a Special Enterprise Award for its overseas expansion by Japanese business circles in 1979 (Yakushin 1980:14), while Kazuo was elected several times as vice-chairman of the Japan Chain Store Association in the 1980s. So in spite of his subsequent withdrawal from Brazil, Kazuo continued his overseas strategy and started to build stores in Singapore in 1974 and Costa Rica in 1979. Once again, he overcame the overwhelming objections of his colleagues and even his brothers, and decided to invest ¥8,250 million in the Hong Kong project.

On 9 December 1984, Yaohan sponsored a HK$1 million fireworks display to mark its opening at the New Town Plaza in Shatin. The plaza comprises two four-storey buildings which house approximately 200 stores, including small retail clothing outlets, restaurants, and herbal medicine shops. A walkway is built to connect this plaza to the Shatin station of the Kowloon-Canton Railway, a mass transit system going to the New Territories (Philips, Stemquist, and Mui 1992:22).

Yaohan reproduced as a regional supermarket

Having established its first outlet, Yaohan continued to develop its business in Hong Kong according to its pattern in Japan as a supermarket. First, Yaohan organized all outlets as chain stores centrally controlled by its headquarters, and it operated more stores than other department stores (*Table 10.4*). By the end of 1995, it had nine stores in Hong Kong, whereas most department stores had only one or two.

Second, Yaohan adopted a locational strategy typical of Japanese supermarkets. *Table 10.4* shows that department stores generally locate themselves in the centre of major retail districts such as Tsimshatsui

Retailer	No. of outlets	Location
Daimaru	1	Causeway Bay*
Isetan[4]	2	Tsimshatsui*, Aberdeen
Matsuzakaya	2	Causeway Bay
Mitsukoshi[5]	2	Causeway Bay, Tsimshatsui
Tōkyū	1	Tsimshatsui
Sogō	1	Causeway Bay
Seibu	1	Admiralty*
Yaohan	9	Shatin**, Tuen Mun**, Hunghom, Tsuen Wan**, Yuen Long**, Lam Tin**, Tin Shui Wai**, Junk Bay**, Ma On Shan**

Table 10.4 Number and Location of Japanese Retail Stores in Hong Kong, 1995

Note: *denotes major retail district. **denotes new town, i.e. residential highrise development for working class tenants

and Causeway Bay which are also high tourist traffic areas. Department store retail space in these two districts, as well as Central, comprise about 75 per cent of the value of central retail space in Hong Kong (Philip, Sternquist and Mui 1992:21). This locational pattern is the same as that of their parent companies in Japan.

Yaohan, on the other hand, operates its chain stores in the densely populated new towns unchallenged by any other major retailing presence. It was the first large-scale retailer of any origin to venture into the undeveloped shopping climate of new towns in the New Territories (Philip, Sternquist and Mui 1992:22). The Hong Kong government created these new towns to alleviate the problems caused by limited land resources within the urban core (Wong 1982:120), designating Tsuen Wan, Tuen Mun, and Shatin as new towns in the 1960s, and Tai Po, Yuen Long, Fanling, Sheung Shui, and Shek Wu Hui at the beginning of 1979 (Wong 1982:121–4). *Table 10.4* shows that eight of the Yaohan's nine outlets are located in these new towns (*Figures 10.1* and *10.2*).

Finally, Yaohan's locational strategy implies a clientele and a merchandising policy that are different from those of the department stores. Since department stores locate their stores in major, high tourist traffic districts, Japanese tourists and local people of the middle to upper-middle class are their customers. Thus, as we saw with

Figure 10.1 Outside view of Yaohan's Shatin store, showing the name and logo.

Figure 10.2 A 'supermarket' aisle in Yaohan's Shatin store.

department stores in Japanese cities, their merchandising policy emphasizes not daily necessities but luxury consumer goods such as fashion, jewellery, shoes, and handbags. Matsuzakaya, Sogō, and Mitsukoshi in Causeway Bay, for example, market a strong selection of Japanese up-market designer goods, while the vast Tokyū department store and Isetan in Tsimshatsui offer a wide range of quality merchandise, emphasising children's wear, cosmetics, and fashionable clothing and accessories for men and women.

Yaohan's merchandising policy is also closely related to its clientele. Inhabitants of new towns usually reside in public housing (Chan 1981:41), indicating that an overwhelming majority of Yaohan's customers are working class people since there is an income limitation on those who qualify for public housing (Wong 1982:126). A survey carried out by Chow (1988:25) in Tuen Mun in 1988 confirms this point. More than two-thirds of the households interviewed were living in public housing blocks, and generally had total monthly incomes lower than the average in Hong Kong. Such low average incomes do not necessarily imply low purchasing power, however. In fact, the disposable income of most new town residents has increased since their move to the new towns. Chow's survey showed that the majority of households interviewed actually paid lower monthly rents after moving into Tuen Mun, with the mean decreasing by 24.2 per cent from HK$590.7 to HK$447.9. Moreover, for all tenants included in Chow's sample, rent accounted for a mere 10 per cent of their median household incomes. Even for those living in private tenement blocks, rent seldom exceeded 25 per cent of their median household income (Chow 1988:28). In other words, Yaohan's customers are mostly working class dwellers of new towns with moderate disposable incomes.

To match this clientele, the company adopted a merchandising policy which emphasized the sale of groceries and everyday items that had previously and for the most part been available in neighbourhood shops. In other words, 'one-stop-shopping' has been Yaohan's winning recipe since customers can buy almost everything they need within a single store. Although around 40 to 50 per cent of goods stocked are Japanese brands, Yaohan's emphasis is less on up-market goods than in the Causeway Bay or Tsimshatsui stores.

What is clear here is that Yaohan, in its locational strategy, merchandising policy, and customer targeting, reproduced itself as a regional supermarket in Hong Kong. However, Yaohan's history in Hong Kong has not been simply as a regional supermarket for the people of Hong Kong have themselves perceived Yaohan according to a different set of criteria about what constitutes a supermarket as opposed to a department store. It is to these criteria that we now turn.

From supermarket to department store

As in Japan, the retail industry in Hong Kong is extremely diverse. However, local Hong Kong cultural categories of 'supermarket' and 'department store' have meanings different from their counterparts in Japan. The definition of 'supermarket' used by the Census and Statistics Department of the Hong Kong government entails two major elements: selling foodstuffs as a major item and self-service (Ho et al. 1994:6–7). That is to say, 'supermarket' in Hong Kong refers to stores which devote most of their sales floor space to food. A 'department store', on the other hand, is seen to provide a wider range of merchandise, including food, variety goods, and textile products. Therefore, in Hong Kong a general merchandise store is classified not as a supermarket, as it is in Japan, but as a department store.

The historical development of supermarkets in Hong Kong helps account for this cultural categorization. Ho and his colleagues (1994:9) classify the development process of supermarkets in Hong Kong into three stages: innovation, accelerated development, and maturity. The innovation stage refers to the period during which supermarkets were first established in Hong Kong, beginning in the early 1950s and developing very slowly over the subsequent two decades. In this innovation stage, most supermarkets were run by American operators and according to the patterns of American supermarkets. Since at that time supermarkets in the United States did not include general merchandise stores, supermarkets in Hong Kong from the beginning were self-service and offered only food and some daily necessities. Supermarkets established in the subsequent two stages followed this same pattern which is why a general merchandise store is not classified as a supermarket in Hong Kong.

In Japan, Yaohan is classified as a regional supermarket, even though it is a general merchandise store. However, when Yaohan moved to Hong Kong, people saw the new store according to their own, rather than Japanese, cultural categories of supermarkets and department stores. Yaohan's retail style was unprecedented in Hong Kong, but by encompassing it within a pre-existing category, Yaohan was made conceptually familiar. The unintended consequence of the appropriation was that the company was welcomed as a department store! This was not just from shoppers perspectives, for researchers and journalists of the Hong Kong retail business have routinely classified Yaohan as a department store (Leung 1986; Luk 1987; Shin 1987; Cheung and Yau 1988; Yeung 1990). Yaohan thus conveniently rid itself of the appellation 'supermarket' with its connotation of cheapness. Unlike its Japanese operation, the company no longer had to work to attract up-market customers who would never forget that it was just a regional supermarket and for a while Yaohan's shopping bags enjoyed the same social prestige in Hong Kong as the wrapping paper of some department stores did in Japan. The company did not hesitate to capitalize on this cultural difference and made itself a name in the local retail industry, which was generally dominated by Japanese department stores.

This reputation, however, cannot be explained only by the cultural order of the retailing world in Hong Kong, for Kazuo's capitalization on Hong Kong's political uncertainty was also a significant factor in Yaohan's changing status.

Yaohan's initial success: an unpredictable consequence

First, because no one at that time was willing to risk such huge amounts of money in Hong Kong, Kazuo's decision to do so drew considerable attention from the local mass media. Therefore, although Yaohan was a newcomer, Kazuo became the talk of the community, a factor which greatly enhanced the company's reputation.

Subsequent political developments also favoured the company's business in Hong Kong. Ten days after the Shatin store opened, Zhao Ziyang and Margaret Thatcher, after two years of painful negotiations, signed the Sino-British Joint Declaration in Beijing. Based on the concept of 'one country, two systems', the Joint Declaration promised that Hong Kong's capitalist economic system and lifestyle would be permitted to continue for 50 years after 1 July 1997. The initial reaction in Hong Kong to the contents of the Joint Declaration was one of relief.

Confidence in Hong Kong recovered, if temporarily, and the economy started to grow again. Consequently, until the end of May 1985, most macro-economic indicators appeared to suggest that Hong Kong was enjoying a steady recovery. Because Yaohan had reduced its initial costs by taking advantage of a poor property market in 1982, it benefited even more from the subsequent economic recovery. Its great financial success then enabled the company to list its shares on the Hong Kong Stock Exchange in 1988.

The initial success and transformation of Yaohan from regional supermarket to department store point to the fact that the form and extent of Yaohan's initial success cannot be gauged simply from the 'objective properties' of Kazuo's investment, but hinge on the way that those properties – for example, the timing of Yaohan's venture into Hong Kong, and the company's broad merchandising policy – have been part and parcel of the socio-political context of Hong Kong and the local categorization of supermarkets and department stores. The same can be said for Yaohan's business development since 1989.

Yaohan moves group headquarters to Hong Kong

To the people of Hong Kong, 1989 was a year of high anxiety, helplessness, and desperation. After the Tiananmen massacre, the Hang Seng index shed 22 per cent of its value, the value of property tumbled about 20 per cent overnight, and GDP grew by only 2.5 per cent, substantially below the expected rate (Sida 1994:295). According to the independent agency Survey Research Hong Kong, which conducts regular quarterly polls to gauge political and economic confidence in Hong Kong, confidence levels in July 1989 were at their lowest ever. Fear 'was the dominant reaction in Hong Kong' (Hartland-Thunberg 1990:98).

Under such circumstances, it was not surprising that the desire to leave Hong Kong increased (Wong 1992:3). The number of applications for certificates of no criminal conviction, which are required by most countries in the course of visa applications, almost doubled in the second half of 1989 as compared to the first half. The number of applications for visas to the United States in August 1989 was 85 per cent higher than for the same month in the previous year, while the number for September was up by 233 per cent (Skeldon 1990:505–6). Finally, the number who actually left in 1990 reached an all time annual high of 62,000 (Sida 1994:296). This included the poor and unskilled, as well as those young, educated, middle-class professionals who had hitherto dominated among Hong Kong emigrants.

1989 was also a special year for Kazuo who reached the age of 60, and so completed another 12-year zodiac cycle according to Chinese thought. Like the year of his birth, 1989 was the Year of the Snake. Noting that one characteristic of a snake is that it sheds its skin every so often, Kazuo decided to cast off his own old skin and be reborn, by relinquishing the presidency to his brother, Terumasa (Wada 1992:19–22).

Kazuo's departure as chief of his company at the age of 60 was more nominal than real, however. Kazuo's ambition was to build a unique company (Wada 1992:29). Acting from a perspective different from that of his colleagues within the company and from the Japanese retail industry as a whole, and with his ability to carry out his idiosyncratic interpretations, he came to a different conclusion from those foreign companies who withdrew their investments from Hong Kong after the 1989 Tiananmen massacre in Beijing. In May 1990, he moved his residence, some HK$1,150 million worth of assets, and the group's headquarters to Hong Kong, aiming to use Hong Kong as a base from which to develop Yaohan from simply a retailer into an international conglomerate (Wada 1992:28). No other Japanese corporation had ever done that. Kazuo took up a new position as chairman of Yaohan's headquarters and holding company, established in 1990 in Hong Kong to co-ordinate the activities of its affiliated companies in twelve countries, develop large-scale projects, and control all domestic and overseas subsidiaries.

From international retailer to conglomerate

Having moved to Hong Kong, Kazuo wasted no time in starting Yaohan's transformation by branching out into three other businesses in addition to the original retailing and distribution: catering, international development, and food processing and trading.

Yaohan's first big move beyond general merchandising owed much to the fashion for family dining out that swept Hong Kong during the 1980s, a period of high-speed economic growth. Kazuo entered rather late in the game by taking over a chain of restaurants from a local Chinese which was performing well in Hong Kong, but was able to obtain a favourable price, because many restaurant owners wanted to sell out and flee to foreign countries, but were having difficulty in finding purchasers. As Kazuo admits, this difficulty meant that a Hong Kong company could be acquired at one-third of its normal price (Wada 1992:36) and yet because they had the for the most part survived tough competition in Hong Kong, they were likely to be good business propositions (Wada 1992:38). Restaurant owners would not have been keen to sell the goodwill they had built up if the political situation had not been so bad. Kazuo subsequently listed his new company, Yaohan International Catering Limited, on the Hong Kong Stock Exchange in December 1990 (Wada 1992:193).

He further capitalized on the political anxieties of Hong Kong's business community by expanding into different fields. In 1991, Yaohan acquired 90 per cent of the issued capital of Millie's, an established retailer of shoes and handbags in Hong Kong. At the same time, it took over a famous chain of cake shops, a game centre, and a well-known food producer, the last of which was also listed on the Stock Exchange at the end of 1992 (Wada 1992:194–5). Thus, within two years, the chief engines of Kazuo's business legacy in Hong Kong were all on track: a department store, a specialty shop, a cake shop, a game centre and a food processing company. Yaohan was no longer simply a large-scale retailer. It had successfully diversified into other businesses and become an international conglomerate.

Yaohan's China Development: An Unintended Consequence

Of course, Yaohan's destiny was not totally at the whim of its chairman. Moving Yaohan's headquarters to Hong Kong may have been the result of one man's personal decision, but this then acquired a historical significance different from Kazuo's original intent during the internal political crisis of Hong Kong in the early 1990s. Kazuo was embraced as an 'extraordinary' person by Hong Kong because his investment boosted confidence in its future at a time when much capital was being transferred out of Hong Kong to North America, Australia, and

Singapore. The local media widely covered and admired Kazuo's move to Hong Kong, so that he suddenly became the talk of the community once again (Wada 1992:7–8). The Hong Kong government was also duly grateful. Kazuo quotes Sir David Wilson, then Governor, as saying in their meeting:

> That an enterprise like Yaohan should choose to transplant its headquarters to Hong Kong and the chairman himself come to reside here and bring along his whole personal assets to invest, and that other enterprises also choose to follow suit, is a sure sign that the future of Hong Kong is indeed rosy, I believe. This is why I am grateful to you [Kazuo] from the bottom of my heart.
>
> (Wada 1992:3–4)

Kazuo himself did not hesitate to amplify the significance of his move through a series of high-profile activities, repeatedly stressing to the media that the Joint Declaration between China and the United Kingdom would be implemented as promised (Itagaki 1990:17). As evidence of his commitment to investing in Hong Kong, he boasted about the expensive offices of his headquarters in Wan Chai and about his mansion on Victoria Peak, a historic building originally owned by the Chairman of the Hongkong and Shanghai Banking Corporation, and symbolising his new status (Wada 1992:4). In order to show the people of Hong Kong that he was determined to become a 'Hong Kong resident', Kazuo repeatedly told the media that he had already obtained a Hong Kong Identity Card (Wada 1992:3).[6]

He went even further by manipulating the sentiment of local Chinese regarding Japan's invasion of China and Hong Kong before the Second World War. Compared with other Asian societies, Hong Kong is free of rivalry and friction between Chinese and Japanese, but wartime memories still lie just beneath the surface. As a Japanese owner of a public relations firm in Hong Kong has said:

> The Chinese still remember the war, but, being pragmatists, they see the Japanese now as financial, successful business people and so accept them on a business level. Hong Kong needs the Japanese; there is much to learn from the Japanese.
>
> (Thome and McAuley 1992:205)

Yet, Hong Kong's Chinese are particularly angered by the selective memory of the Japanese regarding the events of the war. As a Chinese executive in Hong Kong remarked, '[t]he only thing the Japanese remember of the Pacific War is the Atomic Bomb, never Nanjing'

(Thome and McAuley 1992:205).[7] Moreover, the Japanese government has never apologized to the Chinese for its actions during the war. Kazuo, however, always emphasized publicly that since the Japanese had behaved in a terrible manner towards the Chinese during the Second World War, he would not complain if the Chinese government nationalized his Hong Kong stores after 1997. Indeed, if this did happen, he would feel relieved because it would be an opportunity to compensate the Chinese for what the Japanese had done during the War (Wada 1992:174).

Not surprisingly, perhaps, the Mainland Chinese Government was also impressed by Kazuo, since his investment in Hong Kong could be used to convince both local people and domestic and international investors that Hong Kong still had a promising future, as well as to reaffirm that China would honour the promises made in the Sino-British Joint Declaration. As the official newspaper, the People's Daily, wrote when Kazuo bought his Hong Kong office:

> The reason Mr. Wada selected Hong Kong for setting up his headquarters was not only because Hong Kong is a major centre for international finance, but provided a most advantageous tax system and excellent economic growth. And even more important is that China should develop in leaps and bounds in the future and that the Basic Agreement between China and the United Kingdom be implemented as promised.
>
> (translation quoted in Wada 1992:39)

As a result, the Beijing Government openly welcomed Kazuo's move to Hong Kong. Kazuo and his subordinates met with Ji Pengfei, then head of the Hong Kong and Macau Affairs Office, at the Great Hall of the People when they visited Beijing in October 1990, and Kazuo quotes Ji as saying at that meeting that,

> The Chinese government highly rates the transferring of the Yaohan headquarters from Japan to Hong Kong and that the chairman himself has become the Hong Kong resident along with his family. Our government will continue to maintain the present system in Hong Kong after 1997 and the 'one country, two systems' (communism and capitalism) as well. From 1997, we shall be throwing our full support behind Hong Kong.
>
> (Wada 1992: 176)

For his part, Kazuo recalls that upon arrival at Beijing Airport, he was greeted enthusiastically by representatives of the Chinese government.

It not only suprised but astounded him to see a police car with blinking red lights escort him non-stop all the way to the city centre:

> For China to invite a foreign distribution company is an extremely exceptional case, I understand. We were accorded the same treatment as state guests. The place we stayed at in Beijing was the Diaoyutai State Guest House, where President Bush, Prime Minister Thatcher, Dr Kissinger and other VIPs representing their country had stayed. My mother was allotted the room where Prime Minister Thatcher had stayed.
>
> (Wada 1992: 175)

The Beijing government rewarded Kazuo with business opportunities coveted by many other foreign retailers[8] who, lured by annual 20 per cent sales increases, began moving into China once the government began to ease retail investment restrictions in 1992. By then, Yaohan was well ahead in China's retail market ventures, with a joint venture with the Shanghai No. One Department Store Co. to construct a large shopping complex in Shanghai's new Pudong economic zone. The US$200 million complex opened at the end of 1995. Kazuo could not wait until the completion of the shopping centre in Shanghai in 1995, but opened his first store in Shatoujiao, Shenzhen, in September 1991, and a second store in Beijing in December 1992.[9]

These developments led Kazuo to shift his focus from building an international conglomerate to advancing into the Chinese market under the slogan, 'The 21st Century is the Era of China'. When he first moved to Hong Kong, he had not considered China a profitable market, telling the media that China was not rich enough to support his supermarket, although he then hastily added that he did have a plan to build a chain of stores along China's relatively prosperous coastal regions over the next few decades (Yakushin 1990:115–6). However, this was more a vague vision than a concrete plan, which Kazuo did not have the ability or knowledge to realize at the time. According to Kanke Shigeru, advisor at the Japan Research Institute (*Nihon Sōgō Kenkyūjo*), Kazuo told him at a meeting in March 1990 that he did not have any of the personal connections with senior Chinese officials that were considered vital to success in doing business in China. Kanke then introduced a Chinese friend, Ma Hong, at the time director of the Research Centre for Development of the State Council and the China Development Institute. It was Ma who later arranged Kazuo's October trip to Beijing (Nikkei Business 1994:22).

Kazuo was also completely ignorant of China affairs. According to Kanke, Kazuo said to him during the visit to Beijing that he wanted to tell Chinese officials that he would like to thank Chiang Kaishek (Jiang Jieshi), former head of the Nationalist Party, for not demanding compensation when Japan was defeated in the Second World War – without realizing that Chiang was the arch-rival of the 'great leader' of communist China, Mao (Nikkei Business 1994:23).

Kazuo started seriously to consider investing in China when he visited Beijing because he was encouraged by his enthusiastic welcome from the Chinese government. According to the director of the Japan Research Institute who accompanied Kazuo to Beijing, Kazuo felt as if they were part of a *daimyo* feudal lord's procession (Wada 1992:179), when he saw as many as 100 security guards protect the members of his mission and ensure that they would see the Great Wall properly. Not only this, but Wada recalls that 'four sturdy security guards lifted my mother in her wheelchair onto their shoulders and carried her up to the spot where former Japanese Prime Minister Tanaka had climbed' (Wada 1992:1978–9). It was during this visit that Kazuo became serious about investing in China (Nikkei Business 1994:23), so much so that, after forging several successful joint ventures with Chinese companies, he even quietly dropped the idea of building an international conglomerate. At the end of 1992, according to one Japanese staff member of Yaohan, the chairman made an internal company announcement that from then on China would be Yaohan's major target market. As part of this new strategy, he created a company called *Chūgoku Shitsu* (China Room Ltd.) to co-ordinate Yaohan's China projects (Yakushin 1993:76), and recently, he has channelled most of the company's capital into China, even selling some of the company's Hong Kong assets to fund his enterprise. By May 1994, he had already sold the company's Wan Chai office to raise the US$300 million needed for Yaohan's expansion into China.

In sum, Kazuo's decision to venture into China was the unintended product of his personal decision to move to Hong Kong – a decision which was itself transformed by the local political situation, and so acquired an existence of its own. Having learned from the transformation process, Kazuo took full advantage of developments in his emerging corporate policy and so, in turn, reshaped the destiny of Yaohan.

Concluding Remarks

In this chapter, we have seen how Yaohan's venture into Hong Kong developed as 'a reciprocal movement between higher and lower orders, a translation of each into the register of the other' (Sahlins 1990:47–8). Firstly, broad socio-cultural issues, such as the attitudes of Hong Kong Chinese toward Japanese military actions in China during the Second World War and the anxiety of Hong Kong people about their political future, transformed the strictly economic acts of Yaohan's arrival in and transfer of headquarters to Hong Kong into a considerable success in there. Secondly, Kazuo's personal manipulations of political sentiment in Hong Kong after the Tiananmen 'incident' were, as a result of the political consideration of the Chinese government, translated at a higher level into Yaohan's advance into China in 1991. The result of this mutual translation is what Sahlins calls the historiographic hallmark of the event: 'the disproportions so commonly observed between the incident and the consequent' (Sahlins 1990:48).

In short, while Kazuo's decision to move the company's head-quarters to Hong Kong was based on his perception of how best to realize the personal mission that he had set himself, his action was publicly interpreted as extraordinary in the politically uncertain context of Hong Kong. It was the latter which led to his being rewarded by the Beijing government with business opportunities in China. As a result, having started out with the ambition of becoming an international conglomerate in Hong Kong, Yaohan ended up as a company with 'China fever'. In other words, what the press or even Kazuo himself calls 'Yaohan's China strategy' is not something that was strategically planned – unless, that is, we are prepared to deny and reduce the whole venture from a complex synthesis in which different causal series reciprocally mediated with one another – to a simple episode in which Yaohan rationally advanced into Hong Kong and China in order to maximise its profit.

I have also shown that Yaohan's venture was the product of a process of simultaneous reproduction and transformation. On the one hand, Yaohan reproduced itself in Hong Kong as a regional supermarket thanks to its locational strategy, merchandising policy, and clientele. Kazuo kept to his mission to make Yaohan a unique company, first by extending his overseas expansion to Hong Kong in 1984, and six years later by moving his company's headquarters from Japan to Hong Kong, and by diversifying the company's business there. On the other hand, we have also seen that, by coincidence, the two Japanese cultural categories of 'sūpā' and 'depāto' gained new meanings when transferred to Hong Kong.

So, while Yaohan was busy trying to reproduce itself as a regional supermarket, Hong Kong Chinese welcomed it as a department store.

However, such misunderstandings, distorted perceptions, and fragmented reconstructions can be – and, in this case, were – creatively and successfully adapted to a business situation. Thus, the process of how Yaohan arrived and was received in Hong Kong described in this chapter can be understood as a secondary process within the more general process described in this book of the transfer and reconstruction of department stores from Europe, America, and Australia to Hong Kong, Shanghai, Tōkyō, and elsewhere. As we have seen, the idea of the 'department store' as a new category proved successful as stores were set up one after another throughout East Asia's urban centres. The previous chapters have described the way in which Asia's department stores have often presented the best modern goods and consumer experiences to their respective nations. The processes involved in Yaohan's development and transformation can be seen as continuing this general process *within* Asia, and thus as secondary. In both processes, successful retailers are always the target of competition and hence can become templates for new cultural categories. This is the way business history unfolds itself.

Notes

1 I conducted two years of fieldwork in the company from 1991 to 1993, using participant observation and intensive interviews. I spent my first year of fieldwork rotating among different departments in the company's different outlets in Hong Kong in order to build up the context of the phenomena observed or, in more concrete terms, to observe different aspects of the company and get to know people in different hierarchical and functional positions. Half of the second year was spent conducting intensive research on the Children's Section of one of the company's outlets. The rest of the second year focused on researching Japanese expatriates.
2 The huge Japanese retail industry encompasses a very complex scheme of cultural categories. Japanese retail analysts classify the industry into two sections: one selling without a store and the other selling through a store. The former consists of mail-order houses, telephone sales, and television shopping. The latter comprises shopping centres, discount stores, convenience stores, specialty stores, middle- to small-scale retailers, and large-scale retailers (*Nihon Keizai Shinbun* 1991:52). Large-scale retailers primarily include department stores and supermarkets.
3 Japanese department stores can be classified into two types: those originating from the kimono tradition and those from the railroad tradition. The history of the former can be traced back to the Edo period while that of the latter begins in the early twentieth century. For more detail on these two types of department stores, see Brian Moeran's chapter in this volume.

   Japanese supermarkets cannot boast such long histories. They emerged in Japan only after the Second World War and developed rapidly. In 1953,

Kinokuniya built Japan's first self-service supermarket, and by 1960 Japan already had 1,465 stores (Havens 1994:75). The rapid growth of the supermarket business coincided with the emergence of a standardised consumer market in which everyone with the wherewithal sought the same material goods. Supermarkets successfully capitalized on this market because they could offer the high volume and low profit sales for a limited range of products which best matched this market (Katayama 1986:11–2). At that time, the largest and most prestigious department stores such as Daimaru and Mitsukoshi did not take the supermarket threat seriously. Consequently, the supermarket chain Daiei outperformed Mitsukoshi and became the sales leader among individual retailing companies in 1972. Ever since this symbolic moment, supermarkets have dominated the large-scale retail market (Havens 1994:75).

4 Isetan closed its two stores and withdrew completely from Hong Kong in 1995.
5 Mitsukoshi closed its Tsimshatsui store in 1995.
6 In fact, everyone staying in Hong Kong is required to obtain an identity card.
7 The Nanjing massacre, seen by the Chinese as the main Japanese war atrocity, took place in 1937. It is estimated that more than 300,000 Chinese civilians were killed by the Japanese army at Nanjing.
8 Of course, this is not the only reason for the Chinese government to reward Kazuo with business opportunities. As Carlile demonstrates in the preceding chapter, Yaohan's successful entry into China's retail market has been attuned to the Chinese government's conscious policy of modernising the distribution system. However, I want to suggest here that this policy alone cannot explain why the Chinese government chose Yaohan over other foreign retailers.
9 For more details, please refer to Carlile's chapter in this volume.

REFERENCES

All about Shanghai and Environs: A Standard Guidebook 1934–5, Shanghai: The University Press, 1934–35.

Allison, Anne 1994 *Nightwork: sexuality, pleasure, and corporate masculinity in a Tōkyō hostess club*, Chicago and London: University of Chicago Press.

Andō Yoshio (ed.) 1984 *Kindai Nihon Keizaishi Yoron* (Handbook of Modern Japanese Economic History) 2nd ed., Tōkyō: Tōkyō Daigaku Shuppankai.

Aomen ribao (Macao daily news) 1991, 12–13 March.

Asahi Shinbun 1996 Western Edition, 9 May.

Asia Magazine 1996 Letters to the Editor, 19–21 July.

Asian Finance 1989 'How the Japanese are winning the retailing war', p. 26–7 in 15 (1) (January).

Barth, Gunther 1980 *City People: the rise of modern city culture in nineteenth-century America*, New York: Oxford University Press.

Beijing shangye sishi nian (Forty Years of Commerce in Beijing) 1989, Beijing: Zhongguo caizheng jingji chubanshe (Finance and Economy Press).

Beijing shi diyi shangye ju shiliao huibian (1949–1985) (A Collection of Historical Materials of Bejing's No. 1 Bureau of Commerce [1949–1985]) 1986, n.p.

Beijing Wangfujing Department Store (Group) Ltd. (eds.) 1995 *Celebrating the 40th Anniversary of Beijing Wangfujing Department Store*, n.p.

Bellah, Robert 1957 *Tokugawa Religion: the values of pre-industrial Japan*, Glencoe, Illinois: The Free Press.

Benson, Susan Porter 1986 *Counter Cultures: saleswomen, managers, and customers in American department stores, 1890–1940*, Urbana: University of Illinois Press.

Berger, Brigitte (ed.) 1991 *The Culture of Entrepreneurship*, San Francisco: ICS Press.

Berger, John 1972 *Ways of Seeing*, Harmondsworth: Penguin/BBC Books.

Bergère, Marie-Claire 1989 *The Golden Age of the Chinese Bourgeosie, 1911–1937*, Cambridge: Cambridge University Press.

——1979 'Shanghai ou l'autre Chine, 1919–1949', p. 1039–68 in *Annales, Economies, Societes, Civilisations* (5) (September-October).

Bowlby, Rachel 1985 *Just Looking: consumer culture in Dreiser, Gissing and Zola*, New York: Methuen.

British Foreign Office 1859 'Translation of a Chinese placard in Canton respecting coolie barracoons at Macao', p. 88a-b in FO 97/102A.

Brown, Rajeswany Ampalavanar (ed.) 1995 *Chinese Business Enterprise in Asia*, London: Routledge.

Buck, Pearl S. 1953 *The Man Who Changed China: the story of Sun Yat-sen*, New York: Random House.

Carroll, John 1996 'Japan in the China market', p. 8–21 in *Journal of the American Chamber of Commerce in Japan* (September).

Carlile, Lonny E. 1996 'Economic development and the evolution of Japanese overseas tourism, 1964–1994', p. 11–8 in *Tourism Recreation Research* 20 (1).

Chain Store Age 1988 'Japan: a land of contradictions', p. 25–44 in 64 (3) (March).

Chan, Ming K. 1975 *Labor and Empire: the Chinese labor movement in the Canton delta, 1895–1927*, Ph.D. dissertation, Stanford University.

Chan, Henry Min-Hsi 1995 'Community, culture, commerce: new approaches to the history of the Chinese in Australia', p. 106–17 in J. Ryan (ed.) *Chinese in Australia and New Zealand: a multidisciplinary approach*, New Delhi: New Age International Publishers.

Chan, Wellington K. K. 1994 'The origins and early years of the Wing On Company Group in Australia, Fiji Island, Hong Kong and Shanghai: organization and strategy of a new enterprise', p. 80–95 in R. Brown (ed.) *Essays on Chinese Business Houses*, London: Routledge.

——1993 'Personal styles, cultural values and management: the Sincere and Wing On companies in Shanghai and Hong Kong, 1900–1941', unpublished paper presented at the conference *Urban Progress, Business Development and the Modernization of China*, Shanghai Academy of Social Sciences, 17–20 August.

——1982 'The organizational structure of the traditional Chinese firm and its modern reform', p. 218–35 in *Business History Review* 56 (2).

Chan Ying-keung 1981 'The development of new towns, p. 37–50 in A. King and L. Lee (eds.) *Social Life and Development in Hong Kong*, Hong Kong: Chinese University Press.

Chang, Sidney H. and Leonard H. D. Gordon 1991 *All Under Heaven. . . Sun Yat-sen and his revolutionary thought*, Stanford: Hoover Institution Press.

Chen Duo 1923 *Riyong baike quanshu* (Daily Encyclopedia) 11th ed., vol. 26, Shanghai: Shanghai chubanshe.

Cheng Chu-yuan (ed.) 1989 *Sun Yat-sen's Doctrine in the Modern World*, Boulder, Col.: Westview Press.

Cheng, Allen T. 1996 'Open sashimi', in *Asia Inc.* (August), as posted at <http://www.asia-inc.com/archive/1996/08964yaohan.html> (Asia Inc. Online).

Cheung W. L. and Yau H. M. 1988 'Baihuoye guke dui meiti ji huopin de pianhao' (The prejudice of department store customers against mass media and products), p. 121–4 in *Xinbao yuekan* (Hong Kong Economic Journal Monthly) 134.

Ching, Leo 1996 'Imaginings in the empires of the sun: Japanese mass culture in Asia', p. 169–94 in J. Treat (ed.) *Contemporary Japan and Popular Culture*, Honolulu: University of Hawaii Press.

Choi, C.Y. 1975 *Chinese Migration and Settlement in Australia*, Sydney: Sydney University Press.

REFERENCES

Chow, W. S. Nelson 1988 *Social Adaptation in New Towns: a report of a survey on the quality of life of Tuen Mun inhabitants*, Resource Paper Series no.2, Hong Kong: Department of Social Work and Social Administration, University of Hong Kong.

Clifford, Nicholas R. 1991 *Spoilt Children of Empire: westerners in Shanghai and the Chinese revolution of the 1920s*, Hanover and London: Middlebury College Press.

——1979 *Shanghai 1925: urban nationalism and the defense of foreign privileges*, Ann Arbor: Center for Chinese Studies, University of Michigan.

Coble, Parks M., Jr. 1980 *The Shanghai Capitalists and the Nationalist Government, 1927–1937*, Cambridge, Mass.: Harvard University Press.

Cochran, Sherman 1980 *Big Business in China: Sino-foreign rivalry in the cigarette industry, 1890–1930*, Cambridge, Mass.: Harvard University Press.

Creighton, Millie forthcoming 'From seedling to sophisticated shopper: Japanese store lay-outs and philosophical statements of meaning', in J. F. Sherry (ed.) *Encountering Servicescapes: built environment and lived experience in contemporary marketplaces*.

——1994 '"Edutaining" children: consumer and gender socialization in Japanese marketing', p. 35–52 in *Ethnology* 33 (1).

——1992 'The depāto: merchandizing the west while selling Japaneseness', p. 42–57 in J. Tobin (ed.) *Re-Made in Japan: everyday life and consumer taste in a changing society*, New Haven: Yale University Press.

——1991 'Maintaining cultural boundaries in retailing: how Japanese department stores domesticate "things foreign"', p. 675–709 in *Modern Asian Studies* 25 (4).

——1989 'Japan's department stores: selling "internationalization"', p. 2–7 in *Japan Society Newsletter* 37 (4).

——1988 *Sales, Service, and Sanctity: an anthropological analysis of Japanese department stores*, Ph. D. dissertation, University of Washington.

Cushman, Jennifer 1984 'A "colonial casualty": the Chinese community in Australian historiography', p. 100–13 in *ASAA Review* 7 (3).

Darwent, C. E. 1920 *Shanghai: a handbook for travelers and residents*, Shanghai: Kelly & Walsh.

Ding Ruchu 1992 'Shanghai huazi daying baohuo gongsi de chuangjian wo jingying' (The establishment and operation of Chinese-owned large department stores in Shanghai), unpublished paper presented at *Luce Seminar on Shanghai*, Cornell University, Ithaca, NY, 14–15 August.

Elvin, Mark 1974 'Introduction', p. 1–15 in M. Elvin and G. W. Skinner (eds.) *The Chinese City Between Two Worlds*, Stanford: Stanford University Press.

Endacott, G. B. 1958 *A History of Hong Kong*, Hong Kong: Oxford University Press.

Epstein, J. 1987 *Pioneers in China's Modernization*, Beijing: Heping Publishers.

Ewen, Stuart and Elizabeth Ewen 1982 *Channels of Desire: mass images and the shaping of American consciousness*, New York: McGraw-Hill.

Fairbank, John King et al. 1989 *East Asia: tradition and transformation*, Boston: Houghton Mifflin Company.

Far Eastern Economic Review 1997 'Business briefing', p. 55 (27 February) as posted at <http://www.feer.com/restricted/index_best.html>.

Far Eastern Review 1918 vol. 14 (October).

Ferry, John William 1960 *A History of the Department Store*, American Assembly Series, New York: Prentice-Hall.

Feuerwerker, Albert 1958 *China's Early Industrialization: Shen Hsuan-huai (1844–1916) and mandarin enterprises*, Cambridge, Mass.: Harvard University Press.

Fruin, W. Mark 1982 'From philanthropy to paternalism in the Noda soy sauce industry: pre-corporate and corporate charity in Japan', p. 168–91 in *Business History Review: special issue on East Asian business history* 56 (2) (Summer).

Gan Gu 1987 *Shanghai bainian mingchang laodian* (Famous factories and old shops of Shanghai), Shanghai: Shanghai wenhua chubanshe.

Gargan, Edward A. 1996 'Roots in Japan, vision in China: this retailer finds markets before they're markets', p. C1–3 in *New York Times* (19 June).

Garwood, John 1853 *The Million-Peopled City: or, one-half of the people of London made known to the other half*, London: Westheim and Macintosh.

Glen Innes Guardian 1903, 20 October.

Godley, Michael 1981 *The Mandarin-Capitalists from Nanyang: overseas Chinese enterprise in the modernization of China 1893–1911*, Cambridge: Cambridge University Press.

Goodman, Roger 1993 *Japan's 'International Youth': the emergence of a new class of schoolchildren*, Oxford: Clarendon Press.

Gough, J. W. 1969 *The Rise of the Entrepreneur*, London: T. B. Batsford.

Greenfield, Karl T. 1994 *Speed Tribes: children of the Japanese bubble*, London: Boxtree.

Guangzhou minguo ribao 1930, 21 January.

Guo Le (Kwok Lock) 1949 (dedication date) *Hui'yi lu* (Memoires), n.p.

Guo Quan (Kwok Chin) 1961 (preface date) *Yong'an jingshen zhi fazhan jiqi chengzhang shilüe* (A Brief History of the Origin and Development of the Spirit of Wing On), n.p.

Hahn, Emily 1987 *China To Me*, London: Virago Press.

Hamilton, Gary G. and Lai Chi Kong 1989 'Consumerism without capitalism: consumption and brand names in late imperial China', p. 253–279 in H. J. Rutz and B. S. Orlove (eds.). *The Social Economy of Consumption*, Lanham: University Press of America.

Hannerz, Ulf 1992 *Cultural Complexity: studies in the social organization of meaning*, New York: Columbia University Press.

——1991 'Scenarios for peripheral cultures', p. 108–28 in A. King (ed.) *Culture, Globalization and the World System*, New York: MacMillan.

Hao Yen-ping 1970 *The Comprador in Nineteenth Century China: bridge between east and west*, Cambridge, Mass.: Harvard University Press.

Hartland-Thunberg, Penelope 1990 *China, Hong Kong, Taiwan and the World Trading System*, London: MacMillan.

Hatsuda Tōru 1993 *Hyakkaten no Tanjō* (The Birth of the Department Store), Tōkyō: Sanseidō.

Havens, Thomas R. H. 1994 *Architects of Affluence: the Tsutsumi family and the Seibu-Saison enterprises in twentieth century Japan*, Cambridge, Mass.: Harvard University Press.

——1982 *Artist and Patron in Postwar Japan*, Princeton: Princeton University Press.

He Wenxiang 1989 *Xianggang jiazu shi* (History of Some Powerful Families in Hong Kong), Hong Kong: Shihuatang yinshua youxian gongsi.

Hein, Laura E. 1993 'Growth versus success: Japan's economic policy in historical perspective', p. 99–122 in A. Gordon (ed.) *Postwar Japan as History*, Berkeley: University of California Press.

Hernadi, Andreas 1990 'Consumption and consumerism in Japan', p. 186–191 in A. Boscaro et al. (eds.) *Rethinking Japan. Vol. 2: social sciences, ideology & thought*, Sandgate: Japan Library.

Hidaka, Rokuro 1984 *The Price of Affluence: dilemmas of contemporary Japan*, Tōkyō: Kodansha.

Ho, Kit-yiu Virgil 1991 'The limits of hatred: popular attitudes towards the west in republican Canton', p. 87–104 in *East Asian History* (2).

Ho, Suk-ching et al. 1994 *Report on the Supermarket Industry in Hong Kong*, Hong Kong: The Consumer Council.

Honig, Emily 1986 *Sisters and Strangers: women in the Shangai cotton mills, 1919–1949*, Stanford: Stanford University Press.

Hongqi (Red flag), May 1977.

Horioka, Charles Yuji 1993 'Consuming and saving', p. 259–92 in A. Gordon (ed.) *Postwar Japan as History*, Berkeley: University of California Press.

Huazi ribao 1907, 15 August.

Hung, Humprey Hip-lap 1991 *An analysis of the retailing mix of the Japanese department stores in Hong Kong*, M.B.A. thesis, University of Hong Kong.

Ishihara Takemasa 1993 'Chūshō shōgyō seisaku no kiseki' (The locus of small and medium-sized commerce policy), p. 237–52 in Nikkei Ryūtsū Shinbun (ed.) *Ryūtsū gendai shi: nihongata keizai fūdo to kigyōka seishin* (Modern History of Distribution: Japanese-style economic climate and entreprenuerial spirit), Tōkyō: Nihon Keizai Shinbunsha.

Ishizuka, Hiromichi 1981 'Slum dwellings and the urban renewal scheme in Tōkyō, 1868–1923', p. 169–193 in *The Developing Economies* 19 (2).

Itagaki Hidenori 1990 *Yaohan*, Tōkyō: Pāru.

Ivy, Marilyn 1993 'Formations of mass culture', p. 239–58 in A. Gordon (ed.) *Postwar Japan as History*, Berkeley: University of California Press.

——1989 'Critical texts, mass artifacts: the consumption of knowledge in postmodern Japan', p. 21–46 in H. Harootunian and M. Miyoshi (eds.) *Postmodernism and Japan*, Durham and London: Duke University Press.

——1988 'Tradition and difference in the Japanese mass media', p. 21–30 in *Public Culture* 1 (1).

Jao, Y. C. 1987 'Hong Kong's economic prospects after the Sino-British Agreement: a preliminary assessment, p. 57–94 in Chiu H. et al. (eds.) *The Future of Hong Kong: toward 1997 and beyond*, New York: Quorum.

JETRO China Newsletter 1994 'Retail and wholesale distribution of consumer goods in China', p. 16–8 in 112 (September–October).

Katayama Mataichirō 1993 'Kindaika no katei' (The process of modernization), p. 3–39 in Nikkei Ryūtsū Shinbun (ed.) *Ryūtsū gendai shi: nihongata keizai fūdo to kigyōka seishin* (Modern History of Distribution: Japanese-style economic climate and entrepreneurial spirit), Tōkyō: Nihon Keizai Shinbunsha.

——1986 *Jusco: genba no ei tachi* (Jusco: the heroes on the sales floor), Tōkyō: Hyōgensha.

Katō Kō 1996 'Shikinguri ni kutōsuru Yaohan no akiresu ken' (Yaohan's Achilles heel as it struggles to juggle its financing), p. 12–4 in *Shūkan Daiyamondo* (Diamond Weekly) (2 December).

Kawabata Tai 1986 'Council spells out goals of education', in *Japan Times* 24 April.

Keizai no 'me' (Economic 'Eye') 1996 'Chūgoku ryūtsūgyō no taigai kaihō' (The liberalization of China's distribution industry), p. 24–5 in 44 (May).

Keuh, Y. Y. 1992 'Foreign investment and economic change in China', p. 637–690 in *The China Quarterly* 132 (September).

King, Y. C. Ambrose and Lance P. L. Lee (eds.) 1981 *Social Life and Development in Hong Kong*, Hong Kong: Chinese University Press.

Kinsella, Sharon 1995 'Cuties in Japan', p. 220–54 in L. Skov and B. Moeran (eds.) *Women, Media and Consumption in Japan*, London: Curzon.

Kinoshita Ritsuo and Ashimura Jirō 1980 *Seinenjō o Mukaeru Okada Taisei: Mitsukoshi* (Okada's Youth Targeting Strategy: Mitsukoshi), Tōkyō: Asahi Sonorama.

Knt, A. L. 1833 'Contribution to an historical sketch of the Portuguese settlements in China, principally of Macao; of the Portuguese envoys and ambassadors to China; of the Catholic missions in China; and of the papal legates to China', p. 398–408 in *The Chinese Repository* vol. 1 (May 1832-April 1833).

Kondo, Dorinne K. 1990 *Crafting Selves: power, gender, and discourses of identity in a Japanese workplace*, Chicago: University of Chicago Press.

Lambert, R. A. 1938 *The Universal Provider: a study of William Whiteley and the rise of the London department store*, London: Harrup.

Larke, Roy 1994 *Japanese Retailing*, London and New York: Routledge.

Leach, William 1993 *Land of Desire: merchants, power, and the rise of a new American culture*, New York: Pantheon Books.

Lee Sim Loo 1984 *A Study of Planned Shopping Centres in Singapore*, Singapore: Singapore University Press.

Leung K. Y. 1986 'Riben baihuo gongsi dui Xianggang baihuoye de chongji yu gongxian' (Japanese department stores' impact on and contribution to Hong Kong department stores), p. 29–31 in *Xinbao yuekan* (Hong Kong Economic Journal Monthly) 10 (4).

Levenson, Joseph 1968 *Confucian China and Its Modern Fate: a trilogy*, vol. 1, Berkeley and Los Angeles: University of California Press.

Levy, Marion J., Jr. and Shih Kuo-heng 1949 *The Rise of the Modern Chinese Business Class: two introductory essays*, New York: Institute of Pacific Relations.

Lin Jinzhi 1986 'Aozhou Zhongshan huaqiao zai Shanghai touhuode qiye' (Shanghai enterprises funded by Australian overseas Chinese from Zhongshan), p. 5–19 in *Zhongshan wenshi* 8–9, 25 August.

Liu Huiwu (ed.) 1985 *Shanghai jindai shi* (A Modern History of Shanghai), vol. 1, Shanghai: Huadong shifen daxue chubanshe.

Liu Tianren 1932 'Ben gongsi erhshiwu zhounian ji jiangguo' (The historical records of Wing On in the last twenty-five years), p. 1–12, shilue (History column) in *Xianggang Yong'an youxian gongsi ershiwu zhounian jinian lu* (The Wing On Company Limited, Hong Kong: in commemoration of the 25th anniversary, 1907–1932), Hong Kong: Tianxing yinwu ju.

Liu Yuzun et al. 1982 'Huaqiao Xining tielu yu Taishan' (Overseas Chinese, Xining railways and the Taishan District), p. 304–40 in *Huaqiao lunwenji* (Studies of Overseas Chinese), vol. 1, Guangzhou: Huaqiao lishi xuehui.

Lo Bohua and Deng Guangbiao 1969 'Cong Su-Hang duo baihuo' (From Suzhou and Hangzhou style shops to department stores), p. 228–50 in *Guangzhou wenshi ziliao* (Historical Materials on Guangzhou) (20).

Lord & Taylor 1926 *The History of Lord & Taylor (Centennial Publication)*, New York: Lord & Taylor.

Lu Hanchao 1995 'Away from Nanking Road: small stores and neighborhood life in modern Shanghai', p. 93–123 in *Journal of Asian Studies* (54) 1 (February).

Luk T. K. 1987 'Mofang rizi jingying moshi nengfou niuzhuan lieshi' (Can the imitation of Japanese management by Hong Kong department stores reverse their inferior situation?), p. 12–4 in *Xinbao yuekan* (Hong Kong Economic Journal Monthly) 11 (6).

Ma Bohuang (ed.) 1992 *Zhongguo jindai jingji sixiang shi* (A History of Modern Chinese Economic Thought), vol. 2, p. 71–172, Shanghai: Shanghai Academy of Social Sciences.

MacMillan Allister 1923 *Seaports of the Far East*, London: W. H. L. Collingridge.

MacPherson, Kerrie L. 1987 *A Wilderness of Marshes: the origin of public health in Shanghai, 1843–1893*, New York: Oxford University Press.

MacPherson, Kerrie L. and C.K. Yearley 1987 'The $2\frac{1}{2}$ percent margin: Shanghai's British traders and China's resilence in the face of commercial penetration', p. 202–34 in *Journal of Oriental Studies* (25) 2.

Maruki T. 1992 *Ryūtsū Gyōkai Hayawakari Mappu* (A Map for a Quick Understanding of the Distribution Industry), Tōkyō: Kō Shobō.

Matsudaira Sadayuki 1994 'Trends in consumption and foreign retailers', p. 7–13 in *JETRO China Newsletter* 113 (November–December).

McBride, T. M. 1978 'A women's world: department stores and the evolution of women's employment 1870–1970', p. 664–683 in *French Historical Studies* (10) 4.

McFarland, Neill H. 1967 *The Rush Hour of the Gods: a study of new religious movements in Japan*, New York: MacMillan.

Middlebrook, S. M. 1951 'Yap Ah Loy', p. 1–127 in *Journal of Malayan Branch of The Royal Asiatic Society* 24/2, independent issue.

Miller, Michael 1981 *The Bon Marché: bourgeois culture and the department store, 1869–1920*, Princeton, N.J.: Princeton University Press.

Mitsukoshi 1990 *Kabushiki Kaisha Mitsukoshi: 85 nen no kiroku* (Mitsukoshi Co. Ltd: an 85 year record), Tōkyō: Kabushiki Kaisha Mitsukoshi.

——1986 *Press Release of May 11.* Tōkyō: Mitsukoshi Ltd.

Miyashita Kōichi 1994 'Yaohan chūgoku senryaku no kenkyū: sono kiso chōsa' (Research on Yaohan's China strategy: a basic survey), p. 151–66 in *Obirin Ekonomikkusu* (Obirin Economics) 3 (32).

Miyashita Masafusa 1994 'Nihon to chūgoku: ryūtsū no chigai to wa' (Japan and China: how does distribution differ?), p. 16–8 in *Keizai no 'me'* (Economic 'Eye') 22 (July).

Mo Xiangyi and Mo Yimei 1991 *William J. Liu, O.B.E. – Pathfinder 1893–1983*, Sydney: Australia-China Chamber of Commerce and Industry of New South Wales.

Moeran, Brian 1996 *A Japanese Advertising Agency: an anthropology of media and markets*, London: Curzon.

——1987 'The art world of contemporary Japanese ceramics', p. 27–52 in *Journal of Japanese Studies* 19 (2).

Moeran, Brian and Lise Skov 1996a 'A view from afar', p. 181–205 in P. Asquith and A. Kalland (eds.) *Japanese Images of Nature: cultural perspectives*, London: Curzon.

——1996b 'Images of Spain and Europe in Japanese advertising', unpublished paper presented at the *Japan Anthropology Workshop*, Santiago de Compostela, May.

Morikawa Hidemasa 1992 *Zaibatsu: the rise and fall of family enterprise groups in Japan*, Tōkyō: University of Tōkyō Press.

Morris-Suzuki, Tessa 1995 'The invention and reinvention of "Japanese culture"', p. 759–781 in *Journal of Asian Studies* (54) 3 (August).

——1994 *The Technological Transformation of Japan: from the seventeenth century to the twenty-first century*, Cambridge: Cambridge University Press.

Motz, Earl J. 1972 *Great Britain, Hong Kong, and Canton: the Canton-Hong Kong strike and boycott of 1925–26*, Ph.D. dissertation, Michigan State University.

Mukerji, Chandra 1983 *From Graven Images: patterns of modern materialism*, New York: Columbia University Press.

Murphey, Roads 1974 'The treaty ports and China's modernization', p. 17–72 in M. Elvin and G. W. Skinner (eds.) *The Chinese City Between Two Worlds*, Stanford: Stanford University Press.

Nakamachi H. 1986 'Ginza store war, p. 32–6 in *Japan Quarterly* 33 (1).

Nee, Victor and Herbert Y. Wong 1985 'Asian American socioeconomic achievement: the strength of the family bond', p. 281–306 in *Sociological Perspectives* 28 (3).

Negishi Hirokazu 1994 'Issues on China's distribution system', p. 9–13 in *JETRO China Newsletter* 122 (May-June).

Ng Lun Hai-ha 1981 'The Hong Kong origins of Dr. Sun Yat-sen's address to Li Hung-chang', p. 168–78 in *Journal of the Hong Kong Branch, Royal Asiatic Society* (21).

Nihon Keizai Shinbun Inc. (ed.) 1991 *Ryūtsū Nyūmon* (An Introduction to Distribution), Tōkyō: Nihon Keizai Shinbun Inc.

Nikkei Ryūtsū Shinbun 1993 *Chōsahōhō* (Research Methods), Tōkyō: Nikkei Ryūtsū Shinbunsha.

Nishimura Gōtarō 1996 'Yaohan: kabuka haran no shinkokuna "jijō"' (Yaohan: the dire 'situation' behind the stock troubles), p. 52–3 in *Shūkan Tōyō Keizai* (Oriental Economist Weekly) (14 December).

North-China Herald 1917, 20 October; 1918, 7 September; and 1926, 29 May.

O'Donnell, Peter 1985 'Take a lesson (and more) from retailers in Japan', p. 49–54 in *Stores* 1.

Ohnuki-Tierney, E. 1990 'Introduction, p. 1–25 in E. Ohnuki-Tierney (ed.) *Culture Through Time: an anthropological approach*, Stanford: Stanford University Press.

Okada Yasushi 1994 *Hyakkaten Gyō kai* (The Department Store Industry), Tōkyō: Kyōikusha.

REFERENCES

Okamoto Yoshihiro 1995 'Ryūtsūgyō no kokusaika' (The internationalization of the distribution industry), *Wako Keizai* (Wako Economics) 27 (2) (January).
Ono Hiroshi 1992 *Naze Yaohan no Kourishōhō dake ga Kaigai de Seikō suru no ka?* (Why Does Only Yaohan's Retailing Business Strategy Succeed Overseas?), Tōkyō: Asuka.
Orru, Marco et al. 1997 *The Economic Organization of East Asian Capitalism*, Thousand Oaks: Sage Publications.
Ozawa Kiyoshi 1990 'The vision of Chairman Kazuo Wada, cosmopolitan retailer', *Tōkyō Business Today* 58 (8) (August).
Panglaykim, J. and I. Palmer 1970a *Entrepreneurship and Commercial Risk: the case of a Schumpeterian business in Indonesia*, Singapore: Nanyang University.
——1970b 'Study of entrepreneurship in developing countries: the development of one Chinese concern in Indonesia', p. 85–95 in *Journal of Southeast Asian Studies* 1 (1) (March).
Parco Editorial Board (ed.) 1989 *Ōinaru Meisō* (The Great Diaspora), Tōkyō: Parco Shuppan.
People's Tribune 1956 23 (December).
Philips, Lisa A. et al. 1992 'Hong Kong department stores: retailing in the 1990s, p. 16–24 in *International Journal of Retail and Distribution Management* 20 (1).
Quanguo baihuo hangye xiehui (The Department Store Association of China) (ed.) 1991 *Quanguo shi da baihuo shangdian* (The Ten Large Department Stores of China), n.p..
Rapaport, Carla 1995 'Retailers go global', p. 102–8 in *Fortune* (20 February).
Rawski, Thomas 1975 'The growth of producer industries, 1900–1971', p. 203–34 in D. H. Perkins (ed.) *China's Modern Economy in Historical Perspective*, Stanford: Stanford University Press.
Redding, Stanley Gordon 1991 'Culture and entrepreneurial behavior among the overseas Chinese', p. 137–56 in B. Berger (ed.) *The Culture of Entrepreneurship*, San Francisco: ICS Press.
——1990 *The Spirit of Chinese Capitalism*, New York and Berlin: Walter de Gruyter.
Robertson, Jennifer 1988 'The culture and politics of nostalgia: furusato Japan', p. 494–518 in *International Journal of Politics, Culture and Society* 1 (4).
Robison, Richard and David S. G. Goodman (eds.) 1996 *The New Rich in Asia: mobile phones, McDonald's and middle-class revolution*, London and New York: Routledge.
Sahlins, M. 1990 'The return of the event, again: with reflections on the beginnings of the great Fijian War of 1834 to 1855 between the kingdoms of Bau and Rewa', p. 37–99 in A. Biersack (ed.) *Clio in Oceania*, Washington, D. C.: Smithsonian.
——1985 *Islands of History,* Chicago: University of Chicago Press.
Sakakibara Eisuke 1997 'Reforming Japan', p. 80 in *The Economist*, 22 March.
Satō Hajime 1978 *Nihon no Ryūtsū Kikō* (The Japanese Distributive Mechanism), Tōkyō: Yūhikaku.
Schiffrin, Harold Z. 1970 *Sun Yat-sen and the Origins of the Chinese Revolution*, Berkeley and Los Angeles: University of California Press.

Schivelbusch, Wolfgang 1986 *The Railway Journey: the industrialization of time and space in the 19th century*, Berkeley and Los Angeles: University of California Press.
Schumpeter, Joseph 1947 'The creative response in economic history', p. 149–59 in *Journal of Economic History* 7 (2) (Nov.).
Seibu Department Store 1986 *SEED, Shibuya Seibu Guide*, Tōkyō: Seibu Department Store.
——1985a *Tsukuba Seibu Store Guide*, Tsukuba: Seibu Department Store.
——1985b *Tsukuba Seibu Promotional Film*, Tsukuba: Seibu Department Store.
Seibu Saison Group 1985 *Seibu Saison Group 1985*, Tōkyō: Company Files.
——1986 *SEED Floor Information Guide*, Tōkyō: Company Files.
Seidensticker Edward 1991 *Tōkyō Rising: the city since the great earthquake*, Cambridge, Mass.: Harvard University Press.
——1983 *Low City, High City*, New York: Alfred A. Knopf.
Seiter, Ellen 1992 'Toys are us: marketing to children and parents', p. 232–47 in *Cultural Studies* 6 (2).
Sender, Henry 1995 'Game over: China Venturetech falls from its pedestal', p. 47–8 in *Far Eastern Economic Review* 158 (3) (21 January).
Shanghai baihuo gongsi et. al. 1988 *Shanghai jindai baihuo shangye shi* (The History of General Merchandizing in Modern Shanghai), Shanghai: Shanghai shehui kexueyuan chubanshe.
Shanghai shehui kexueyuan jingji yenjiuso (ed.) 1989 *Shanghai duiwai maoyi* (Shanghai Foreign Trade 1840–1949), vol. 1, Shanghai: Shanghai shehui kexueyuan chubanshe.
Shanghai Yong'an gongsi di shangsheng fazhan wo gaizao (The Birth, Development, and Reconstruction of the Shanghai Wing On Company) 1981, Shanghai: Shanghai shehui kexueyuan chubanshe.
Shanghai Yong'an gongsi, see also Wing On and Xianggang Yong'an youxian gongsi.
Sherry, John F., Jr. (ed.) forthcoming *Encountering Servicescapes: built environment and lived experience in contemporary marketplaces.*
Shin Y. M. 1987 'Baihao gongsi shibie "jingchang guke" de shizheng zhiyin' (An empirical guideline for distinguishing regular customers of department stores), p. 125–9 in *Xinbao yuekan* (Hong Kong Economic Journal Monthly) 11 (6).
Shiono H. 1989a *Kaimawari Hin* (Luxury Merchandise), p. 73–4 in Shōgyōkai (ed.) *Shōgyō Yōgo Jiten* (Dictionary of Commercial Vocabulary), Tōkyō: Shōgyōkai.
——1989b *Moyori Hin* (Daily Necessities), p. 314 in Shōgyōkai (ed.) *Shōgyō Yōgo Jiten* (Dictionary of Commercial Vocabulary), Tōkyō: Shōgyōkai.
Shirouzu Noriko and Fara Warner 1997 'Yaohan Group pauses to take inventory', p. 1, 4 in *Asian Wall Street Journal* (17–18 January).
Shūkan Tōyō Keizai (Oriental Economist Weekly) 1996 (14 December).
——1994 'Daiei no chūgoku shinshutsu: mazu shanhai daga uyokyokusetsu' (Daiei's entry into China: Shanghai first but with complications), p. 37 (9 July).
Sida, Michael 1994 *Hong Kong Towards 1997: history, development and transition*, Hong Kong: Victoria Press.

Silverman, Debra 1986 *Selling Culture: Bloomingdale's Diana Vreeland, and the new aristocracy of taste in Reagan's America*, New York: Pantheon Press.

Sincere n.d. *The Sincere Company, Limited, Hong Kong: diamond jubilee 1900–1975*, Hong Kong: n.p.

Sincere, see also Xianshi gongsi.

Sinn, Elizabeth 1989 *Power and Charity: the early history of the Tung Wah Hospital, Hong Kong*, Hong Kong: Oxford University Press.

Skeldon, Ronald 1990 'Emigration and the future of Hong Kong, p. 500–23 in *Pacific Affairs* 63 (4).

Skov, Lise and Brian Moeran (eds.) 1995 *Women, Media and Consumption in Japan*, London: Curzon.

Smith, Henry D. II 1978 'Tōkyō as an idea: an exploration of Japanese urban thought until 1945', p. 69–71 in *Journal of Japanese Studies* 4 (1) (Winter).

Solinger, Dorothy J. 1984 *Chinese Business under Socialism: the politics of domestic commerce in contemporary China*, Berkeley: University of California Press.

South China Morning Post 1997:9:19.

Sun Yatsen 1884 'Shang Li Hongzhang shu' (Petition to Li Hongzhang), in *Wanguo gongbao* (Review of the Times), vols. 69 and 70 (September-October), reprinted by Huawen, Taibei (n.d.), pp. 14703–14715;14787–14793.

——1918 (preface date) *Memoirs of a Chinese Revolutionary: a programme of national reconstruction for China*, London: Hutchinson & Co.

Takaoka Sueaki and Koyama Shūzō 1991 *Gendai no Hyakkaten* (Modern Department Stores), Tōkyō: Nihon Keizai Shinbun.

Tang, Victoria Chung-man 1990 *A study of the business strategies of Japanese department stores in Hong Kong*, M.B.A. thesis, University of Hong Kong.

Tang Zhenchang (ed.) 1989 *Shanghai shi* (A History of Shanghai), Shanghai: Shanghai renmin chubanshe.

Taniguchi, M. 1962 *The Truth of Life*, vol. 7, California: Seichō-no-Ie.

Thomsen, Harry 1963 *The New Religions of Japan,* Tōkyō: Tuttle.

Tobin, Joseph J. (ed.) 1992a *Re-Made in Japan: everyday life and consumer taste in a changing society*, New Haven and London: Harvard University Press.

Tobin, Joseph J. 1992b 'Japanese preschools and the pedagogy of selfhood', p. 21–39 in N. R. Rosenberger (ed.) *Japanese Sense of Self*, Cambridge: Cambridge University Press.

Treadgold, Donald 1973 *The West in Russia and China: religious and secular thought in modern times*, vol. 2: 'China, 1582–1949', New York: Cambridge University Press.

Tsuchiya Takanori 1991 *Yaohan Wada Kazuo* (Yaohan Wada Kazuo), Tōkyō: Kyōbunsha.

Tsuda Sōkichi 1970 *An Inquiry Into the Japanese Mind as Mirrored in Literature*, Tōkyō: Japan Society for the Promotion of Science.

Uemura Junz 1993 ' Ōgata kouri-gyō no kaigai shutten' (The overseas expansion of large-scale retailing), p. 88–116 in Nikkei Ryūtsū Shinbun (Nikkei Distribution Newspaper) (ed.) *Ryūtsū Gendai Shi: nihongata keizai fūdo to kigyōka seishin* (Modern History of Distribution: Japanese-style economic climate and entrepreneurial spirit), Tōkyō: Nihon Keizai Shinbunsha.

Ueno Chizuko 1991 'Image no shijō – taishū shakai no "shinden" to sono kiki' (The image market: the "sanctuary" of mass society and its dangers), p. 5–136 in Saison Group-shi Henshū Iinkai (ed.) *Saison no Hassō* (The Development of Saison), Tōkyō: Libro Porto.

——1987 *'Watashi' Sagashi Game – yokubō shimin shakairon* (Looking for My 'Self': on privatization and consumerism), Tōkyō: Chikuma Shobō.

Underwood, Laurie 1995 'The lure of luxury', p. 54–61 in *Free China Review* (45) 6 (June).

Upham, Frank 1993 'Privatizing regulation: the implementation of the large-scale retail stores law', p. 264–94 in G. D. Allinson and S. Yasunori (eds.) *Political Dynamics in Contemporary Japan*, Ithaca and London: Cornell University Press.

Wada Katsu 1988 *Yaohan: inori to ai no shōnin michi* (Yaohan: prayer and love as the way of merchants), Tōkyō: Kyōbunsha.

Wada Kazuo 1995 *Yaohan Chūgoku de Katsu Senryaku* (Yaohan's Winning Strategy in China), Tōkyō: TBS Buritanika.

——1994 'Thinking big on China', p. 38–40 in *Asian Business* 30 (7) (July).

——1992 *Yaohan's Global Strategy: the 21st century is the era of Asia*, Hong Kong: Capital Communications Corporation Ltd.

Wada Kazuo et al. 1994 *Yaohan Runessansu* (Yaohan Renaissance), Tōkyō: Kyōbunsha.

Wada Naomi 1994 'Naze, watashi wa "Barajiru" ni shippai shitaka?' (Why I was defeated in Brazil?), p. 92–117 in K. Wada et al. 1994 *Yaohan Runessansu* (Yaohan Renaissance), Tōkyō: Kyōbunsha.

Wang Zhiyuan 1958 *Ye Delai zhuan* (A Biography of Yap Ah Loy), Kuala Lumpur: Yihua chuban yinshua yixian gongsi.

Wang Gungwu 1991 *The Chineseness of China: selected essays*, Hong Kong: Oxford University Press.

——1988 'The life and times of William Liu: Australian and Chinese perspectives', p. 109–24 in J. Hardy (ed.) *Stories of Australian Migration*, Sydney: NSW University Press.

Wangfujing 1993, Beijing: Beijing Chubanshe.

Weber, Adna 1899 *The Growth of Cities in the Nineteenth Century*, New York: Macmillan Co.

Wei, Betty P.T. 1987 *Shanghai: crucible of modern China*, London and Hong Kong: Oxford University Press.

Wiedemann, Elizabeth 1981 *World of its Own: Inverell's early years*, Inverell: Devill Publicity.

Williams, Rosalind 1982 *Dream Worlds: mass consumption in late nineteenth century France*, Berkeley: University of California Press.

Wilton, Janis 1994 'Identity, racism and multiculturalism: Chinese-Australian responses', p. 85–100 in R. Benmayor and A. Skotnes (eds.) *International Yearbook of Oral History and Life Stories*, vol. 3: 'Migration and identity', Oxford: Oxford University Press.

——1991 'Remembering racism, p. 32–8 in *Oral History Association of Australia Journal*, vol. 13.

——1989 'The Chinese in New England: the necessity of fieldwork, the fragility of memory, p. 42–57 in *Oral History Association of Australia Journal* 11.

——1988 *Hong Yuen: a country store and its people*, Armidale: Armidale College of Advanced Education and NSW Department of Education, Multicultural Education Coordination Committee.

Wing On 1975 *The Wing On Life Assurance Company Limited: golden jubilee book 1925–1975*, Hong Kong: Wing On Company Ltd.

Wing On, see also Xianggang Yong'an youxian gongsi and Shanghai Yong'an gongsi

Wong, J.Y. 1986 *The Origins of an Heroic Image: Sun Yatsen in London, 1896–1897*, Hong Kong: Oxford University Press.

Wong K. Y. 1982 'New towns: the Hong Kong experience, p. 118–30 in J. Cheng (ed.) *Hong Kong in the 1980s*, Hong Kong: Summerson (HK) Educational Research Centre.

Wong Siu-lun 1992 *Emigration and Stability in Hong Kong*, Occasional Paper #7, Social Sciences Research Centre, Hong Kong: The University of Hong Kong.

——1988 *Emigrant Entrepreneurs: Shanghai industrialists in Hong Kong*, Hong Kong: Oxford University Press.

——1986 'The Chinese family firm: a model, p. 58–72 in *British Journal of Sociology* 26 (1).

Wright, Arnold 1908 *Twentieth Century Perceptions of Hong Kong, Shanghai and Other Treaty Ports of China*, London: Lloyd's Greater British Publishing Co.

Wright, Mary 1969 *The Last Stand of Chinese Conservatism: the T'ung-Chih restoration, 1862–1874*, New York: Atheneum.

Wu Xin et al. 1936 (preface date) *Minguo Shanghai xian zhi* (Gazetteer of the Shanghai County of the Republican Era), Shanghai: n.p.

Xianggang Yong'an youxian gongsi 1934 *Xianggang Yong'an youxian gongsi minguo ershian nianfen zongjie ce* (The Balance Sheet of the Wing On Company of Hong Kong for the Year 1934), Hong Kong: Xianggang Yong'an youxian.

——1932 (preface date) *Xianggang Yong'an youxian gongsi: ershiwu zhounian jinian lu* (The Wing On Company Ltd. of Hong Kong: commemoration of the 25th anniversary, 1907–1932), Hong Kong: Tianxing yinwu ju.

Xianggang Yong'an youxian gongsi, see also Wing On and Shanghai Yong'an gongsi.

Xianshi gongsi 1924[?] *Xianshi gongsi ershiwu zhounian jinian ce* (The Sincere Company: twenty-fifth anniversary commemorative issue), Hong Kong: Shangwu yinshu guan.

Xianshi gongsi, see also Sincere.

Xiao Fanbo 1972 'Guangzhou Xianshi gongsi ershidou nian di sheng'ai' (The rise and fall of Guangzhou's Sincere Company during its twenty-odd years), p. 126–43 in *Guangzhou wenshi ziliao* (Historical Materials on Guangzhou) (23).

Xin Tan 1994 'Chūgoku no shōhin ryūtsū no kaikaku' (The reform of product distribution in China), p. 12–5 in *Keizai no 'me'* (Economic 'Eye') 22 (July).

Xu Dixin (ed.) 1988 *Zhongguo qiyeji liezhuan*, vol. 1 (Biographies of Chinese Industrialists), Beijing: Jingji ribao chubanshe.

Yamamoto Taketoshi 1984 *Kōkoku no Shakaishi* (A Social History of Advertising), Tōkyō: Hōsei Daigaku Shuppankyoku.

Yaohan Department Store Ltd. 1993 *Yakushin* (Leap Forward) 109, Japan: Yaohan Department Store Ltd.

——1990 *Yakushin* (Leap Forward) 102, Japan: Yaohan Department Store Ltd.

——1980 *Yakushin* (Leap Forward) 81, Japan: Yaohan Department Store Ltd.

Yaohan International Group 1993 *Yaohan International Group*, Hong Kong: Yaohan International Holdings Ltd.

Ye Xian'en 1987 'Ming-Qing zhujiang sanjiaozhou shangren yu shangye huodong' (Merchants and commercial activities in the Pearl River Delta), p. 41–56 in *Zhongguo shi yenjiu* (Research on Chinese History) 2.

Yen Ching-hwang 1995 *Studies in Modern Overseas Chinese History*, Singapore: Times Academic Press.

——1991 'The Wing On Company in Hong Kong and Shanghai: a case study of modern overseas Chinese enterprise', p. 77–117 in *Proceedings of Conference on Eighty Years History of the Republic of China*, vol. 4, Taipei: Academia Sinica.

——1985 *Coolies and Mandarins: China's protection of overseas Chinese during the late Ch'ing period 1851 –1911*, Singapore: Singapore University Press.

——1984 'Chang Yu-nan and Chaochow Railways, 1904–1908', p. 119–35 in *Modern Asian Studies* 18 (1).

——1982 'The overseas Chinese and late Ch'ing economic modernization', p. 217–32 in *Modern Asian Studies* 16 (2).

Yeung K. K. 1990 'Riben ningshouye zhe huizhan xiangjiang (Japanese retailers head for decisive battle in Hong Kong), p. 38–9 in *Next Magazine* (March).

Yong, C. F. 1977 *The New Gold Mountain: the Chinese in Australia, 1901–1921*, Adelaide: Raphael Arts Pty. Ltd.

——1965–66 'The banana trade and the Chinese in New South Wales and Victoria, 1901–1921', p. 28–35 in *A.N.U. Historical Journal, 1965–1966* 1 (2).

Yoshimi Shunya 1987 *Toshi no Dramaturgy – Tōkyō, sakariba no shakaishi* (Urban Dramaturgy: a social history of the pleasure quarters of Tōkyō), Tōkyō: Kōbundō.

Young, John D. 1985 'Reform versus revolution: a re-appraisal of Sun Yat-sen's early thoughts on national salvation', p. 133–45 in *Journal of the Institute for Chinese Studies* 22 (2).

Yung Wing 1909 *My Life in China and America*, New York: Henry Holt and Company.

Zhang Haoruo 1994 'Shijō keizaika no kagi nigiru ryūtsū kaikaku' (Distribution holds the key to the shift to market economy), p. 72–7 in *Shūkan Tōyō Keizai* (Oriental Economist Weekly) (21 May).

'Zhongguo guohuo youxian gongsi jianjie' (Brief introduction to the China Products Company Ltd.), p. 28–31 in *Zhongguo guohuo youxian gongsi chengli 50 zhounian* (50 year anniversary of founding of the China Products Company, Ltd.) 1988, Hong Kong.

Zhongguo shangbao (China Business Daily) 1996:3:1.

Zhongguo zhengquan bao (China Securities) 1996:4:23.

Zhongguo zhengquan bao (China Securities) 1996:4:19.

Zhou Shixun 1933 *Shanghai daguan* (The Grand Sights of Shanghai), Shanghai: Wenhua meishu tushu gongsi.

REFERENCES

Zhu Longzhan 1988 'Shuaixian yinjin qiaozidi Guo Le (Guo Le – the industrialist who used overseas Chinese capital), p. 20–8–15 in Xu D. (ed.) *Zhongguo qiyejia liezhuan*, vol. 2 (Biographies of Chinese industrialists), Beijing: Jingji ribao chubanshe.

LIST OF CONTRIBUTORS

Lonny E. CARLILE is an Assistant Professor of Japanese Studies at the Asian Studies Program, University of Hawai'i at Manoa. His interests range across all areas of Japan-related political economy, broadly defined. He has published articles on labour politics, labour movement ideology, deregulation, the overseas travel industry, Taishō period big business associations, and Russo-Japanese economic relations. He is currently working on an edited volume on deregulation and a sole authored work on labour politics.

Wellington K. K. CHAN (Ph.D. Harvard) is Professor of History at Occidental College, USA. He has published extensively on the socio-economic history of modern East Asia. Currently, he is completing two studies, the first on the historiography of the Chinese family firm, the second on modern Chinese commercial culture as exemplified by Shanghai's Nanjing Road. Both will appear as chapters in forthcoming volumes. His book *Merchants, Mandarins and Modern Enterprises in Late Ch'ing China* (Harvard U. P., 1977) has been translated into Chinese and is to be published by the Institute of Modern History, the Chinese Academy of Social Sciences, Beijing.

Millie CREIGHTON is Associate Professor in the Department of Anthropology and Sociology, and a faculty member of the Japan Centre at the University of British Columbia. She has conducted lengthy and extensive research on department stores in Japan. In addition to Japanese department stores, she has also published the results of research in Japan on advertising, children's marketing, tourism, traditional craft seminars, work and leisure, gender roles, and concepts of the self.

GUO Hongchi, Professor, graduated from Beijing Furen University in 1948 and now teaches in the graduate programme at the Beijing Institute of Business. His research field is retail management. Main works are *Retail Management, Commercial Management, Total Quality Control*; *The Theory and Practice of Modern Commerce Management*; and *The Business of Circulating Enterprise*. Guo Hongchi is an executive director of the China Commerce Enterprise Management Association and a consultant for the Beijing Commerce Enterprise Management Association.

LIU Fei, Associate Professor, graduated from the Beijing Institute of Business in 1983, and then joined the BIB faculty. She worked in commercial enterprises for eight years before pursuing her graduate studies. Her main research areas are retail management and hotel marketing. Her key works are *Market Information Management and Practice*; *The Collection of Market Information*; and *The Handbook of Commerce Enterprise*. She often works as an advisor for large-scale stores in Beijing and devises business strategies and operating programmes for them.

Kerrie L. MACPHERSON is an Associate Professor of History, and Fellow of the Centre of Urban Planning and Environmental Management at The University of Hong Kong. Her main research interests are urban history, urban planning and infrastructural development as well as urban public health, the focus of her book *A Wilderness of Marshes: the origins of public health in Shanghai, 1843–93* (1987). Recent publications include 'Designing China's urban future: The Greater Shanghai Plan, 1927–37' in *Planning Perspectives* (1990); 'The head of the dragon: the Pudong New Area and Shanghai's urban development' in *Planning Perspectives* (1994); 'The Shanghai model in historical perspective' in Y. M. Yeung and Sung Yun-wing (eds.) *Shanghai Transformation and Modernization under China's Open Policy* (1996); and 'A conspiracy of silence: a history of sexually transmitted diseases and HIV/AIDS in Hong Kong' in M. Lewis et al. (eds.) *Sex, Disease and Society* (1997).

Brian MOERAN is a social anthropologist who has published widely on various aspects of advertising, media and consumption in Japan. Recent books include *Women, Media and Consumption in Japan* (edited with Lise Skov), *A Japanese Advertising Agency: an anthropology of media and markets*, and *Folk Art Potters of Japan*. He is currently the Swire Professor of Japanese Studies at The University of Hong Kong.

UENO Chizuko holds a Professorship in the Graduate School of Humanities and Sociology at the University of Tōkyō. She finished her Ph.D. course at Kyoto University. She has published widely in Japanese and English on gender issues, sexuality, family, and Japanese consumer society, including department stores. Among her major publications are *Patriarchy and Capitalism* (1990) and *The Rise and Fall of the Japanese Modern Family* (1994).

Janis WILTON is a Senior Lecturer in the Department of History at the University of New England, Armidale, Australia. She has a particular interest in oral history, and in researching and recording the histories and experiences of Australians from non-English-speaking backgrounds. She is the author of a beginner's handbook on oral history, a past editor of the *Oral History Association of Australia Journal*, co-author of *Old Worlds and New Australia* (Penguin) and editor of *Internment: the diaries of Harry Seidler* (Allen and Unwin). She also researched and compiled *Immigrants in the Bush*, an oral history based resource package for schools. She is currently extending her research on immigrants in rural Australia through an oral history of the Chinese in twentieth century New England.

WONG Heung Wah is a social anthropologist and Assistant Professor of Japanese Studies at the University of Hong Kong. His research interest lies in the study of Japanese culture and its relation to Japanese corporations. As one of the few Chinese anthropologists studying Japan, he studies Japanese corporations in Chinese cultural contexts, especially those of Taiwan, Mainland China, and Hong Kong. He has completed two years of fieldwork in a Japanese department store-cum-supermarket in Hong Kong and received his D. Phil. degree from the Institute of Social and Cultural Anthropology, University of Oxford.

YEN Ching-hwang obtained his Ph.D. degree from the Department of Far Eastern History, Australian National University, Canberra, in 1970. He was Professor of History at the University of Hong Kong, and is now Reader/Associate Professor of History at the University of Adelaide, South Australia. His major publications in English include *The Overseas Chinese and the 1911 Revolution* (Oxford U.P., 1976), *Coolies and Mandarins* (Singapore U.P., 1985), and *A Social History of the Chinese in Singapore and Malaya*, 1800-1911 (Oxford U.P., 1986). All these major works have been translated into Chinese. More recent publications in English are *Studies in Modern Overseas Chinese*

History, and *Community and Politics: the Chinese in colonial Singapore and Malaysia* (both Times Academic Press, 1995).

John D. YOUNG received his Ph.D. degree in history from the University of California, Davis, in March 1976; he taught in universities in North America, Australia and Hong Kong, where he lectured in legal translation at the Chinese University of Hong Kong. His major areas of interest were the history of Christianity in China, modern Chinese intellectual history, and Hong Kong studies. At his untimely death in 1996, he was working on a book-length manuscript of Sun Yatsen's early revolutionary programme.

INDEX

Note: References to illustrations are in bold type.

Pan Xulun 87
Parco 180, 203n, 204n; see also Seibu
    Saison Group
paternalism 108
Po Leung Kuk 61
Pudong 246–7

racial discrimination see 'white
    Australia policy'
railroads, 7–8, 167, 206, 267;
    exposition 150; the 'Five Great
    Department Stores by Subway'
    166; Hankyū Dentetsu 162–4;
    Keihin Kyūkō Railway 178; Minoo
    Arima Railway 162, 164; terminal
    depāto 8, 162–6, 171–2, 174n;
    Tokyo-Yokohama Railway 167–8;
    and Sun Yatsen 34, 37, 43
Rawski, Thomas 47
Red Guards 122
remittance banks 15, 59–61, 62, 80,
    83; see also Wing On and Sincere
Rong Hong see Yung Wing

Sahlins, M., 253
san duo yi shao ('three numerous and
    one less') 123; see also Wangfujing
    Department Store
Science City 225
Schivelbusch Wolfgang, 171–2
Schumpeter, Joseph 14, 47, 65, 88
SEED see Seibu Saison Group
Seibu Retailing Group 204n; see also
    Seibu Saison Group
Seibu Saison Group, 21, 177, 181,
    204n; advertising campaigns of
    178, 185–7, 188–96, **190**, **191**, **193**,
    194; art museum and exhibitions of
    181, 187–8, 209–19; corporate
    culture of 200–1; diversification of
    179–80, 183; educational support
    of 209, 230 n.15; history of
    178–81; Ikebukuro store 178–9,
    180–1, 213–4; image marketing of
    183–7; innovation of 199; Habitat
    188; health promotion of 217–8;
    LoFt 203; in Los Angeles 234,
    236; marketing of 'a meaningful
    life' 206–30; philosophy of 215–9;

and postwar consumer market
    178–84; and railroads 178–9; sales
    promotion department 195–6;
    SEED 22, 204n, 219, 225–9;
    separation from department store
    business 197–203; Shibuya store
    179–80; specialized shops in 197;
    Sports 188; theme Stores 219–29;
    Tsukuba store 22, 219, 222–5, 230
    n.2; Yurakuchō store 22, 219–20,
    222–5; see also Tsutsumi Seiji and
    Tsutsumi Yasujirō
Seichō-no-Ie 257, 259, 261–3, 264–5;
    see also Wada Kazuo and Yaohan
Seiyū Group 25, 179–80, 257, 265;
    see also supermarkets
Shansi Bankers 40
Shanghai 1–2, 8–9, 67; bombing of 81,
    109–10, 112; General Chamber of
    Commerce 73; Product Exhibition
    Hall 73; Sincere in 76; stock
    exchange of 126; see also Nanjing
    road and Pudong and Yaohan
Shanghai Tang Department Store 30n
Shih Kuo-heng 47
Shirokiya 1, 10, 146, 151, 234
si-door 42
Sincere 1, **4**, **73**, **77**, **78**, 80, 100;
    Australian connections of 112;
    banking and savings of 83;
    branches of 15; boycott of 15, 81;
    compared to Wing On 48, 68,
    70–8, 84; corporate culture of 82–9
    passim; entertainment in 72–3;
    financial crisis of 81; Guangzhou
    store 72, 78–9, 87; incorporated
    72; manufacturing of 74;
    remittance business of 15,
    reorganization in Hong Kong 77;
    see also Ma Yingbiao
Sino-British Joint Declaration 263,
    272
Sogō 23, 237–8, 269
Song Ailing 39
Song Qingling 33
Sony, gap theory of 265–6
state-owned enterprises 123, 124–7
Stewart, Alexander T. 71; see also
    Marble Palace

266; in the China market 242,
243–8, 274–8; China strategy of
245–7; and CITIC 242; as a
conglomerate 273–4; domination
by Wada family 257–61;
globalization strategy of 248–52;
as a Hong Kong department store
253–81, **268**, **269**; and IMMs 240,
246–8; and the internationalization
of Japanese retailing 233–8; in
Japanese retail market 251–2, 257;
NEXTAGE Complex in Shanghai
246–7, 277; as a religious group
261–3; reproduced as a regional
supermarket in Hong Kong
267–70; retail outlets of **259**;
shareholders of **260**; in Singapore
239–40, 247, 260; and Venturetech
Investment Corporation 246; *see
also* Seichō-no-Ie *and* Wada Kazuo
Yap Ah Loy 47
yi tuan huo *see* 'blazing spirit'

Yongsheng Zhuang *see* Wing Sang &
Co.
Young, Percy 95–7, **110**; *see also*
Kwong Sing
Yung Wing 49
Yong'an gongsi *see* Wing On
Yong'an Guolan 83–4
Yuan Shikai 38
Yurakuchō Seibu *see* Seibu Saison
Group

zahuo dian 67
za-uri sales 146
Zeng Guo-fan 35
Zhang Binggui **136**, 136–8; *see also*
'blazing spirit' *and* Wangfujing
department store
Zhang Bishi 47
Zheng Guanying 34, 49
Zhongshan 49, 71, 74,82, 83, 98; *see
also* Sun Yatsen *and* Xiangshan
Zhuxiuyuan *see* Chuk Sau Yuen